A FIERCE AND
FRACTIOUS FRONTIER

A FIERCE AND FRACTIOUS FRONTIER

The Curious Development of Louisiana's Florida Parishes, 1699–2000

EDITED BY
Samuel C. Hyde Jr.

WITH A FOREWORD BY
Hodding Carter III

LOUISIANA STATE UNIVERSITY PRESS
BATON ROUGE

Published by Louisiana State University Press
Copyright © 2004 by Louisiana State University Press
All rights reserved
Manufactured in the United States of America

DESIGNER: AMANDA MCDONALD SCALLAN
TYPEFACE: MINION
TYPESETTER: COGHILL COMPOSITION CO., INC.
PRINTER AND BINDER: THOMSON-SHORE, INC.

Library of Congress Cataloging-in-Publication Data

A fierce and fractious frontier : the curious development of Louisiana's
Florida parishes, 1699–2000 / edited by Samuel C. Hyde Jr.
      p.   cm.
Includes index.
   ISBN 978-0-8071-2923-4 (pbk. : alk. paper)
   1. Florida Parishes (La.)—History.   I. Hyde, Samuel C., 1958–
F377.F6F54   2004
976.3′3—dc22
                                                            2003022746

The paper in this book meets the guidelines for permanence and durability of the Committee on Production Guidelines for Book Longevity of the Council on Library Resources. ♾

For Clay and Andrew, a seventh generation in the piney woods

CONTENTS

Louisiana's Florida Parishes: *A Sense of Place and History*
HODDING CARTER III   ix

Acknowledgments   xiii

Introduction: *Discovering a Neglected Southern Subregion*
SAMUEL C. HYDE JR.   1

I | A CONVOLUTED COLONIAL IDENTITY

    1 A Geography of Power: *French and Indian Alliances on the Southeast Louisiana Frontier*
       CHARLES N. ELLIOTT   15

    2 Boom in the Bayous: *Land Speculation and Town Planning in the Florida Parishes under British Rule*
       ROBIN F. A. FABEL   44

    3 Slavery in Louisiana's Florida Parishes under the Spanish Regime, 1779–1803
       GILBERT C. DIN   60

II | CONFRONTING THE CHALLENGE OF AMERICA

    4 Giving Jackson Victory: *Thomas ap Catesby Jones, the Battle of Lake Borgne, and British Frustration along the Gulf*
       GENE A. SMITH   91

    5 A Threshold of Unobtainable Commitment: *Irregular Operations in Louisiana's Florida Parishes, 1862–1865*
       SAMUEL C. HYDE JR.   109

6 The Ongoing Agricultural Credit Crisis in the Florida Parishes of
  Louisiana, 1865–1890
  RICHARD H. KILBOURNE JR.   125

7 The Legendary Longleaf Pine Forests of the Florida Parishes:
  Historic Character and Change at the Hand of Man
  LATIMORE SMITH   140

III | CHALLENGES LESS SPOKEN

8 African American Lumber Workers in the Florida Parishes
  Lumber Industry, 1900–1925
  BILL WYCHE   161

9 Washington Parish and Its Black Community: *Horace Mann
  Bond's Study of 1934–1935*
  ADAM FAIRCLOUGH   174

10 Environment, Economy, and Quality of Life in Louisiana's
  Florida Parishes
  PAUL H. TEMPLET   191

Contributors   223
Index   225

LOUISIANA'S FLORIDA PARISHES
A Sense of Place and History

$\mathscr{I}$T HAS BEEN MANY YEARS BETWEEN VISITS TO LOUISIANA'S FLORIDA Parishes for me, decades really, though it was long my habit while Greenville, Mississippi, was still my home to pull off the Interstate while passing down to New Orleans and take a quick drive past my grandfather's old farmhouse outside Hammond.

It has been a long time primarily because it has been twenty-four years since I was truly rooted in a community and in close communion with the past, my family's past and my own. I left Greenville in 1976 to work for Jimmy Carter's election and then his administration, fully expecting to be back home in four years. Instead, the Carter years turned out for me to be a farewell trip, a permanent remove from the towns and regions that had been formative in every way.

Much as I have loved aspects of my life since then, the removals remain a cause of abiding sadness. A sense of place was central to my sense of self, sometimes in embrace of its mores and history, sometimes in rejection, but always in active engagement. Perched since leaving southeast Louisiana and northwest Mississippi in two areas that define the outermost limits of our much-changed Southland—the Northern Virginia suburbs of Washington, D.C., and the center of metropolitan Miami in South Florida—my perspective has changed from that of participant to observer. It is not an inconsequential change.

In fact, I would argue that this purely personal account of extraction from place and its effects on one person have something larger to say about contemporary life in the mass society of our country. To put it plainly, the disconnect of growing tens of millions of Americans from place, from the history of their place and their sense of place, has proceeded in tandem with their disconnect from civic enterprise and identity.

And that disconnect, I am increasingly persuaded, carries within it a poison that already sickens and can ultimately kill the fundamental virtues and essential institutions of this democratic republic.

But let me go back in time a bit. Southeastern Louisiana University, where the conference "Louisiana's Florida Parishes: Continuity and Change, 1699–2000" was held, looms large in my family's notion of place, in large part because it was the product of the vision held by my grandfather, Will Carter, and three other men who founded it as a tiny junior college in a high school building in 1925. They knew their community needed a portal to higher education for those who could not afford the jump to a four-year institution, public or private. Thirty years later, one of my cousins graduated from the four-year institution Southeastern Louisiana College had become, not long after Dad had given the commencement address during her freshman year. One of the campus buildings is named after Granddad.

But the point about Will Carter's foresight was less any particular result and more the instinct that drove it. If you lived in a place, it was your responsibility to make it better. It was not so much that each impulse of each participant was going to be judged benignly by history. Granddad was, like virtually every white man in the Deep South of his day, a bone-deep white supremacist and acted accordingly, occasionally in ways that seem inexplicable today. What mattered (and still matters) was that you could not, should not, be a neutral in the events affecting your time and place. A community was shaped by the memories and activities of its inhabitants. That was their unavoidable responsibility.

My dad captured all of that, as defined by Granddad's life, in a *Reader's Digest* piece originally titled "Someone Has to Do It." In anecdote after loving anecdote, written for the "My Most Unforgettable Character" section, Dad recounted the multiple times his father had stepped forward to do the hard but necessary thing in his Florida Parishes community.

It was a family legacy, and a great one. It was more than that, however. It was also a direct statement of what it takes to create a decent place, whether town, parish, region, state, nation, or world. You grow where you are planted. You give back to that which has nourished you. You stand up to be counted, and to be counted on, when the hard times come.

Dad took it with him from Louisiana to Mississippi, in both states using the community newspapers he owned (and ran) to speak what he understood to be the truth to his fellow citizens and to give them as clear a picture of their time and place as he could, in order that they might fashion their own truths and answers. He taught his sons that the family was the center of the universe and the community was the vital center of civilized society. He loved those local communities, as well as the larger one that was the South of his day, too much to remain silent as his own beliefs about racial segregation increasingly deviated from those of his fellow white southerners.

So it was that I grew up in a family that was both at the center of its community and at war with one of that community's central themes. Lessons were learned from that strained existence, some of them hard ones, all of them valuable. The most valuable of all was that each person has a responsibility to participate fully in the public debate of the time in which he or she lives, less because anyone can be certain of the undying validity of his views than because no one should default to others the right to define the nature of their time and place.

Dad was clear about the debt he owed his mentors. One was his own father. Another was William Alexander Percy, the poet, planter, and lawyer who was chiefly responsible for bringing him to Greenville in 1936 to start a newspaper after Dad's squabble with Huey Long. As recounted in his 1952 autobiography, *Where Main Street Meets the River,* Dad and Will Percy were talking about what could be done to remake whatever could be saved from the changes they both felt were coming. At some point, Percy said:

> You can't do anything on the grand scale. But when this comes to an end, you can work again for your own people in your own town. It isn't national leaders we need so much as men of good will in each of the little towns of America. So try to keep Greenville a decent place by being a correct citizen yourself. The total of all the Greenvilles will make the kind of country we want or don't want.

But how many live for long in neighborhood or community or even region today? We are increasingly a nation of nomads. Even in the contemporary South, once the most rooted of regions, we move to and fro like so many migratory birds, though unlike them not going back and forth from known destination to known destination. We are a nation of perpetual immigrants, internal as well as external, in a world economic system that places little value—but massive strains—on local customs, local autonomy, and local economy. We barely know the identity of those who are elected to serve our interests at any level, often because we do not stay in any one place long enough to get to know them, and a huge majority of us shun the ballot boxes as religiously as we shun all forms of public service.

Perhaps we cannot go home again. There was never a Golden Age, not in Louisiana's Florida Parishes and not in the United States, for us to return to. On balance, our present seems better than our past, but at least in large part those predecessors who lived with a sense of place distilled a sense of purposeful involvement from their rootedness. The tattered history of southeast Louisiana offers concrete proof of that proposition.

It is precisely because these physical connections are so tenuous in our time that the intellectual ones must be cultivated, encouraged, and nourished. The active engagement Dad and Granddad preached by word and example as the way to make a place better starts by knowing its history and appreciating its heritage. *A Fierce and Fractious Frontier: The Curious Development of Louisiana's Florida Parishes, 1699–2000* provides such a beginning. The essays in this book stress the curious, even peculiar, sense of *regional* place rooted in southeast Louisiana and puts our neglected regional history within the context of greater southern and national experiences. Reconnecting with our past, our regional past, helps encourage the civic enterprise and identity necessary to nourish the fundamental virtues and essential institutions of our democratic republic. The past *is* prologue.

HODDING CARTER III

ACKNOWLEDGMENTS

Planning a conference designed to correct a historical imbalance and guiding the product through the course of production for both film and book serve as the very ideal of a "splendid misery" that most do not often wish to repeat. Such a project can prove an enduring burden to the best-intentioned as well as the unwilling victims. But it can also offer a variety of rewards, not the least of which is the opportunity to encounter those dedicated to a like-minded vision willing to cheerfully share the burden in commitment to its purpose.

The eleven essays included in this volume reveal that cutting-edge research has finally visited the Florida Parishes in a substantive sense. But the contents of this book reflect merely a fraction of the work that supported the program, just as the contributors represent but a few of those who contributed to the success of the overall project. As the program advanced from idea to reality, scores of individuals assisted in its planning, support, and performance. The Louisiana Endowment for the Humanities along with the College of Arts and Sciences and Department of History and Government at Southeastern Louisiana University provided crucial financial assistance. Sally Clausen, Randy Moffett, John Miller, Bill Robison, and Roman Heleniak provided the administrative and hands-on support necessary to coordinate the conference at SLU. Faye Phillips, Bill Brockway, and Mark Martin enhanced the comprehensive nature of the program through their presentations highlighting the photographic and architectural legacy of the region.

The immersion into the folkways and cultures of the Florida Parishes that served as the core of the three-day conference resulted from the contributions of many artistically inclined individuals. Bryan Gowland and Mary Howell facilitated the inclusion of the dynamic Piney Woods Opry Roadshow. The Hank Jones Band, Reggie Sanders Quartet, and the Hungarian Folklife Dancers each demonstrated the cultural mélange that sustains the region's musical heritage. The Fifth Company Washington Artillery along with Hollis Gill, James Jenkins, Tom Colvin, Annabelle Servat, Julia Chan, Edward Carr, Ruby Petho, John Magee, Gary Cyrix, and Myrlene Pertuit's quilting circle offered realistic glimpses of our cultural roots. L. E. Wallace provided a recorded visual record of the entire program. Bonnie Lewis and Rick Samson, of the Florida Parishes Social Science Research Center, used their impressive statistical analysis of prevailing socioeconomic conditions in the area to remind us to consider the implications for the future as we reflect upon the past.

Finally, but far from least, the staff of the Center for Southeast Louisiana Studies proved tireless in their dedicated support of this project. Vicky Mocsary, Lois Wagner, Reggie Span, David Kubilus, Anna Clark, and Melissa Chauvin answered far and above the call to ensure the success of the program and accompanying activities. As always, the kind consideration and courteous attention provided by the staff at LSU Press make the most burdensome portion of any project a pleasure. The contributions of each of these individuals remain visibly evident as we continue to pursue the challenge of discovering a neglected southern subregion.

A FIERCE AND
FRACTIOUS FRONTIER

INTRODUCTION

Discovering a Neglected Southern Subregion

SAMUEL C. HYDE JR.

"Desperate determination" may best describe the prevailing spirit characterizing the explorations of southeastern Louisiana and surrounding environs in 1699 by Pierre LeMoyne, sieur d'Iberville. Commanding impressive credentials, which included an unblemished record of ruthless victories over the English, and standing as the first Canadian-born recipient of one of France's highest honors, the Cross of the Order of Saint-Louis, Iberville enjoyed a reputation as the first Canadian hero. Despite his military prowess, Iberville faced a challenge in 1699 that none before him had overcome. Charged by the French king Louis XIV to identify the mouth of the Mississippi River and secure the region for France, Iberville chafed under the burdens imposed by inconsistent information, poor logistics, and the demands for haste occasioned by the growing threat of English and Spanish encroachment.[1]

When he finally located the fabled "east fork" of the Mississippi, along the course of present-day Bayou Manchac, Iberville concluded that he had at last identified the position of the great waterway his predecessor La Salle considered critical to securing and developing central North America. As he entered the Amite River and traveled across the two lakes he later named Maurepas and Pontchartrain, Iberville recorded in his journal, "The place where I am is one of the prettiest spots I have seen, fine level ground, beautiful woods, clear and bare of canes." Continuing his observations of the region, he added, "This looks like fine country to live in. The mainland north of the lakes is a country of pine trees mixed with hardwood. The soil is sandy, and many tracks of buffalo and deer can be seen." Iberville concluded that the region he was exploring, now known as the Florida Parishes of Louisiana, remained absolutely critical to any scheme designed to control the lower Mississippi Valley.[2]

Iberville was not the only adventurer to appreciate the area's significance. Explorers and early pioneers from three different nations recognized the strategic importance the Florida Parishes commanded. Yet those familiar with the published history of Louisiana over the past century will know that the region's relevance has somehow become abbreviated, if not forgotten, over time. Tales of Cajuns, Creoles, and the debauchery of New Orleans have come to dominate both popular and professional impressions of Louisiana. While Acadiana and the Crescent City are significant in their own right, popular interest in these locales has undoubtedly distracted attention from the region that arguably experienced the most dramatic pattern of development in Louisiana, if not the entire Gulf South. The eight modern parishes of East Baton Rouge, East and West Feliciana, Livingston, St. Helena, St. Tammany, Tangipahoa, and Washington collectively form a distinct region linked by geography and a peculiar common heritage. On the eve of the bicentennial of the Louisiana Purchase, it seems fitting that this unique area be afforded proper consideration.[3]

So what contributes to the Florida Parishes' extraordinary significance? Following more than a decade of personal research concentrated on the area, I remain most impressed by the curious combination of intense consistency and uncompromising aberration the region shares with, or maintains from, the rest of the state. More precisely, the Florida Parishes enjoy close association with all the elements that make other areas of the state distinctive but also include aspects of development identifiable *only* in southeastern Louisiana. Indeed, in their eagerness to underscore the peculiar attributes of Louisiana, historians have neglected certain conditions evident in the Florida Parishes while absorbing qualities unique to the region into a larger discussion of Louisiana's distinctiveness. Some obvious examples of the misrepresentation characterizing historical treatments of Louisiana and its relationship to the Florida Parishes highlight this pattern.[4]

For generations historians have boasted of Louisiana's ten flags. One prominent author even named his book about the state *Ten Flags in the Wind*. In reality, Louisiana's ten flags enjoy association exclusively with the Florida Parishes; only eight flew over the remainder of the state. The flag disparity suggests that a more curious, colorful, and perhaps contentious pattern of development may have prevailed in southeastern Louisiana.[5]

Another prevailing misconception, which is linked to the flag issue, concerns Louisiana's relationship with Britain. For years historians, tourism officials, and others have encouraged the belief that much of Louisiana's distinctiveness related to its absence of identification with the British empire. Remarkably, the first page in chapter one of the most widely circulated Louisiana history text currently in print declares, "Louisiana never existed as a British colony, giving it a very different heritage from that of many other states in the nation." While true that most of Louisiana never experienced British domination, this historical interpretation completely omits the Florida Parishes' brief tenure under British overlordship. The British era continued from 1763 to 1783 and proved critical to the territory's development.[6] Even more significant, their brief association with Britain ensured that the Florida Parishes would emerge as one of the few regions of our nation that can claim association with every major power that established colonies in North America.

The changing cycle of governing powers highlights yet another overlooked characteristic contributing to the region's distinctiveness, specifically, the peculiar blend of ethnic groups inhabiting the Florida Parishes. Like the remainder of Louisiana, the region has served as home to significant numbers who claim an American Indian, African, French, German, Isleño, or Scotch-Irish ancestry. Less frequently mentioned remains the Florida Parishes' role as home to the largest rural Italian and Hungarian communities in America. What is more unusual is that a significant proportion of the white population in the Florida Parishes boasts an English heritage, unlike the white population throughout the rest of the state and the Gulf South. In the wake of the American Revolution substantial numbers of British loyalists, fleeing persecution along the eastern seaboard, migrated to then Spanish West Florida in an effort to escape the overlordship of their former rebel enemies. Their presence established in the area a pocket of so called "Tories," many of English descent, who remained intensely suspicious of most forms of authority.[7]

Suspicion, if not contempt, for authority emerged as one of the most identifiable characteristics common to the people of West Florida, and it contributed directly to an explosive event that also advances the region's singularity. Despite the efforts of Thomas Jefferson's emissaries to secure the region and complete American control of the entire east bank of the Mississippi River, the Florida Parishes were *not* included in the 1803 Louisiana Purchase; instead the territory remained subject to the control of Spain. Following an abortive 1804 insurrection, local residents initiated a revolution in 1810 that successfully overthrew Spanish domination. Through force of arms the residents established the original Lone Star Republic, which endured for seventy-four days before William C. C. Claiborne arrived to claim the territory as a part of the United States. Popular support for the revolt, as well as American absorption of the territory, nonetheless remained far from universal. Many residents actively opposed the West Florida rebels, while others openly voiced their distaste for American overlordship. Such animosities fueled isolated incidents of brutality that accompanied the revolt and contributed to the sustained pattern of instability that has characterized the region.[8]

The violence that accompanied the West Florida Revolution proved but a shadow of a much more ominous tradition evident in the Florida Parishes. While warfare and brutality have been common to most regions of America during the course of national development, southeastern Louisiana has endured more than its fair share. Fierce tribal warfare between the indigenous native peoples, specifically the Bayougoula and the Houma Indians, contributed to one of the most identifiable sites in Louisiana. Early French explorers reported of a "red stick," or *bâton rouge*, that traditionally served as the dividing line between the warring tribes. Moreover, the Florida Parishes are the only area of the state to have witnessed military operations in every major war occurring within the territory of the United States, with the exception of the French and Indian War, which involved little if any direct action in the Gulf South. Governor Bernardo de Gálvez's 1779 assault on the British outposts in West Florida constituted the only significant action occurring in the state during the course of the American Revolution. Likewise, the naval engagements on lakes Borgne and Pontchartrain as well as Andrew Jackson's logistical operations on the north shore of the lakes kept the region in the thick of the local action during the War of 1812, while the violent destruction occasioned by the Civil War ensured the region's place as a sustained victim of the costs of warfare.[9]

The Florida Parishes have experienced a remarkably turbulent pattern of development that necessarily contributed to a legacy of instability and exceptional violence in the area. Each of the four governing powers, including the Americans, provided liberal land grants to their adherents and supporters that often conflicted with previously established tracts, furthering suspicion and mistrust among neighbors. The devastating consequences of the Civil War and a brutal Reconstruction period contributed to unprecedented levels of violence in the late nineteenth and early twentieth centuries that earned for the region the reputation as a dark and bloody ground. Exploiting an ineffective legal system functioning amid a population committed to a vision of individual rights that endorsed violent resolution of interpersonal conflict, lawless elements threatened the triumph of utter chaos. From the close of Reconstruction through the advent of World War II the region consistently sustained some of the highest rural homicide rates in the nation, an ominous distinction that remains evident even into the present.[10] Throughout the course of regional development, peace has proven an elusive dream.

The challenges of history have in no way dampened the prevailing enthusiasm for life typically assigned all residents of the Bayou State. The cultural color and seemingly carefree abandon that characterize Louisiana in the popular imagination can be found in varying degrees across the state, including the Florida Parishes. The region nonetheless maintains a distinct identity that may be among the most peculiar in the nation. As an acknowledgment of the territory's special status, in September 2000, on the eve of the Louisiana Purchase bicentennial, some of the foremost researchers identified with the area came together at Southeastern Louisiana University to explore and celebrate the region's singular identity. The fifteen presentations included in the conference, appropriately titled "Louisiana's Florida Parishes: Continuity and Change," were designed not only to fill gaps in the historical record but also to highlight the circumstances of life common to the area that helped shape its traditions and character.

This book is a result of that conference. The first section, "A Convoluted Colonial Identity," concentrates on the curious cycle of colonial governance that characterized the region in the wake of the European intrusion. In the first essay, Charles Elliott examines an issue central to development during the French period. Those familiar with settlement patterns in early America recognize the self-imposed limitations that inhibited French colonization efforts. Specifically, the French demand that all colonists adhere strictly to Catholicism contributed to markedly depressed population statistics as French settlers confronted the challenge posed by growing numbers of English colonists who enjoyed that nation's more liberal emigration policy. As a result of the population imbalance, the French sought to augment their numbers through alliances with the native population. In the first geopolitical examination of the *petites nations*, the indigenous peoples of the Florida Parishes, Elliott demonstrates that the native tribes' association with the French led to their utter destruction, a development that provided unexpected benefits for their European benefactors. With the territory cleared of the *petites nations*, the far more numerous Tunica and Choctaw migrated to the region, establishing a more formidable buffer to protect French New Orleans from attack by the fierce, English-allied Chickasaw and Natchez.

In the end, the protection native alliances afforded the French could not save them from their old nemesis, Great Britain. The enormity of the British victory over France and its ally Spain in the French and Indian War produced extensive consequences for North America in general and the Florida Parishes in particular. Determined to solidify control over their new territory, the British offered liberal land grants that serve as the focus of Robin Fabel's study highlighting England's brief tenure in southeastern Louisiana. Fabel describes a land speculation scheme that led dozens of people, in what may be characterized as "irrational exuberance," to apply for thousands of acres in what was then the Wild West of frontier environs. Fueled in the belief that indigo and furs, brought to market over a series of nonexistent clear flowing streams, would reap vast profits for the speculators, the plan ultimately proved little more than another "bayou bubble." No vast profits were realized, and the paucity of British loyalists in the area made the region ripe for conquest from an aggressive neighbor.

Britain's troubles in North America were not limited to her new holdings in the Gulf South. With the outbreak of armed revolution in the British colonies along the Atlantic seaboard, Spanish governor Bernardo de Gálvez directed a military offensive from New Orleans that overwhelmed the British in West Florida, initiating the third, and final, colonial period in the territory. In the last selection of part I, Gilbert Din examines the circumstances afforded the involuntary labor force during the Spanish period. Regardless of who served as the governing power, slavery remained a cornerstone of the economy. In analyzing the practice during the Spanish period, Din discovers a general continuity in the treatment of slaves under the various powers, although he suggests that in many regards Spanish law remained milder than that of the French or British. Din concludes that the slave system reflected a peculiar attribute of Spanish governance—namely, a consistent determination to secure reconciliation with the different factions under its authority, from ruling masters to oppressed slaves.

The essays included in part II, "Confronting the Challenge of America," concentrate on some of the most dramatic changes and events that characterized the region during its first century of association with the United States. Following the absorption of the West Florida republic by the young American nation in 1810, the residents struggled with their newfound identity. During the course of the nineteenth century representatives of the territory twice petitioned to be detached from Louisiana and made a part of Mississippi. Yet shared misfortune often makes for newfound friends. The severity of the challenges that confronted Louisiana during the next half century, and the suffering they produced, served to assuage problems of identity and encourage popular affection for the Bayou State among the residents.[11]

If the critical eye discerns an omission of notable consequence in this compilation, it likely centers on the antebellum period. None of the included essays highlights the pattern of social, economic, and political development that characterized the antebellum Florida Parishes. The social and cultural transformation of the region that accompanied the emergence of the cotton economy and its concomitant, the slave system, contributed to a bifurcation of the territory that institutionalized distinctions separating the plantation parishes along the Mississippi from those in the eastern piney woods. Such distinctions undergirded the cultural and political tensions that separated the plain folk from the planters in each area, furthering the region's peculiar identity. Far from an omission of choice, the absence of an antebellum essay instead reveals fertile ground for further research. With the exception of my own previously published surveys of the antebellum Florida Parishes, little scholarship has centered exclusively on the region's peculiar relationship with the state and nation during the antebellum period.[12]

The region did nonetheless enjoy a relatively prosperous antebellum period despite some ever-present turbulence. Andrew Jackson's defense of southeastern Louisiana during the War of 1812 served as one of the first major steps in the region's cautious move toward identification with both Louisiana and the United States. Jackson's advance across the Florida Parishes on the way to New Orleans secured the construction of a new route of market access along the Jackson Military Road, the emergence of a new term in the regional nomenclature—that is, "Free Jack," used to describe the slaves freed by Jackson in return for assistance in cutting the roadway—and some recruits for the American cause. Perhaps most significant, as outlined by Gene Smith, the American decision to defend New Orleans resulted in the only naval battle of significance to occur in the lakes that separate the Florida Parishes from the Isle of Orleans. Focusing on the role of the American naval commander, Thomas ap Catesby Jones, Smith demonstrates that though seldom seriously treated by historians, the fighting in the lakes proved a critical component of America's greatest victory during the war.

Just as the War of 1812 helped initiate integration of the region with the state and nation, the outbreak of hostilities during the Civil War furthered identification with Louisiana and the South. In the second essay in this section, my own research reveals the utter catastrophe the war occasioned in southeastern Louisiana. With regular Confederate forces unable to effectively defend the region, and Union troops determined to subjugate the area at all costs, by the final year of the fighting a vicious war of sustained brutality and destruction had emerged, pitting the increasingly aggressive Federals against determined bands of guerrillas. The results provide a microcosm for examining the long-debated potential Confederates may have enjoyed from reliance on guerrilla operations, rather than regular tactics, in their effort to secure independence.

The destruction occasioned by the Civil War and the political climate that prevailed in its wake contributed to yet another catastrophe in the Florida Parishes. The oft-quoted remark attributed to George C. Wallace, that no Marshall Plan was enacted to assist the defeated South, suggests the difficulty the residents of the region encountered in their efforts to recover from war and Reconstruction. In his contribution, Richard Kilbourne demonstrates that an enduring crisis in agricultural credit rendered recovery virtually impossible for most. Like much of the rest of the South, scores of common people, black and white, were forced into the vicious cycle of debt commonly known as sharecropping. Yet unlike in some other regions of the South, Kilbourne argues, the prevailing circumstances in the Florida Parishes ensured that financial hardship knew no parameters of class, subjecting both the elite and the impoverished to an uncertain future of economic woes.

Among the Florida Parishes' natural resources that could be tapped to stimulate economic revival during the late nineteenth and early twentieth centuries were its vast stands of virgin longleaf pine. As stands of timber were depleted in the northeast, southern pines assumed an intensified significance that attracted the attention of northern firms as well as a fledgling local industry. In the final selection of part II, Latimore Smith details the complete destruction of the once ubiquitous regional pine trees. According to Smith, poorly coordinated harvesting and a complete absence of conservation or reforestation efforts ensured dramatic consequences for the forests and their inhabitants. Wealth derived from the timber flowed out of the region into the hands of those who cared little about the ultimate consequences of the forest's destruction. When conservationists finally did encourage reforestation, they suggested, not the indigenous trees, but a new, more rapidly maturing variety that forever altered the delicate natural balance of the regional forests. Smith reminds us that however well-intended, our actions can provoke enduring repercussions that command devastating ecological consequences.

Reconciling the legacies of the past with the values of the present has proven a continuing challenge for many southerners, and the residents of the Florida Parishes are no exception. Identifying a means to harmonize the demands of progress with the need for an improving quality of life remains central to current regional planning as well. The essays included in the final section, "Challenges Less Spoken," concentrate primarily on the painful process of racial accommodation and the emerging controversy between industrial development and environmental quality.

In the first selection, Bill Wyche examines the role and relevance of black laborers in the crucial lumber industry. In the first decades of the twentieth century, many areas of the South experienced significant black emigration as the descendants of the region's previously enslaved population sought a better life in the North. Long accustomed to life as second-class citizens, many blacks fled in the face of overt racial oppression and extreme poverty occasioned by the institutionalized belief that certain jobs should be reserved for whites only. While such circumstances may have been the norm across the South, Wyche argues that it was not the case in Washington Parish. Not only did Washington Parish witness a significant increase in black residents in response to the demands of the timber industry, but perhaps most unusual, Wyche identifies a remarkable willingness to cooperate among black and white workers that challenges the prevailing premise of incompatibility between racially diverse labor forces in the South.

Wyche's survey of timber laborers may reveal the existence of a stream of opportunity, as well as cooperation, between whites and blacks in Washington Parish. Despite the presence of such possibilities, the second essay in part III cautions us to avoid the temptation to assign Washington Parish a distinctive identity in contrast to conditions prevailing across the South. Adam Fairclough's study of black historian and activist Horace Mann Bond reveals that the dark side of life in the South remained abundantly evident in the same Washington Parish, albeit with some curious twists.

The violent suppression of an indigenous labor movement and the brutal lynching of a young black man did color Bond's understanding of the region, yet it was the absence of racial tension that most impressed him. Perhaps most significant, Fairclough demonstrates that Bond himself considered the shared ancestry of many local whites and blacks as a direct contributor to the prevailing racial peace. In those portions of the parish where miscegenation appeared highest, racial animosity proved remarkably low. Ultimately, Fairclough employs the example of Washington Parish to remind us that just as current social sensitivities discourage generalizing about peoples and places, serious scholars should embrace the same consideration in their studies of specific regions, as well as the wider South.

The challenges that continue to confront the South are many. One of the most poignant, if not passionate, to recently emerge in the Florida Parishes involves the difficult process of balancing economic growth with an improving quality of life. In the final selection, Paul Templet addresses the dispute centered on industrial development versus a healthy environment. For more than a generation the champions of industry have argued that environmental restrictions make for bad business. Not so, says Templet. Relying on impressive statistics derived from recent analysis, as well as from his personal tenure as the director of the Louisiana Department of Environmental Quality, Templet disputes the rhetoric of those in opposition to environmental regulations, arguing instead that a clean environment actually encourages economic development. As do all areas of the country, Louisiana needs more jobs, and in the southeastern region of the state, chemical and other industries have proven a bulwark of employment opportunities. Yet Templet's analysis suggests even greater opportunity in a diversified economy, one that accommodates the needs of industry while also expecting that they too should contribute to the emergence of an economically diverse, ecologically healthy, and increasingly productive Louisiana.

The essays included in this volume are in no sense designed to serve as a definitive statement of regional historical development. Instead, they serve to encourage the emergence of a new era in the study of Louisiana and, perhaps, the wider South, one that abandons generalizations and stereotypes through inclusiveness and a broader awareness of diversity. A primary strength of local history is that it permits the revelation of the previously less considered. The essays included in this survey suggest the relevance of subregional studies. We hope they will provide a starting point for further research that abandons preconceptions in celebration of our differences.

NOTES

1. For a detailed account of Iberville's mandate and explorations, see Richebourg Gaillard McWilliams, ed., *Iberville's Gulf Journals* (Tuscaloosa: University of Alabama Press, 1981).

2. Ibid., 80, 112–13.

3. Although the numbers pale in comparison to the volumes examining some other regions of the state, numerous primary-researched studies highlighting the history of the Florida Parishes, published by major academic presses or journals, remain available. Among the most useful are: Edward Bacon, *Among the Cotton Thieves* (Detroit: The Free Press, 1867); John V. Baiamonte, *Spirit of Vengeance: Nativism and Louisiana Justice, 1921–24* (Baton Rouge: Louisiana State University Press, 1986); Edwin C. Bearss, "The Battle of Baton Rouge," *Louisiana History* 3, no. 1 (1962): 77–128; Powell A. Casey, "Military Roads in the Florida Parishes of Louisiana," *Louisiana History* 15, no. 3 (1974): 229–42; Edwin A. Davis, ed., *Plantation Life in the Florida Parishes, 1836–1846: As Reflected in the Diary of Bennet H. Barrow* (New York: Columbia University Press, 1943); Lawrence Estaville Jr., "A Strategic Railroad: The New Orleans, Jackson, and Great Northern in the Civil War," *Louisiana History* 14, no. 2 (1973): 117–36; Albert W. Haarman, "The Spanish Conquest of British West Florida, 1779–81," *Florida Historical Quarterly* 39, no. 2 (1960): 107–34; Samuel C. Hyde Jr., *Pistols and Politics: The Dilemma of Democracy in Louisiana's Florida Parishes, 1810–1899* (Baton Rouge: Louisiana State University Press, 1996); Samuel C. Hyde Jr., "Mechanisms of Planter Power in Eastern Louisiana's Piney Woods," *Louisiana History* 39, no. 1 (1998): 19–44; Samuel C. Hyde Jr., "Bushwhacking and Barnburning: Civil War Operations and the Florida Parishes Tradition of Violence," *Louisiana History* 36, no. 2 (1995): 171–86; William E. Perrin Jr., "Civil War Operations in and around Ponchatoula, Louisiana," *Louisiana History* 12, no. 2 (1971): 123–36; Amy Quick, "The History of Bogalusa: The 'Magic City' of Louisiana," *Louisiana Historical Quarterly* 29, nos. 1, 2 (1946): 73–201; Milton Rickels, "Thomas Bangs Thorpe in the Felicianas, 1836–1842," *Louisiana Historical Quarterly* 39, no. 2 (1956): 169–97; F. Jay Taylor, ed., *Reluctant Rebel: The Secret Diary of Robert Patrick, 1861–1865* (Baton Rouge: Louisiana State University Press, 1959); E. Russ Williams Jr., "Slave Patrol Ordinances of St. Tammany Parish, Louisiana, 1835–1838," *Louisiana History* 13, no. 4 (1972): 399–412. Many general studies of Louisiana include substantive coverage of the Florida Parishes. See Adam Fairclough, *Race and Democracy: The Civil Rights Struggle in Louisiana, 1915–1972* (Athens: University of Georgia Press, 1995); William Ivy Hair, *Bourbonism and Agrarian Protest: Louisiana Politics, 1877–1900* (Baton Rouge: Louisiana State University Press, 1969); George Rable, *But There Was No Peace: Violence and Reconstruction Politics* (Baton Rouge: Louisiana State University Press, 1978); Joe Gray Taylor, *Louisiana Reconstructed, 1863–1877* (Baton Rouge: Louisiana State University Press, 1974). For a comprehensive bibliography of other studies, including folklife and other unpublished or self-published studies highlighting the region until 1983, see C. Howard Nich-

ols, *Louisiana's Florida Parishes: A Bibliography* (Hammond, La.: Center for Regional Studies, 1983).

4. Among the most useful comprehensive surveys of Louisiana history are: François Marquis de Barbe-Marbois, *History of Louisiana, Particularly of the Cession of that Colony to the United States of America* (Baton Rouge: Louisiana Bicentennial Commission in cooperation with Louisiana State University Press, 1977); Henry E. Chambers, *A History of Louisiana: Wilderness, Colony, Province, Territory, State, People* (New York: American Historical Society, 1925); Edwin A. Davis, *Louisiana: A Narrative History* (Baton Rouge: Claitor's, 1976); Charles L. Dufour, *Ten Flags in the Wind* (New York: Harper and Row, 1967); Alcée Fortier, *A History of Louisiana* (New York: Exposition Press, 1949); Charles Gayarré, *History of Louisiana* (New Orleans: Pelican, 1965); Grace King, *History of Louisiana* (New Orleans: F. F. Hansell, 1903); François-Xavier Martin, *The History of Louisiana* (Gretna, La.: Pelican, 1963); Garnie W. McGinty, *The History of Louisiana* (Baton Rouge: Louisiana Bicentennial Commission in cooperation with Louisiana State University Press, 1975); Harriet Magruder, *A History of Louisiana* (Boston: D. C. Heath, 1909); Bennett H. Wall, ed., *Louisiana: A History*, 3rd ed. (Wheeling, Ill.: Harlan Davidson, 1997).

5. Dufour, *Ten Flags in the Wind*. The British Union Jack and the Lone Star Flag of the West Florida Republic flew exclusively over the Florida Parishes.

6. Wall, *Louisiana*, 3.

7. John Baiamonte Jr., *Immigrants in Rural America: A Study of the Italians of Tangipahoa Parish, Louisiana* (New York: Garland, 1990); Victoria Mocsary, *Arphadon: The Largest Rural Hungarian Settlement in the United States* (Hammond, La.: Center for Regional Studies, 1990); Hyde, *Pistols and Politics*, 4–5, 18–19.

8. Stanley Arthur, *The Story of the West Florida Rebellion* (Baton Rouge: Claitor's, 1975); Isaac Cox, *The West Florida Controversy: A Study in American Diplomacy* (Baltimore: Johns Hopkins Press, 1918); Hyde, *Pistols and Politics*, 20–21.

9. Paul du Ru, *Journal of Paul du Ru (February 1 to May 8, 1700): Missionary Priest to Louisiana* (Chicago: Caxton Club, 1934), 7; Charles Elliott, "Bienville's English Turn Incident: Anecdotes Influencing History," *Gulf South Historical Review* 14 (spring 1999): 6–32; Hyde, *Pistols and Politics*, 19, 102–38; John D. Winters, *The Civil War in Louisiana* (Baton Rouge: Louisiana State University Press, 1963).

10. Hyde, *Pistols and Politics*, 102–262; Taylor, *Louisiana Reconstructed*, 114–313; William B. Bankston and David H. Allen, "Rural Social Areas and Patterns of Homicide: An Analysis of Lethal Violence in Louisiana," *Rural Sociology* 45 (1987): 223–37.

11. "Report of the Select Committee Making an Apportionment of Representation in the House of Representatives," *Louisiana House Journal*, 2nd sess., 1833, 17–18; *Clinton (La.) Patriot-Democrat*, August 28, 1880; *Amite City Democrat*, April 1, 1876; Hyde, *Pistols and Politics*, 21, 185.

12. For a discussion of antebellum development see Hyde, *Pistols and Politics*, 17–91; Hyde, "Mechanisms of Planter Power in Eastern Louisiana's Piney Woods," 19–44.

I | A CONVOLUTED COLONIAL IDENTITY

1

A GEOGRAPHY OF POWER

French and Indian Alliances on the Southeast Louisiana Frontier

CHARLES N. ELLIOTT

The French and Indian presence in those portions of southeast Louisiana north of Lake Pontchartrain, south of the thirty-first degree north latitude, east of the Mississippi, and west of the Pearl River remains the most understudied aspect of a generally neglected region. A historiographical survey reveals local aficionados dismissing and academic specialists overlooking the history of the Florida Parishes before 1763. Admittedly, the term *Florida Parishes* evolves from the British, Spanish, and American military occupations of 1764, 1779, and 1810 respectively and does not officially apply before those dates, but the region's critical role in establishing and maintaining French colonial Louisiana merits greater consideration and interpretation.

Beginning in 1699, the Florida Parishes assumed a position of geographical relevance and political importance by offering control of alternative backwater approaches to the Mississippi River from the Gulf of Mexico. When the first French regime in Louisiana ended with the secret Treaty of Fontainebleau of 1762 and the surrender Treaty of Paris of 1763, the region was firmly linked to New Orleans and possessed a geopolitical significance surviving intact under shifting colonial and territorial allegiances well into American statehood. These continual national conflicts over the Florida Parishes' strategic location, which contributed to the region's peculiar culture of violence, began with the initial French exploration. In the formative eight-year period from Iberville's arrival in 1699 to his departure in 1706, France formed Louisiana's Florida Parishes into a geography of power capable of protecting crucial transportation routes and key portages through a system of political alliances with mutually antagonistic resident and transient Indian nations. While these diplomatic relationships at first appeared beneficial and helped create a defensive frontier between the Louisiana colony, strategically located Native American allies, and their common enemies, the French presence soon proved lethal and the small Indian republics original to the Florida Parishes quickly disappeared from the region and from history.

Extensive remains of shell middens and earth mounds indicate powerful and prosperous Native American polities occupied the Florida Parishes for more than 3,000 years before the French arrived in Louisiana. Certain archaeological excavations paralleling the region's southern boundary reveal local prehistoric cultures evolved primarily along the rivers and lakes connecting the Mississippi River to the Gulf Coast. The Bayou Jasemine site in lower Tangipahoa Parish near the western end of Lake Pontchartrain reflects the simple itinerant hunting, gathering, and agriculture-less lifestyle of early Indians in the Pontchartrain Basin from around 1500 B.C. upwards. From 600 B.C. to A.D. 200 the appearance of small scattered settlements of the Tchefuncte Culture, named for sites on the north shore of Lake Pontchartrain inside Tchefuncte (present-day Fontainebleau) State Park, evidences an intensive harvesting of brackish-water clams and a lavish pottery construction as well as squash and gourd cultivation. Two now-destroyed shell middens within the park, one measuring 100 x 250 feet and the other 100 x 150 feet, contained more than 50,000 pieces of the distinctive Tchefuncte footed-pottery and 43 sets of human remains. At the Kleinpeter site, currently on the grounds of the Country Club of Louisiana in southwestern East Baton Rouge Parish and slightly above the intersection of Bayou Fountain, Bayou Manchac, and Alligator Bayou, a Tchefuncte occupation began about 250 B.C., but between A.D. 400 and 1100 the Coles Creek Culture introduced the bow and arrow and flat-topped pyramidal temple mounds. By 1500, the location featured six sizable earthen mounds, four of which were arranged in the cardinal directions and enclosed a central plaza covering 14,000 square feet.[1]

The development of this Florida Parishes ceremonial complex within the dynamically evolving Mississippian Culture remains conjectural. Beginning around A.D. 700 to 900 in the area along the river between the modern-day cities of St. Louis and Vicksburg, the Mississippian Tradition came to represent the highest prehistoric cultural achievement in North America. By A.D. 1200, the simultaneous introduction of beans and the new variety of eastern flint corn (which thrived in the moist soils and relatively cool climate of the Southeast) created greater, more dependable agricultural yields and caused a population explosion. Increased populations resulted in additional farming communities, larger and more distinctive ceremonial centers with pyramidal mounds supporting both temples and the houses of secular elites, and territorial expansion of the successful Mississippian system and its aggressive chiefdoms. An established regional center at the Kleinpeter site in southeastern Louisiana may have matured as Mississippian developments spread southward from the central Mississippi Valley or entered the lower Mississippi Valley from the Gulf Coast. If the location twenty-five miles to the east near Ponchatoula in Tangipahoa Parish of the contemporary but smaller Hoover site, consisting of four compass-directed platform mounds surrounding a central plaza, implies cultural influences flowing along a shared Bayou Manchac–Amite River waterway, the arrangement of the largest mound on the western side of the Kleinpeter plaza displays a clearly Mississippian characteristic with no precedent from earlier cultural periods. Given its size, proximity to the Mississippi River, and ease of connection to the Gulf Coast along the watery southern edge of the Florida Parishes, the Kleinpeter site in all probability represents an important regional center of southeastern Louisiana and the greater Mississippian Culture.[2]

The impressive scale of the Kleinpeter and Hoover sites strongly argues for a large prehistoric Indian population. The region's geography in the early sixteenth century featured numerous outlying settlements focused on intensive and extensive corn-growing with natives seasonally assembling for religious instruction and celebration in the plazas before the temple mounds; but by 1699 southeast Louisiana presented a dramatically altered landscape. Across the American South from the mid-sixteenth century onward, the flourishing Mississippian chiefdoms, where hereditary elites ruled densely populated regions of ceremonial centers and productive cornlands, began to dissolve or disperse in the wake of Hernando de Soto's four-thousand-mile march of death and destruction. If Indians in the Florida Parishes avoided direct, ruinous encounters with *conquistadores,* the indirect effects of the Spanish expeditions still proved catastrophic. Smallpox, measles, influenza, and other European-introduced diseases traveling along a complex southeastern trade network quickly and continually caused severe population losses, perhaps as high as 80 percent of an estimated 1.3 million southern Indians, and destroyed the social, political, and economic fabric of the autocratic chiefdoms. True to the larger pattern, both the Hoover and Kleinpeter sites appear to have been vacant in the period following the brief campaigns through Louisiana by de Soto and his successor Luis de Moscoso. After this Native American holocaust, remnant peoples moved, regrouped, and reorganized into smaller, more egalitarian tribes hunting, farming, and gathering on the abandoned ceremonial mounds and grown-over Mississippian oldfields.³

Migrating descendants of these southeastern survivors became the *petites nations* of French colonial Louisiana's Florida Parishes and superimposed their new tribal systems on a diverse environment. While the region's upper piney woods and lower cypress swamps awaited future harvesting, numerous southern-flowing, creek-fed rivers, "narrow but deep, swift and clear . . . running over a bed of sand and pebbles," produced fresh, clean water, provided cherty gravel for Stone Age tools and weapons, and created optimum fishing conditions where they emptied into a series of shallow lakes. Creek and river bottoms proved fertile enough for the Indians' communal cornfields and vegetable patches and extensive enough to supply ample white-tailed deer and other wild game for communal cooking fires. These natural opportunities combined with navigable waterways, convenient portages linking those waterways, and a complementary system of trails connecting the region with the Gulf Coast to mandate Native American settlement patterns in the Florida Parishes before 1699.⁴

A multitude of place-names commemorates a widespread Indian heritage from Chubby Bottoms down to Ponchatoula and from Bogalusa across to Baton Rouge, but the historical record identifies and locates several small, yet distinct, late-seventeenth-century resident nations. Between 600 and 700 Acollapissas, scattered over six villages eleven miles above the mouth of the Pearl River, settled the north shore of Okwa-ta, later called Lake Pontchartrain, in the vicinity of modern Slidell. In a seventh, related village, smaller numbers of Tangipahoas lived along their namesake river and astride three Indian trails connecting the upper Florida Parishes to the lakefront west of Madisonville. Still farther west, fewer than 500 Quinipissas-Mugalashas, probable offshoots of the Acollapissas, occupied lands generally on and above the Lake Maurepas–Amite River–Bayou Manchac waterway but freely intermixed with an equal number of Bayougoulas living below. Around 1,000 Houmas controlled the east bank of the Mississippi above Bayou Manchac's natural boundary, up past the modern artificial border at the thirty-first degree north latitude, and along the western edge of Wilkinson County, Mississippi. Two river landings, one above and one below a great meander near the intersection of the Red River, led in-country to their main villages near the present site of Angola State Penitentiary in the far northwest corner of the Florida Parishes.⁵

The region's 3,000 or so Indians, sparsely inhabiting nearly 5,000 square miles of swamps, fields, and forests, huddled under the neighboring territories of three larger Native American nations. Immediately to the northwest, 4,000 Natchez, formidable holdovers from an earlier Mississippian culture, dominated the east bank of the Mississippi River near the modern city bearing their name. North of the Florida Parishes and the Natchez, 2,000 Tunicas occupied the south side of the lower Yazoo River above present-day Vicksburg. To the northeast, 20,000 Choctaws occupied south central Mississippi and farmed the terraces of streams flowing into the upper Pearl, Tombigbee, and Chickasawhay Rivers. As the third largest, most densely populated, and only corn-surplus-producing Indian nation in the South, the Choctaws undeniably exerted considerable regional influences. Their sacred Nanih Waiya, once a prominent temple-mound of a particularly important Mississippian chiefdom, remained the spiritual center of the Choctaw universe and served as the source of the southward-flowing Pearl River. Since all Native American place-names and every resident nation's proper name in the Florida Parishes derive from words or phrases in the academically designated Longfellow dialect of the Choctaw language, a dialect spoken in the western part of the Choctaw republic, evidence suggests cultural and possible political associations with this *grand nation*.[6]

Beyond linguistics, Florida Parishes Indians shared values common to the Native American South. All remained a hunting, fishing, gathering, and farming people, tracing descent from the mother's bloodline and dividing labor along strict gender lines. Women managed the farmlands and raised the principal crops of corn, beans, and squash while foraging for a wide variety of supplemental wild plants. Men, clearing the fields the women farmed, hunted the forests for game. By definition "brave," Indian men lived a life determined primarily by the ethics of the warpath. Perpetual conflict formed their reality and created a Native American culture of violence where Indians "fought to gain prestige and power, to demonstrate their courage and martial skills, to resist aggression, to dominate weaker neighbors, to exhort tribute, to gain hunting territory and fishing rights, to control trade, and to avenge real or imagined wrongs."[7]

Certain events occurring slightly before and after 1699 indicate the *petites nations* of southeast Louisiana practiced or endured endemic violence, openly pursuing policies and secretly harboring agendas frequently hostile toward and often ruinous to their mutually antagonistic neighbors. In the 1680s, Tangipahoas, occupying a small satellite village on the far western end of the great curve of Acollapissa settlements along the north shores of

Lake Pontchartrain and Lake Maurepas between the Pearl and Mississippi Rivers, intruded on Houma hunting territories and were killed or carried off as prisoners by that larger tribe. Ten years later and in the same general area, the Quinipissas-Mugalashas vanished from history when Bayougoulas attacked, exterminated the men, and captured the majority of the women and children.[8]

If a tradition of violence persisted, the focus of this regional warfare apparently began to change around 1699 based on events begun in New France some thirty years earlier. With wide-brimmed felt hats the fashion of the seventeenth century, high quality Canadian beaver pelts commanded higher prices than the inferior and diminishing European variety, fueling a lucrative luxury trade and sparking penetration into the interior of the North American continent. Throughout the 1670s and 1680s, René Robert Cavalier de La Salle, assisted by his able lieutenant, Henri de Tonti, expanded the beaver market by establishing forts and trading posts in the Great Lakes region. Cautioning that English enemies were already pressing up from New England and down from Hudson Bay, he continually called attention to the necessity of not letting rival nations outmaneuver France and inevitably bring about the downfall of the colony. By 1682, La Salle explored and descended the Mississippi to its mouth, taking ceremonial possession of "this country of Louisiana, the seas, harbors, ports, bays, adjacent straits, and all the nations, people, provinces, cities, towns, villages, mines, minerals, fisheries, streams and rivers comprised in the extent of said Louisiana.... along the River Colbert, or Mississippi, and rivers which discharge themselves therein ... as far as ... the ... Gulf of Mexico."[9]

While La Salle's discovery allowed him to claim vast midcontinental territories for Louis XIV, it also offered an alternative warm-water route to supplement Canada's sole artery, the St. Lawrence River, vulnerable year-round and icebound in winter, and provided new military approaches flanking Spanish America. La Salle's expedition also revealed French America's grave strategic weakness: Trade and warships, including those of rival powers, could move both up and down the Mississippi, threatening New France and diverting the flow of furs away from Canada and the French treasury. By 1688, a second expedition, ordered to find the mouth of the river from the Gulf and construct there a fortified settlement, dissolved in failure. The colony was mislocated near Matagorda Bay, La Salle murdered in the East Texas hinterland, and his colonists abandoned along the Texas coast.[10]

For the next ten years, Louis XIV's European concerns focused royal attention away from Louisiana until the Peace of Ryswick allowed the king the leisure to consider reestablishing a military colony and the publication of English editions of certain La Salle journals forced the king to consider protecting La Salle's legacy. In 1698, Dr. Daniel Coxe, holder of the largest grant of land in America ever given by the English crown to a private individual, launched a diverse program to promote and develop his colonial property, a vast wilderness called *Carolana*, which by the grace of royal favor ran westward from behind the Carolina coast across the entire continent to the Pacific Ocean. He issued revised accounts of La Salle's first expedition to induce popular and financial enthusiasm for colonizing his grant and in October dispatched two small brigantines under the command of Captain William Bond on a preliminary survey of the region from the Gulf. Bond wintered at Charles Town and, by May 1699, sailed off in the twelve-gun *Carolina Galley* for the Mississippi after arranging to meet deep-country English and renegade French fur-traders at the Chickasaw Bluffs, a landing on the river near present-day Memphis where the Chickasaw Indians maintained a trail to their towns at Tupelo in northwest Mississippi.[11]

La Salle's ceremonial possession of Louisiana and Coxe's land-grant claims to Carolana threatened the security of Spain's Mexican silver mines and colonial treasure fleets, but imperial economy and more pressing commitments delayed action until rumors of an English expedition to the Mississippi made occupation a priority. Leaving Veracruz the same month Bond left England, a Spanish expedition naturally arrived in the Southeast first, winning the race to the Gulf, but not to the river. In November 1698, three hundred soldiers, slaves, and convicts under the command of naval officer Andres de Arriola began constructing a fort at Pensacola, the finest deep-water bay in the Gulf South, from which Spanish officials hoped to control the northern Gulf Coast and any approaches to the mouth of the Mississippi River.[12]

French authorities, acutely aware of the dangers of English and Spanish expeditions to the Gulf, responded by choosing Pierre LeMoyne, sieur d'Iberville to command a simultaneous expedition to secure La Salle's achievement. The Ministry of the Marine picked the thirty-eight-year-old Canadian naval captain because of his qualities as a navigator, his experience in the wilderness and with the Indians, and his splendid military reputation. For more than ten years, the uncommonly brave and utterly ruthless Iberville won virtually every battle he fought on land and sea against the English.[13] On 23 July 1698, he was instructed to rediscover the Mississippi, establish a fort at its mouth to "prevent other nations from entering the river," and make a careful geographical survey of Louisiana.[14] By late October 1698, Iberville's small fleet of the thirty-gun frigates *Badine* and *Marin* accompanied by two sail- and oar-powered *traversiers,* the coastal longboats *Precieux* and *Biscayenne,* left Brest for Cap François on the northern coast of Santo Domingo, where he enlisted a pilot familiar with Caribbean waters but unfamiliar with the location of the Mississippi River. Sailing away on New Year's Eve, the expedition rounded the western tip of Cuba and entered the northeastern Gulf of Mexico.[15] Encountering their Spanish rivals at Pensacola in late January 1699, the French evasively hid their true intentions behind diplomatic correctness and continued along the coast in search of a suitable harbor.[16] Using Spanish maps, Iberville located Mobile Bay and carefully examined an Alabama river he thought might possibly be a southern branch of the Mississippi. Sailing westward along the southern shore of the Iberville-named Massacre Island, the French expedition carefully tested the passages between several coastal islands and anchored within the shelter of aptly named Ship Island. Landing at Biloxi Bay on 13 February, Iberville began exploring the mainland, looking for informative natives and "making ready to ... discover the Myssysypy."[17] Indians on the Gulf Coast approached warily, singing the calumet of peace for Iberville, accepting gifts, and exchanging visits.[18]

Here Iberville heard mention of the Chozeta, a powerful Gulf South nation soon considered "the key to this country."[19] On 16 February 1699 he first met Indians from Louisiana's Florida Parishes when "a chief of the Bayougoula with twenty-one of his men and some Mougoulascha, who ... live on the bank of the Myssysypy and, being on the hunt on this side, came on at the noise of the cannon to see who we were."[20] This face-to-face contact proved crucial for Iberville, since before constructing a fort at the mouth of the river as Louis XIV commanded he must of course find the right river. This was no easy task, as shown by La Salle's fatally misplaced colony and by Iberville's progressive examination of the Gulf Coast. Available maps remained problematical, and with no Frenchmen ever having seen the river from the Gulf, Iberville relied on earlier descriptions of the mouth and on assertions of a large distributary fork identifying the Mississippi in some published accounts of La Salle's voyages.[21] Amid elaborate Indian calumet ceremonies and generous French gifts of tobacco, pipes, axes, knives, blankets, shirts, and glass beads, southeast Louisiana's natives casually mentioned they routinely "went to the Myssysypy by way of rivers that connect with one another,"[22] comforting news for rediscovery but disturbing information which, if true, might compromise Iberville's instructions to fortify the mouth to "prevent other nations from entering the river." These Indians soon vanished, reportedly heading for home by their familiar western route, and missed a promised rendezvous with the French. Left on their own, Iberville, two officers, one priest, a pilot, and forty Canadian frontiersmen and Santo Domingan buccaneers shifted aboard the two *traversiers* and began blindly exploring southwest in search of the mouth of the river. Passing along the Mississippi, Chandeleur and Breton Sounds, the expedition negotiated a confusing maze of marshy coastal islands and endured ferociously bad weather. Unable to find an opening in the shoreline indicating the mouth of the missing Mississippi, Iberville finally headed for the open sea before perceiving what appeared to be a rocky coastal prominence.[23]

On 2 March 1699, the *traversiers,* each with a birchbark canoe in tow, reached and penetrated this immense, stony-looking barrier of hardened mud and petrified logs obstructing a breach in the Mississippi delta, eventually known as the North Pass, and crossed into a large, strong, and unidentified roux-brown river. Continually moving upstream, Iberville met a wandering party of Biloxis and Bayougoulas, who reported the Indians "whom I had seen at the . . . bay, near the ships, to whom I had given presents and a calumet of peace, were (already) back at the village of the Bayougoula,"[24] a clear implication of a faster backwater approach to the river. An obliging guide soon "pointed out to me the place through which the Indians make their portage to this river from the back of the bay where the ships are anchored. They drag their canoes over a rather good road, at which we found several pieces of baggage owned by men that were going there or were returning."[25] Here, at the future location of New Orleans, the riverbend formed a muddy crescent flanked by swampland with *Bayuk choupic* seeping from behind the natural levee to drain away into a brackish lagoon.[26] Skirting this first portage site, Iberville journeyed upriver from Indian village to Indian village, uncertain of his location and unable to verify his rediscovery of La Salle's Mississippi, since "I could not get from them any information about the fork mentioned in the relations."[27]

Passing the head of modern-day Bayou Lafourche, "a great arm of water coursing toward the southwest,"[28] the explorers received welcoming chants and howls at a Mugalasha village, but when "Monsieur d'Iberville asked them if the fork in the river was still far away; they gave us to understand that there was none."[29] The French pressed their inquiry with a mix of sign language and trade jargon augmented with crude map-making, but the Mugalashas "kept on arguing with us to the contrary, and asserted that there was no fork. Finally, tired of our insistence, they gave us to understand that there was one (fork) toward which they had once ascended, but that there was no depth of water there, and that they had to portage their canoes several times."[30] Since the presence at the village of the distinctive "calumet of peace" presented by the French to the Indians earlier at Biloxi seemed to prove they "went to the Mississippi by way of rivers that connected with one another," Iberville doubted Mugalasha veracity and continued upriver to a Bayougoula village where he wrote that "they pointed out to me the stream they take to go to . . . Bylocchy . . . and it flows to the sea, into the bay where the ships are. The Myssysypy flows into it. That is the only branch they are acquainted with."[31]

Noting this second portage site at *Bayuk imashank,* the future Bayou Manchac, the French rowed up past the Houmas' lower hunting grounds and stopped at their Istrouma settlement to see the *bâton rouge,* "a maypole with no limbs, painted red, several fish heads and bear bones being tied to it as a sacrifice,"[32] before continuing upriver to the main village. To arrive there, Iberville used and improved an Indian-advised shortcut called Pointe Coupée, which saved a day's journey but required clearing a 350-foot-long path through a 30-foot-high logjam obstructing a little bayou leading to the upper channel.[33] The most populous and powerful nation in southeast Louisiana, Houmas dominated two important Mississippi River portages. The small outpost at Baton Rouge hovered above Bayou Manchac, while the principal landing for their main village faced the westbank intersection of the Red River and provided a convenient passage into north central and northwest Louisiana. Since Iberville made no mention of the standard welcoming calumet ceremony at the Istrouma site, the lower deferential settlement probably consisted of simple palmetto-roofed huts, but the upper village with 140 cabins circling a 200-yard-wide communal square impressed the French.[34] Here in the vicinity of modern Angola, the Houmas welcomed the French with calumets, a feast, and a lively dance of nearly naked young Indian men and women.[35] Leagues away from his ships at Biloxi, short on supplies, unable to find the fork, and suspecting earlier recollections were a hoax, a discouraged Iberville, fearing "people would tell me in France that I had not gone up the Mississippi,"[36] ordered a retreat back down the river.[37]

Puzzled if Bayou Manchac, true to Mugalasha and Bayougoula consensus, might be an identifying southeastern fork, Iberville became curious of the bayou's condition and exact route to the Gulf of Mexico. Seeing no possibility of getting his longboats through the Indians' narrow and alleged alternate passage, Iberville ordered the expedition downriver and, with the two bark canoes, four Frenchmen, and a Mugalasha guide, traveled and explored the bayou himself. With the annual spring rise flushed by the snowmelt and heavy rains of the Upper Mississippi and its Ohio, Missouri, and Red River tributaries, the meandering lower Mississippi normally jumped the riverbank across from Manchac Point, cut a notch in the natural levee of the eastern bend, flooded the Manchac channel-head, and transformed the sluggish water into a rushing torrent, but in the last days of March 1699, the bayou remained a shallow, slow-flowing stream.[38] "The river or creek . . . no more than 8 to 10 yards wide, being full of uprooted trees, which obstruct it,"[39] forced the party to portage their canoes sixty times in the first two days.[40] Abandoned by his overworked guide (probably close to the present-day intersection of Bayou Manchac, Bayou Fountain, and Alligator Bayou), an exhausted Iberville nevertheless found himself charmed by his surroundings and made the encouraging prediction that "it would be easy to clear out this stream during low water and make it navigable all the way to the Myssysypy."[41]

Determined to "show the Indians that, without a guide, I go wherever I want to go,"[42] Iberville doggedly portaged and canoed through the obstructed bayou into the more user-friendly Riviere Amite and paddled successively over two lakes later named in honor of ministers of the marine, the Comte de Maurepas and the Comte de Pontchartrain. He "came to the way out of the (larger) lake, which is a pass one-eighth of a league wide, between islands of grass and meadows . . . and found a freshwater river 300 yards wide and 3 fathoms deep, which branches into two steams, one flowing into the main pass and the other running among islands."[43] Hugging the north shore slightly east of modern Slidell, Iberville kept the Pearl River on his left, exited by way of Lake Borgne, and arrived at Biloxi Bay to board his ships some two hours before the larger expedition returned via the mouth of the Mississippi. Surprisingly, the tardy arrivals brought with them written evidence verifying they had in fact found La Salle's river. Floating downstream, Iberville's younger brother, Jean Baptiste Lemoyne, sieur de Bienville, stopped at a Mugalasha-Bayougoula village and was presented with a hoarded letter for La Salle dated 20 April 1685 that the loyal Henri de Tonti left at the "Village of the Quynypyssa" when he canoed south searching in vain for the earlier misplaced colony. This letter and Iberville's explorations of the Bayou Manchac waterway, a seasonal distributary fork of the Mississippi, confirmed the river's identity and located La Salle's lost Louisiana.[44]

After rediscovering the Mississippi and after uncovering two alternative routes indirectly connecting the river and the Gulf, Iberville established French colonial Louisiana by first constructing a military post at Biloxi Bay. He certainly fulfilled Louis XIV's instruction to find the mouth of the Mississippi and began the assignment to make a careful geographical survey of Louisiana, but in building this small palisaded stronghold, Iberville clearly disobeyed the central element of the royal directive. Fort Maurepas, undeniably built on the Mississippi Gulf Coast and not on the Mississippi River or even in the Mississippi Valley, did not and could not "prevent other nations from entering the river" at its mouth, and Iberville essentially failed to fulfill the expedition's mission, unless the southeastern Louisiana portage sites, navigable confluences, and complementing trails are factored into his decision. French exploration for and of the Mississippi disclosed the risky conditions at the dangerously obstructed mouth and revealed a tediously long lower channel flowing with powerful currents. The discovery of two unforeseen, shorter, and commonly used entrees to the river at the southern boundary of the Florida Parishes qualified the relevance of any fort at the mouth of the river in protecting Canada and its fur trade. Bay-side Fort Maurepas, logically chosen for naval reasons and safely located within the shelter of coastal islands, effectively guarded the extreme eastern approaches of preferable ways from Pensacola, Mobile, and Biloxi to the Mississippi River. Fully securing those alternative backwater routes presented new challenges to French colonial administrators.[45]

In May 1699, Iberville sailed back to France without even sighting the feared English expedition or establishing any program or procedures to obstruct its anticipated upriver challenge and left his younger brother to continue the king's assignment to carefully explore Louisiana. Leaving Fort Maurepas, Bienville scouted eastward to examine Mobile Bay, investigated rumors of Pensacola's abandonment, canoed westward taking the shorter route through the Louisiana lakes, crossed easily at the lower portage, entered the river, and visited Indian villages. Mid-September and fifteen miles below Bayou Choupic, the nineteen-year-old Frenchman with five men in two birchbark canoes surprised and was surprised by the English expedition's twelve-gun *Carolina Galley* struggling upriver. With a vigorous *ruse de guerre,* Bienville adamantly claimed the Mississippi for France by right of La Salle's discovery and bluffed Captain Bond into halting, turning back, and exiting the river.[46] Before they grudgingly withdrew from the bend humorously known afterward as the English Turn, the crew voiced their intentions to "establish a settlement on the Mississippi" of "more than four hundred Protestant families then living in Carolina,"[47] and Bond questioned Bienville "at length about whether he had got any information about the English that were in the direction of the Chicachas and were to come and join him."[48] Inadvertently revealing additional overland and upriver dangers to French control of the Mississippi, the English threatened "to come back and settle this river . . . ; there was land for them and land for us, one on one side, and the other on the other side; . . . and it was as much theirs as ours."[49]

Returning from France in December 1699, Iberville brought the king's renewed instructions to locate a fort near the mouth of the river. Accordingly, he led an expedition to the *Bayuk choupic* portage (now renamed in honor of Bienville), traveled fifty miles downriver, and, by January 1700, constructed a small earthworks fort amid a grove of river birches. While cannons and soldiers of the *Compagnies franches de la Marine* at Fort de la Boulaye (sometimes called Fort du Mississipy) might effectively prevent further English advances from the mouth, the newly discovered alternative approaches remained unguarded and the recently revealed backcountry threats unchallenged. Since rival powers from Charles Town and Pensacola could tactically circumvent Boulaye by using the more convenient routes to the Mississippi from the east while other combinations upriver at Memphis and upcountry at Tupelo could flank Boulaye from the north, French colonial officers began crafting a geopolitical response to protect their presence on the Gulf and the river. Political alliances with certain strategically located Native Americans, particularly the *grand nation* of Choctaws and the *petites nations* occupying the Florida Parishes, might create the safety zone of a defendable southeastern frontier between France and her enemies and form a geography of power capable of establishing and maintaining the Louisiana colony.[50]

These chosen Indians may have appeared remarkably receptive to French overtures because of a dramatic increase in unprecedented endemic violence. Since 1690, South Carolina slavers and their Chickasaw allies repeatedly attacked the Choctaws, burned their towns and villages, and marched thousands to Charles Town as slaves.[51] By century's end, resident Florida Parishes nations suffered raids as well. In late May 1699, when Bienville

> embarked with a Bayougoula chief and twelve Canadians to visit the Colapissa nation, who lived on the right bank of lake Pontchartrain . . . he found . . . upwards of three hundred warriors, all armed and waiting to attack him. He kept a distance, and sent the Bayougula chief to hold a parlay with them, and to ascertain their object. He learned from them that two days before, two Englishmen, with two hundred Chicachas, had surprised their village, and carried off a number of their men, and they supposed . . . (Bienville) to be of the same nation. The Bayougoula chief having undeceived them, advised them to form an alliance. They accordingly laid down their arms and received M. de Bienville peaceably.[52]

Such unprovoked Anglo-Chickasaw incursions indicated a major shift in power across the Native American South involving a peculiar evolution in the Carolina-Carolana Indian trade. When Iberville planted his first settlements at Forts Maurepas and de la Boulaye, the English aggressively dominated Middle and Deep South commerce, and Frenchmen everywhere found evidence of the Charles Town traders. Although Georgia colonizer James Oglethorpe traced an English-Chickasaw economic connection back to 1680, the germ of that relationship arguably began a century and a half earlier. The general decline of the Mississippian chiefdoms in the period after initial contacts with Spanish explorers and conquistadors left a legacy of unusual demographic and ecological change in the Southeast. Severe population losses, while obviously reducing the numbers of sixteenth- and seventeenth-century Indian hunters and farmers, correspondingly caused an abandonment of the extensive cornfields required to support the estimated 1.3 million Mississippians. When these fallow fields were naturally covered over with second-growth vegetation, they provided the ideal browse for white-tailed deer. Drastically decreasing human competitors and predators, combining with dramatically increasing food supplies, launched an explosion in the southeastern deer population. By the end of the seventeenth century, a seemingly unlimited supply of deer merged with an English commercial interest in leather to create a lucrative trade in deerskins between the Carolana backcountry and Charles Town. Existent records show the annual export to England from Carolina averaged nearly 54,000 deerhides, which, even as late as the mid-eighteenth century, exceeded in value the combined returns from indigo, cattle, beef, pork, lumber, and naval stores. As the voracious demands of Charles Town leather markets thinned out the white-tailed deer in the Chickasaw lands of northern Mississippi and southwestern Tennessee, Chickasaw hunters, their wood bows and flint-tipped arrows replaced by English-supplied muskets, invaded the hunting grounds of their rival Indian neighbors. With English Carolina venturing deeper into indigo, rice, and tobacco production, planters increased their demands for Indian slaves until ongoing tribal animosities over hunting rights developed into a regional Indian war. Chickasaws, with English encouragement, expanded their poaching activities into massive, wide-ranging, and commercially based slave raids against Gulf South tribes armed only with native weapons.[53] The French arrival in Louisiana at this precise moment must have appeared as fortuitous to the hard-pressed Indians as the discovery of two backwater approaches to the lower river and a threatened upriver English colony in Chickasaw territory appeared challenging to the French. By mid-September 1700, when "a party of Chactas arrived at Biloxi to demand of the French some troops to assist them to fight the Chicachas,"[54] the survival instincts of traditionally armed Indians meshed with the colonial interests of France to encourage reciprocal alliances against their mutual enemies, the Chickasaws and the English.

Adjusting to new demands, Iberville in 1701 began moving the center of the colony slightly eastward, abandoning Fort Maurepas for a new site at Mobile offering better water, a more protected bay, and a network of rivers, creeks, and trails leading northwest to the main Choctaw villages near present-day Philadelphia, Mississippi. Seizing the initiative, he invited the principal warring nations to Mobile. Offering the Chickasaws French trade goods and the Choctaws French muskets, Iberville skillfully negotiated a tenuous peace that put an end to the slave raids promoted by the English and ensured the security of the French forts and posts recently established on the Gulf Coast and up the Mississippi River.[55]

Nullifying the Chickasaw threat was only the first step in establishing a southeast Louisiana frontier protecting the crucial Florida Parishes transportation routes and key portages against enemy attacks. France next sought to make peace and alliances among the region's mutually antagonistic resident Indian nations, but soon found traditions of short-range hostility toward neighbors often overcame wishes for long-range security from Chickasaws. To ease his journey upriver, Iberville earlier brokered peace between the Houmas, who "have . . . the reputation of being warriors and are feared by the neighboring tribes,"[56] and the Bayougoulas, only to find the conflict renewed when the larger nation surprised the smaller at work in the fields, killing several and taking twenty-five prisoners, during his first return trip to France.[57] Iberville's Jesuit chaplain Father Paul du Ru recorded a meeting with a Bayougoula elder at Fort de la Boulaye, where "we talked politics chiefly, more by gesture than by words. He declared that his tribe expected us to avenge them for the wrongs which they have suffered from the Oumas. He did everything he could to animate us against them, but I do not believe that we are likely to fight in the pay of the Bayougoulas for their benefit. War is by its nature always a bad trade and it would be especially so in this country."[58] Renegotiating with the "more civilized and honest" Houmas,[59] Iberville freed the captives and reestablished peace above and below the Bayou Manchac portage. Within a year, however, the Bayougoulas returned to their hostile proclivities by utterly destroying their Mugalasha neighbors. Jesuit Father Jacques Gravier lamented the massacre of the French-friendly nation: "The blood of so many Innocents cries for vengeance; consequently God is beginning to punish them [the Bayougoulas] by famine and disease, and they must fear that the houmas and the Kolapesssas will avenge the murder of all their allies."[60]

With a fragile peace made at Mobile and an imperfect peace in the Florida Parishes, Iberville apparently felt French Louisiana secure enough to plan an offensive operation against English North America. Leaving Bienville in nominal charge of the colony, he left for France to report to the Ministry of the Marine, promoting Louisiana and proposing a joint French and Indian campaign against New England. During his absence, Bienville began extending the political geography of their Louisiana colony. Development of the alternative lake-bayou-river routes from the Gulf required assessments of both the lower and upper portages. Iberville's initial enthusiasm, prophesying "it would be easy to clear out this stream [Bayou Manchac] during low water and make it navigable all the way to the Myssysypy," rested on certain private and national assumptions. He could immediately recall his own little clearing project at Pointe Coupée, easily remember France's huge domestic Canal du Mide achievement, where twelve thousand men dug a 162-mile channel connecting the Atlantic Ocean and Mediterranean Sea, and realistically muse that clearing 18 miles of an obstructed colonial bayou might be neither beneath consideration nor beyond accomplishment. However, the potential opportunities of the upper portage were submerged by the existing opportunities at the lower. The 120-mile open-water route from Mobile to Bayou St. John proved easier, shorter, and safer than the 170 miles to the river by the upper approach with its western end obstructed at Bayou Manchac. Personal preferences may have played a factor as well. If reference to the Bayou Manchac–Amite River confluences on early maps as Riviere d'Iberville identified the waterway with its French explorer, Bayou St. John enjoyed a longer and deeper association with its namesake, the younger Lemoyne brother. Although few Indians originally lived between the shallow lake and the river's muddy crescent, Bienville recognized present conveniences and possible enhancements, using the portage as his favorite route to the upper and lower Mississippi and promoting the low-lying area along Bayou St. John despite its tendency to flood.[61]

Construction of a small defensive stockade, prefiguring Fort St. John as early as 1701, on an old Indian mound near Bayou St. John's intersection with Lake Pontchartrain signaled a growing French interest in southeastern Louisiana. The presence of a fortified campsite at the bayou's mouth helped launch a series of migrations as nations within and without the Florida Parishes adjusted to the geographical pull of the new political reality.[62] André Pénicaut's Narrative for the Year 1705, referring to events transpiring in 1702, reported "during that same time, the Collapissas, who dwelt on the back of the Taleatcha [Pearl], a little river four leagues from the shore of Pontchartrain, came to the shore of that lake and settled at a place named Castein Bayouque,"[63] directly across from Bayou St. John. Within the year, the Natchitoches, after suffering crop failures, abandoned their North Louisiana villages and traveled down the Red and Mississippi Rivers to petition the commander of Fort de la Boulaye for relief. At his request, the recently relocated Acollapissas cordially welcomed these transient Caddo people into their new north-shore homes east of Mandeville, and both tribes participated in joint actions with the French against Chitimachas from Bayou Lafourche on the west bank of the river who had murdered a missionary and four other Frenchmen.[64] When provisions ran short at Mobile, Bienville "gave permission to several persons of the garrison to go hunting or to live as best they could among the savage nations friendly to the French."⁶⁵ "When we got to their village . . . , they embraced us, the men as well as the women and girls, all being delighted to see us come to stay with them."⁶⁶ As one of the twelve French refugeeing among the Acollapissas, Pénicaut thought "the Nassitoches are handsomer and have better figures than the Colapissas, because the Colapissas' bodies, men's and women's are all tattooed,"⁶⁷ and while his comments make curious ethnographic reading, an aside about hunting practices reveals a subtle change in the southeastern arms race: "When they go hunting, they go dressed in deer-skin with the antlers attached. They make the same motions that a deer makes; and when the deer notices this, he charges them; and when he gets in good musket range, they shoot at him and kill him. With this method they kill a great many deer; and it should be acknowledged that in hunting buffalo as well as bear and deer they are more skillful than the French."⁶⁸ With this description, Pénicaut details more than just Acollapissa hunting prowess. Florida Parishes Indian nations, traditionally armed with bows and arrows before Iberville's arrival in Louisiana, had quickly acquired French muskets and readily mastered the new firearms technology.

As resident and transient Indian nations jockeyed closer to the French, who offered alliances, trade goods, and muskets, the fragile peace between Choctaws and Chickasaws began to fail and endemic violence returned to the southeast. In late 1704, Bienville noted: "The English came . . . with three thousand Indians to raid the Choctaws who having been warned of it retired to the woods. The English ravaged their cabins and their corn and went back home. These Choctaws attacked their rear-guard and destroyed many of their men. They returned to Louisiana very proud of this feat, attributing this advantage to the guns he had given them."⁶⁹ On 7 January 1706, the Choctaws reported an attack "by four thousand [Chickasaw] Indians, led on by the English, who had carried off upwards of three hundred of their women and children."⁷⁰ The French quickly renegotiated a cessation of hostilities, but "on the 5th March, two Chactas came to the fort to inform M. de Bienville, that notwithstanding the promise of peace, the Chicachas had carried off from one of their villages upwards of one hundred and fifty persons, and asked for assistance and some ammunition."⁷¹

Soon other nations fleeing the renewed attacks of Anglo-Chickasaw slavers entered the Florida Parishes looking for French protection and alliance. Far-roving Tensas, "well-built men that live on the deer, the bear, and the game they hunt"[72] on the west bank of the Mississippi across from the Natchez, "were forced to abandon their villages by the . . . Chicchas, and to retire [downriver] among the Bayagoulas, and that not long afterwards the Taensas attacked the Bayagoulas, and had nearly exterminated them; a punishment they deserved for destroying . . . the Mongoulachas. The Taensas fearing the vengeance of the Colapissas, the Houmas, and other nations . . . they did not dare to return to their ancient villages."[73] Wishing to remain in southeast Louisiana, the Tensas courted French favor by inviting "many families of the Chitimachas . . . to come and eat the grain of the Bayougoula, and that by this ruse they had surprised many of these savages, whom they had carried away as slaves."[74] Mauled by the Tensas, and under continual attacks from French-allied Acollapissas and Natchitoches, the Chitimachas retreated deeper into inaccessible bayous until they were "almost entirely destroyed; the few that remain are slaves in the colony."[75] Needing the two hundred Tensas warriors for further frontier defense, the French chose not to punish them for destroying Bayougoulas and instead allowed Tensas resettlement at Bayou Manchac.

In October 1706, Tunicas, enemies of the Tensas, began to move from the lower Yazoo, down the east bank of the Mississippi, and into the northwestern Florida Parishes near the intersection of the Red River.[76] A former English captive of theirs, resentful of ill-treatment, instigated a Chickasaw raid in reprisal, and "the Tonicas, not feeling themselves strong enough to resist, abandoned their villages and collected again among the Houmas, who received them trustingly. While reposing on their good faith, the Tonicas surprised them and killed more than one-half of their nation."[77] Pénicaut, however, reported no such hostile takeover but simply stated "the Oumas deserted their settlement and . . . Another savage nation named the Tonicas . . . went to settle in the location that the Oumas had vacated,"[78] and Iberville recorded the Houmas lost half their population to a fatal diarrhea, not to war.[79] Whether reduced by disease or killed by treacherous transients, the Houmas migrated as well, abandoning their Florida Parishes homelands to settle on Bayou St. John. The incoming Tunicas, pledging peace with the neighboring Tensas, assumed control of the former upper Houma territories (soon renamed the Tunica Hills) and became "very much attached to the French, and have even been our auxiliaries in war."[80]

By 1706, a Louisiana frontier, maintained by alliances with resident, relocated, and replacement Indian nations, protected the small colony of forts, posts, and small holdings along the Gulf, up the river, and on the lake. In south central Mississippi, French-armed Choctaws created a strong barrier preventing Chickasaw attacks southeast to Mobile and southwest to the lower Mississippi Valley. South Carolina Indian agent Thomas Nairne admitted "to these [Choctaws] being unarmed the Chicasaws did great Damage but they begin now to have gunes plenty and are better able to defend themselfs."[81] In southeastern Louisiana, a deep defensive perimeter protected the alternative backwater routes to the Mississippi. Tunica occupation turned the western Florida Parishes into a buffer zone between the Natchez territories and Bayou Manchac, while Tensas settlement of the Manchac area provided on-site security for the river-to-lake confluences and complementing trail systems. In the eastern Florida Parishes, Acollapissas and Natchitoches in their common northlake villages defended overland approaches to Bayou St. John from the north and the east, while south across the lake a reduced population of Houmas protected the portage itself. Both upriver defenses at Manchac and St. John covered the flank of downriver Fort de la Boulaye guarding the mouth of the Mississippi.[82]

If Iberville's arrival in 1699 began the formation of a successful defensive frontier inhabited by strategically located Native American allies, his death by fever in Havana in 1706 ended his ongoing plans for an offensive against New England and helped cripple the developing Louisiana colony. Boulaye decayed until "there is neither fort nor bastion, nor intrenchments, nor redouts,"[83] and without Iberville's support and ministerial connections, Bienville struggled under the burden of logistical neglect caused by French reversals in the War of Spanish Succession until Antoine de la Mothe Cadillac replaced him as governor in 1713. Cadillac represented a new Louisiana, which was changing from a small royal military province protecting the river and the coast into an expanded commercial trading and agricultural settlement committed to making a profit for Antoine Crozat's new proprietary colony. One of the first steps in this evolution involved the relationships of relocated resident and transient Florida Parishes Indians established during the Iberville regime.

In 1714, "M. de St. Denis, who was a very courageous officer and venturesome man on war parties as well as in the discovery of mines, was summoned down to Mobile by M. de la Mothe. When he got there, M. de la Mothe engaged him to go to the Nassitoches and from the Nassitoches by land to Mexico among the Spaniards to sound out the freedom of trade in that direction."[84] Exiled Natchitoches, living peacefully among Acollapissas on the north shore of Lake Pontchartrain, were ordered to accompany St. Denis back to their original North Louisiana home, but "the Colapissas were seized with jealousy or, rather, with rage. Seeing that the Nassitoches women, too, were leaving and were going away with their husbands, they fell upon the Nassitoches with blows of guns, arrows, and hatchets and killed seventeen. . . . They seized more than fifty women or girls—the others having fled right and left into the woods, wherever they could."[85] Fearing St. Denis's anger and revenge, the Acollapissas fled as well, moving across the lake to settle along the Mississippi River, the last of the original resident nations to abandon their Florida Parishes homelands. A subsequent migration of Tensas from Bayou Manchac, south to a point on the Mississippi River near the modern town of Edgard, and eventually to villages near the French fort at Mobile, opened the Florida Parishes to an almost exclusive occupation by Tunicas in the west and Choctaws in the east.[86]

Tunicas grew in importance as their control of the portages between the Red and Mississippi Rivers linked the Gulf and lower Mississippi with the fort and the community St. Denis established at Natchitoches. They persistently resisted any French religious appeals[87] but proved loyal allies, rejecting all Natchez attempts

> to incite the Chiefs of the Tonicas to put the missionary to death and all of us Frenchmen that were in the village, promising him that all the Natchez savages would unite with them later on to make war on the French, adding that it was much better to deal with the English, who let them have their merchandise cheaper. The Chief of the Tonicas—as level-headed a man as a savage could be, but incapable of treachery, a virtue very rare among the savages—was quite astonished at such a speech. The first thing he wanted to do was have their heads broken.[88]

Choctaws, drifting down from their densely populated Mississippi heartland to the unoccupied eastern Florida Parishes, increasingly became the "key to this country," especially after John Law's Company of the West assumed control of Louisiana and founded New Orleans below Bayou St. John's headwaters in 1718. Staunch allies "who will never depart from the fidelity that they owe to the French,"[89] Choctaws helped protect the Crescent City from rebellious Natchez, conspiring slaves, and raiding Chickasaws and established a north-shore trade in venison, prefiguring a later Florida Parishes backcountry trade in beef and pork.[90]

Loss of Canada in the French and Indian War nullified the need of a Louisiana colony protecting the Mississippi River. France could logically and secretly cede New Orleans and Louisiana west of that river to Spain in 1762 and surrender everything east of the Mississippi, including the Florida Parishes, to England in 1763. The loyal but French-abandoned Indian nations who supported the colony adjusted to the new regional and national situations. Tunicas migrated westward across the river into Spanish Louisiana, remaining near their Red River portage, and settled areas in modern Avoyelles Parish.[91] Choctaws negotiated with successive English, Spanish, and American regimes, endured or avoided the Trail of Tears, maintained a presence near Bayou Lacomb and on the Pearl River in St. Tammany Parish until the early 1900s, and continue to occupy their traditional homeland in Neshoba County, Mississippi.[92] Both tribes survived to scalp the incautious at their reservation-based casinos at Marksville and Philadelphia.

Native Americans resident in the Florida Parishes during the initial French explorations have not fared as well. Acollapissa, Tangipahoa, Quinipissa-Mugalasha, and Bayougoula remnants merged with reduced numbers of Houmas on Bayou St. John before leaving the New Orleans environs after 1718 to relocate on both sides of the Mississippi near the headwaters of Bayou Lafourche. They left the Donaldsonville area in the late 1790s to move deeper into marginal lands along Bayou Terrebonne in present-day Terrebonne Parish. Blending with other refugees of declining Gulf South nations, intermarrying with Frenchmen and free people of color, Houmas retained their cultural identity but have been unable to obtain official recognition as an Indian nation from the U.S. government and therefore have no reservation and no casino.[93]

Interpreting the French and Indian presence in southeast Louisiana by considering the interplay of Native American geography and European colonial politics during the formative eight-year period from Iberville's arrival in 1699 to his departure in 1706 reveals the peculiar geopolitical significance of the Florida Parishes. To control critical alternative backwater approaches to the Mississippi River from the Gulf of Mexico, France created a defensive southeastern frontier by cultivating alliances with and brokering peace among mutually antagonistic resident and transient Indian nations. These diplomatic developments between sovereign French and Indian powers driven by their own agendas evolved into reciprocal relationships successfully protecting all regional partners from their mutual English and Chickasaw enemies. The new political reality encouraged migrations of the Indian people original to the Florida Parishes in 1699 and shuffled interdependent native settlements along the Mississippi River, Bayou Manchac, and the north shore of Lake Pontchartrain. At first the alliances proved beneficial, but new shifts in locations and continued traditions of violence, combining with changes in the colony's commander in 1706 and its directors after 1713, eventually doomed the *petites nations* increasingly interacting with New Orleans. When French Louisiana ended in 1763, the Florida Parishes retained the strategic importance established by Iberville's initial explorations and possessed a geographical relevance that survived intact under shifting colonial and territorial allegiances well into American statehood. All national powers succeeding the first French regime in the Gulf South cast covetous eyes on New Orleans while crafting various initiatives to defend, destroy, or develop Bayou Manchac.[94] Unlike the political conflicts typically erupting between Native Americans and hostile Spanish, English, and American cultures, friendly relationships between the French and Indians in southeast Louisiana developed in part because of the area's unique geopolitical circumstances, but the outcome remained the same: The distinctive Acollapissa, Tangipahoa, Quinipissa-Mugalasha, Bayougoula, and Houma nations of the Florida Parishes that helped maintain French colonial Louisiana by forming a geography of power capable of protecting crucial transportation routes and key portages disappeared first from the region and then from history.

NOTES

1. Darrell A. Posey, "A Resume of the Sharp-Gehegan Collection of Artifacts from Bayou Jasemine, Tangipahoa Parish, Louisiana" (Chicago, 1980), 1–3, in the Wiley Sharp Collection, Center for Southeast Louisiana Studies, Southeastern Louisiana University Archives and Special Collections, Hammond, La.; J. Richard Shenkel, "Early Woodland in Coastal Louisiana," in *Perspectives on Gulf Coast Prehistory,* ed. Dave D. Davis (Gainesville, 1984), 43; Robert W. Neuman and Nancy W. Hawkins, *Louisiana Prehistory* (Baton Rouge, 1993), 10–16; Coastal Environments Inc., *An Assessment of Prehistoric Cultural Resources within the Coastal Zone of Tangipahoa Parish* (Baton Rouge, 1983), 14–21; Richard Beavers, Malcolm C. Webb, Teresia R. Lamb, and John R. Greene, *Archaeological Survey of the Upper Tangipahoa River, Tangipahoa Parish, Louisiana* (New Orleans, 1985), 9–10; Andrew C. Albrecht, "The Origin and Early Settlement of Baton Rouge, Louisiana," *Louisiana Historical Quarterly* 28 (January 1945): 24–26; Dennis Jones, Carl Kuttruff, Malcolm Shuman, and Joe Steveson, *The Kleinpeter Site*

(16EBR5): The History and Archaeology of a Multicomponent Site in East Baton Rouge Parish, Louisiana (Baton Rouge, 1994), xvii, 2, 89, 202; Charles A. Dranguet and Roman J. Heleniak, "Backdoor to the Gulf: The Pass Manchac Region, 1699–1863," *Regional Dimensions* 3 (1985): 5–6; Coastal Environments Inc., *Cultural Resource Survey of the Bayou Fountain Channel Enlargement Area, East Baton Rouge Parish, Louisiana* (New Orleans, 1997), 15.

2. Charles Hudson, *The Southeastern Indians* (Knoxville, 1982), 77–82; Jones et al., *The Kleinpeter Site*, 206, 212–13; Coastal Environments Inc., *An Assessment of Prehistoric Cultural Resources within the Coastal Zone of Tangipahoa Parish*, 30–31; Dennis Jones and Malcolm Shuman, *Archaeological Atlas and Report of Prehistoric Indian Mounds in Louisiana* (Baton Rouge, 1988), 3:157–63.

3. Charles Hudson, *Knights of Spain, Warriors of the Sun: Hernando de Soto and the South's Ancient Chiefdoms* (Athens, Ga., 1997), 394–97, 417–40; Jones et al., *The Kleinpeter Site*, 213; Tennant S. McWilliams, "Armadas on the Mississippi, 1543," *Louisiana Studies* 7 (1968): 213–27; Peter H. Wood, "The Changing Population of the Colonial South: An Overview by Race and Region, 1685–1750," in *Powhatan's Mantle: Indians in the Colonial Southeast*, ed. Peter H. Wood, Gregory A. Waselkov, and M. Thomas Hatley (Lincoln, 1989), 36–102; James Axtell, *The Indians' New South: Cultural Change in the Colonial Southeast* (Baton Rouge, 1997), 5–24; Helen Hornbeck Tanner, "The Land and Water Communications System of the Southeastern Indians," in *Powhatan's Mantle*, 6; Marvin T. Smith, *Archaeology of Aboriginal Cultural Change in the Interior Southeast: Depopulation during the Early Historic Period* (Gainesville, 1987), 13, 54–61, 86, 112, 146–47; Hudson, *Southeastern Indians*, 102–19; Richard White, *The Roots of Dependency* (Lincoln, 1988), 3–7.

4. *New Orleans Daily Picayune*, August 1, 1854; C. Howard Nichols, ed., *Tangipahoa Crossings: Excursions into Tangipahoa History* (Baton Rouge, 1979), 5; Hodding Carter, "The Amite to the Tangipahoa," in *The Rivers and Bayous of Louisiana*, ed. Edwin A. Davis (Baton Rouge, 1968), 153–54; Fred B. Kniffen, Hiram F. Gregory, and George A. Stokes, *The Historic Indian Tribes of Louisiana: From 1542 to the Present* (Baton Rouge, 1987), 49; William E. Myer, "Indian Trails of the Southeast," in *Forty-Second Annual Report of the Bureau of American Ethnology to the Secretary of the Smithsonian Institution, 1924–1925* (Washington, 1928), 735–48, with accompanying map following p. 748.

5. William A. Read, *Louisiana Place-Names of Indian Origins* (Baton Rouge, 1927); David I. Bushnell Jr., *The Choctaw of Bayou Lacomb, St. Tammany Parish, Louisiana* (Washington, 1909), 6–7; Cyrus Byington, *A Dictionary of the Choctaw Language* (Washington, 1915); André Pénicaut, *Fleur de Lys and Calumet: Being the Pénicaut Narrative of French Adventure in Louisiana* (Baton Rouge, 1953), 16; M. De Sauvole, *The Journal of Sauvole* (Mobile, 1969), 31, 37; Evelyn Benham, "Pearl River 'Talcatcha,'" *Journal of Mississippi History* 38, no. 2 (1976): 214; John R. Swanton, *The Indians of the Southeastern United States* (Washington, 1946), 82–83, 190, 176–77, 95, 139–40; John R. Swanton, *Indian Tribes of the Lower Mississippi Valley and Adjacent Coast of the Gulf of Mexico* (Washington, 1911), 274–92.

6. Swanton, *Indians of the Southeastern United States*, 158–61, 197–99, 121–23; Swanton, *Indian Tribes of the Lower Mississippi Valley*, 45–46, 306–10; Jeffrey P. Brain, *On the Tunica Trail* (Baton Rouge, 1988), 6; Jeffrey P. Brain, *Tunica Archaeology* (Cambridge, Mass., 1988), 25–30; White, *Roots of Dependency*, 2, 12–13; Read, *Louisiana Place-Names*, viii; Benham, "Pearl River," 213.

7. Hudson, *Southeastern Indians*, 185, 272, 289–313; Kniffen, Gregory, and Stokes, *Historic Indian Tribes of Louisiana*, 186–207, 224–26; Paul A. Kunkel, "The Indians of Louisiana, about 1700," in *Carnivals and Conflicts: A Louisiana History Reader*, ed. Samuel C. Hyde Jr., C. Howard Nichols, and Charles N. Elliott (New York, 2000), 31–33; Patrick M. Malone, *The Skulking Way of War* (Baltimore, 1991), 9–10.

8. Swanton, *Indians of the Southeastern United States*, 95, 176–77, 190; Swanton, *Indian Tribes of the Lower Mississippi Valley*, 274, 277, 280, 284; Henri de Tonti, "Memoir by the Sieur de la Tonty," in *Historical Collections of Louisiana*, ed. Benjamin Franklin French (New York, 1846), 1:63.

9. Isaac J. Cox, ed., *The Journeys of René Robert Cavelier, sieur de La Salle* (New York, 1973), 167–68.

10. "Memoir of Robert Cavelier de la Salle, on the necessity of fitting out an expedition to take possession of Louisiana," in *Historical Collections of Louisiana*, ed. French, 1:25–34; "Memoir of Robert Cavalier, Sieur De La Salle, Addressed to Monseigneur De Seingnelay," in *Historical Collections of Louisiana and Florida*, ed. Benjamin Franklin French (New York, 1875), 2:12; Marcel Giraud, *A History of French Louisiana* (Baton Rouge, 1990), 1:11; Edmund Robert Murphy, *Henry De Tonty: Fur Trader of the Mississippi* (Baltimore, 1941), 10–14; Anka Muhlstein, *La Salle: Explorer of the North American Frontier* (New York, 1994), 90–125, 192–217; David Roberts, "Sieur de La Salle's Fateful Landfall," *Smithsonian* (April 1997): 40–52; Robert S. Weddle, ed., "La Salle Shipwreck," *Medallion* (May 1996): 1–12; William E. Dunn, *Spanish and French Rivalry in the Gulf Region of the United States, 1678–1702: The Beginnings of Texas and Pensacola* (Austin, 1917), 59–109.

11. John E. Omfret, *The Province of West New Jersey, 1609–1702* (Princeton, 1956), 150; G. D. Scull, "Biographical Notice of Doctor Daniel Coxe, of London," *Pennsylvania Magazine of History and Biography* 7 (1883): 317–19; Daniel Coxe, *A Description of the English Province of Carolana, by the Spanish call'ed Florida and by the French La Louisiana* (Gainesville, 1976), viii–ix; Werner W. Crane, *The Southern Frontier: 1670–1732* (Ann Arbor, 1956), 50; Daniel Coxe, "Coxe's Account of the Activities of the English in the Mississippi Valley in the Seventeenth Century," in *The First Explorations of the Trans-Allegheny Region by the Virginians, 1650–1674*, ed. Clarence W. Alvord and Lee Bidgood (Baltimore, 1996), 246–47; *Journals of the Board of Trade*, February 14–16, 1700, quoted in Crane, *Southern Frontier*, 56–57; Robert S. Weedle, *The French Thorn: Rival Explorers in the Spanish Sea, 1692–1762* (College Station, 1991), 135; James Troy Robinson, "Fort Assumption: The First Recorded History of White Man's Activity on the Present Site of Memphis," *West Tennessee Historical Society Papers* 5 (1951): 62–63; William A. Klutts, "Fort Prudhomme: Its Location," *West Tennessee Historical Society Papers* 4 (1950): 37. For general location of the Chickasaw landing place see Ruth Lapham Butler's note in Paul Du Ru, *Journals of Paul Du Ru (February 1 to May 8, 1700): Missionary Priest to Louisiana* (Chicago, 1934), 22.

12. Lawrence Carrol Ford, *The Triangular Struggle for Spanish Pensacola, 1689–1739* (Washington, 1939), 37–41; Weedle, *French Thorn*, 117–18, 132–33; Dunn, *Spanish and French Rivalry in the Gulf Region*, 146–91; William S. Coker and R. Wayne Childers, "The Presidio Santa Maria de Galve," in *Santa Maria de Galve: A Story of Survival*, ed. Virginia Parks (Pensacola, 1998), 11–20.

13. Giraud, *History of French Louisiana*, 1:20; Dunn, *Spanish and French Rivalry in the Gulf*

Region, 189; Ford, *Triangular Struggle*, 35–36; Nellis M. Crouse, *Lemoyne d'Iberville: Soldier of New France* (Ithaca, 1954), 14–162; Howard H. Peckham, *The Colonial Wars: 1689–1763* (Chicago, 1954), 44–50; Thomas E. Burke Jr., *Mohawk Frontier: The Dutch Community of Schenectady, New York, 1661–1710* (Ithaca, 1991), 103; Kenneth McNaught, *The Penguin History of Canada* (New York, 1988), 35; Desmond Morton, *A Military History of Canada* (Toronto, 1992), 17; French, *Historical Collections*, 2:31–33; Ian McCulloch, "A Hero of New France," *Beaver* (June/July 1995): 14–22.

14. "Instruction to Iberville, July 23, 1698," in *Découvertes et établissements des Français . . . 1614–1754*, ed. Pierre Margry (Paris, 1878), 4:73; Jay Higginbotham, *Fort Maurepas: The Birth of Louisiana* (Mobile, 1968), 20; Crouse, *Lemoyne d'Iberville*, 166.

15. Crouse, *Lemoyne d'Iberville*, 164–69.

16. Pierre Lemoyne d'Iberville, *Iberville's Gulf Journals* (Tuscaloosa, 1991), 35.

17. Ibid., 43.

18. Ibid., 39, 43–44; Crouse, *Lemoyne d'Iberville*, 172–73.

19. "Bienville to Maurepas," in *Mississippi Provincial Archives: The French Dominion*, ed. Dunbar Rowland and A. G. Sanders (Jackson, 1929) 3:159–60.

20. Iberville, *Gulf Journals*, 45–46.

21. Ibid., 61; Dennis Jones, Joann Mossa, and Todd Smith, *Cultural Resources Survey of Fort Adams Reach Revetment, Mile 312.2 to 306.0-L, Mississippi River, Wilkinson County, Mississippi* (Baton Rouge, 1993), 31.

22. Iberville, *Gulf Journals*, 48.

23. Ibid., 48–52; Crouse, *Lemoyne d'Iberville*, 175–77.

24. Iberville, *Gulf Journals*, 55.

25. Ibid., 57.

26. Edna B. Freiberg, *Bayou St. John in Colonial Louisiana, 1699–1803* (New Orleans, 1980), 11, 13–14; W. Adolphe Roberts, *Lake Pontchartrain* (Indianapolis, 1946), 11; Daniel H. Usner Jr., "American Indians in Colonial Louisiana," in *Powhatan's Mantle*, ed. Wood, Waselkov, and Hatley, 105.

27. Iberville, *Gulf Journals*, 60.

28. Henri de Ville Du Sinclair, ed., *Journal of the Frigate "Le Marin," September 5th, 1698–July 2, 1699* (Biloxi, 1974), 37; Fred Kniffen, "What Iberville Saw," *Louisiana Heritage* 1, no. 2 (1969): 19; Philip D. Uzee, "Bayou Lafourche," in *Rivers and Bayous of Louisiana*, 122.

29. Du Sinclair, *Journal of the Frigate "Le Marin,"* 39.

30. Ibid., 39–40.

31. Iberville, *Gulf Journals*, 65.

32. Ibid.; William A. Read, *Istrouma* (Baton Rouge, 1946), 3–15.

33. Iberville, *Gulf Journals*, 66.

34. Ibid., 69.

35. Ibid., 68.

36. Ibid., 60.

37. Ibid., 79.

38. David C. Johnson and Elaine G. Yodis, *The Geography of Louisiana* (New York, 1998), 9–11; Fred B. Kniffen, "Bayou Manchac: A Physiographic Interpretation," *Geographical Review* 25 (1935): 462–63; John R. McKenna Jr., "The Role of Water Transportation in the Settlement

of Bayou Manchac and the Amite River" (M.A. thesis, Louisiana State University, 1975), 9–11; Christopher Goodwin & Associates, *Underwater Cultural Resources Survey of the South Entrance Channel, Pass Manchac, Louisiana* (New Orleans, 1994), 15.

39. Iberville, *Gulf Journals*, 80.
40. Ibid.
41. Ibid.
42. Ibid., 81.
43. Ibid., 84–85.
44. Ibid., 82–85; Marc de Villers, "A History of the Foundation of New Orleans, 1717–1722," *Louisiana Historical Quarterly* 3 (1920): 162; Pierre-François de Charlevoix, *Charlevoix's Louisiana: Selections from the History and the Journal* (Baton Rouge, 1977), 123; Jones, Mossa, and Smith, *Cultural Resources Survey of Fort Adams*, 31.
45. Jay Higginbotham, *Fort Maurepas: The Birth of Louisiana* (Pascagoula, 1971), 66; Giraud, *History of Louisiana*, 1:34.
46. Quoted by Phinias Lyman to Lord Shelburne, 31 October 1766, in Clarence W. Alvord and Clarence E. Carter, eds., *The New Regime, 1765–1767* (Springfield, Ill., 1917), 417; Iberville, *Gulf Journals*, 107–9; Jean Baptiste Lemoyne, Sieur de Bienville, "Memoir of the Services of Sieur de Bienville, Commandant General of Louisiana," in *Mississippi Provincial Archives*, 3:489; "Sauvole to (Pontchartrain?)," in *Mississippi Provincial Archives*, 2:15; Pénicaut, *Fleur de Lys and Calumet*, 30; Jean Delanglez, "Tonti Letters," *Mid-American* 12 (1939): 215; Jean-Baptiste de la Harpe, *Historical Journal of the Settlement of the French in Louisiana* (Lafayette, 1971), 25.
47. La Harpe, *Historical Journal*, 25.
48. Iberville, *Gulf Journals*, 108.
49. Ibid., 109.
50. Crouse, *Lemoyne d'Iberville*, 209; Giraud, *History of French Louisiana*, 1:38; Maurice Ries, "The Mississippi Fort, Called Fort de la Boulaye," *Louisiana Historical Quarterly* 19 (1936): 829–99; Powell A. Casey, *Encyclopedia of Fort, Posts, Named Camps, and Other Military Institutions in Louisiana, 1700–1981* (Baton Rouge, 1983), 29–30; Rene Chartrand, "The Troops of French Louisiana, 1699–1769," *Military Collector & Historian: Journal of the Company of Military Historians* 25 (summer 1973): 58; Freiberg, *Bayou St. John*, 17, 23.
51. Henry Woodhead, ed., *Tribes of the Southern Woods* (Alexandria, Va., 1994), 54; White, *Roots of Dependency*, 35; Thomas Nairne, *Nairne's Muskhogean Journals: The 1708 Expedition to the Mississippi River* (Jackson, 1988), 73–78.
52. French, *Historical Collections*, 3:15–16.
53. Joel W. Martin, "Southern Indians and the English Trade in Skins and Slaves," in *The Forgotten Centuries: Indians and Europeans in the American South, 1521–1704*, ed. Charles Hudson and Carmen Chaves Tessier (Athens, Ga., 1994), 306; Philip M. Brown, "Early Indian Trade in the Development of South Carolina: Politics, Economics, and Social Mobility during the Prosperous Era," *South Carolina Historical Magazine* 76 (July 1997): 118–28; Crane, *Southern Frontier*, 23, 39, 45; Axtell, *Indians' New South*, 41–44; Arrel Gibson, *The Chickasaws* (Norman, 1971), 34, 39–41; Dayna Browker Lee, "Indian Slavery in Lower Louisiana during the Colonial Period, 1699–1803" (M.A. thesis, Northwestern State University, Natchitoches, La., 1989), 16–19; White, *Roots of Dependency*, 35; Kathryn E. Holland Braud, *Deerskins and Duffles*

(Lincoln, 1993), 125; Don LeFave, "Time of the Whitetail: The Charles Town Indian Trade, 1690–1715," *Studies in History and Society* 5, no. 1 (1973): 5–15.

54. La Harpe, *Historical Journal*, 20.

55. Jay Higginbotham, *Old Mobile: Fort Louis de la Louisiana, 1702–1711* (Mobile, 1977), 24–25, 53–68, 78–81; Giraud, *History of French Louisiana*, 1:41–42, 83; Iberville, *Gulf Journals*, 171–73; Daniel H. Usner Jr., *Indians, Settlers, and Slaves in a Frontier Exchange Economy* (Chapel Hill, 1992), 18.

56. Father Jacques Gravier, *The Jesuit Relations and Allied Documents* (Cleveland, 1901), 55:153.

57. Swanton, *Indian Tribes of the Lower Mississippi Valley*, 277.

58. Du Ru, *Journal*, 7.

59. Du Sinclair, *Journal of the Frigate "Le Marin,"* 50.

60. Gravier, *The Jesuit Relations and Allied Documents* (New York, 1959), 65:157–58; Swanton, *Indian Tribes of the Lower Mississippi Valley*, 278.

61. James K. Finch, *The Story of Engineering* (Garden City, 1960), 138–60; F. L. Carsten, ed., *The Ascendancy of France* (Cambridge, 1961), 244.

62. Freiberg, *Bayou St. John*, 24–25; Sauvole, *Journal*, 38; Casey, *Encyclopedia of Forts, Posts*, 197; Mortimer F. Kelly, "Fort St. John," *Southeast Louisiana Historical Papers* 2 (1975): 54; Joseph H. DeGrange, "Historical Data of the Spanish Fort," *Louisiana Historical Quarterly* 2 (January–October 1919): 268; W. O. Hart, "New Orleans," *Louisiana Historical Quarterly* 1 (April 1918): 353–54.

63. Pénicaut, *Fleur de Lys and Calumet*, 100.

64. Ibid., 100–102.

65. Ibid., 105.

66. Ibid., 106.

67. Ibid., 110.

68. Ibid., 112.

69. "Bienville to Pontchartrain," in *Mississippi Provincial Archives*, 3:159–60.

70. La Harpe, in *Historical Collections*, ed. French, 3:34.

71. Ibid.

72. Iberville, *Gulf Journals*, 122.

73. La Harpe, in *Historical Collections*, ed. French, 3:35.

74. Ibid.

75. Charlevoix, *Charlevoix's Louisiana*, 268.

76. La Harpe, in *Historical Collections*, ed. French, 3:35; Swanton, *Indian Tribes of the Lower Mississippi Valley*, 311.

77. La Harpe, in *Historical Collections*, ed. French, 3:35.

78. Pénicaut, *Fleur de Lys and Calumet*, 129–30.

79. Iberville, *Gulf Journal*, 122.

80. Antoine Simon Le Page du Pratz, *The History of Louisiana or of the Western Parts of Virginia and Carolina* (London, 1763), 2:144.

81. Nairne, *Muskogean Journals*, 37.

82. Joseph Zitomerskey, "The Form and Function of French-Native American Relations in Early Eighteenth-Century French Colonial Louisiana," *Proceedings of the Annual Meeting of the French Colonial Historical Society* 15 (1992): 154–77.

83. Ruben G. Thwaites, ed., *The Jesuit Relations and Allied Documents* (Cleveland, 1901), 65:161.

84. Pénicaut, *Fleur de Lys and Calumet*, 145.

85. Ibid., 146.

86. Ibid., 219; Swanton, *Indian Tribes of the Lower Mississippi Valley*, 270–71.

87. Antoine Simon Le Page du Pratz, *The History of Louisiana or of the Western Parts of Virginia and Carolina* (London, 1774), 25.

88. Pénicaut, *Fleur de Lys and Calumet*, 174.

89. "Father Beaudouin, S.J., to Gen. Salmon," in *Mississippi Provincial Archives*, 1:156–57.

90. Usner, "American Indians in Colonial New Orleans," 119–20.

91. Swanton, *Indian Tribes of the Lower Mississippi Valley*, 315; Brain, *Tunica Archaeology*, 42–44.

92. Swanton, *Indians of the Southeastern United States*, 120; Angie Debo, *The Rise and Fall of the Choctaw Republic* (Norman, 1961), 30–79; Arthur H. DeRosier Jr., *The Removal of the Choctaw Indians* (Knoxville, 1970), 16–20, 129–48; Jesse O. McKee, *The Choctaw* (New York, 1989), 28–45, 86–95; Bushnell, *The Choctaw of Bayou Lacomb*, 190.

93. Swanton, *Indian Tribes of the Lower Mississippi Valley*, 290; Brian L. Guevin, "Grand Houma Village: An Historical Houma Indian Site (16AN35) Ascension Parish, La.," *Louisiana Archaeology* 11 (1984): 89–110; Kniffen, Gregory, and Stokes, *Historic Indian Tribes of Louisiana*, 78; Bruce N. Duthu, "The Houma Indians of Louisiana: The Intersection of Law and History in the Federal Acknowledgment Process," *Louisiana History* 38, no. 4 (1997): 409–36; Greg Bowman and Janel Curry-Roper, *The Houma People of Louisiana: A Story of Indian Survival* (Houma, 1982), 5–52; Bruce Duthu and Hilde Objibway, "Future Light or *Feu Follet*? Louisiana Indians and Federal Recognition," *Southern Exposure* 13, no. 6 (1985): 24–32.

94. For the continual national interest in and rivalry over Bayou Manchac after 1763 see: Bettie Jones Conover, "British West Florida's Mississippi Frontier Posts, 1763–1779," *Alabama Review* 29 (July 1976): 177–207; Douglas S. Brown, "The Iberville Canal Project: Its Relations to Anglo-French Commercial Rivalry in the Mississippi Valley, 1763–1775," *Mississippi Valley Historical Review* 32 (1946): 491–516; Philip Pittman, *The Present State of the European Settlements on the Mississippi* (London, 1770); Margaret Fisher Dalrymple, ed., *The Merchant of Manchac: The Letterbooks of John Fitzpatrick, 1768–1790* (Baton Rouge, 1978); V. M. Scramuzza, "Galveztown, A Spanish Settlement in Colonial Louisiana," *Louisiana Historical Quarterly* 13 (1930): 553–609; John W. Caughy, "Willings Expedition down the Mississippi," *Louisiana Historical Quarterly* 15 (1932): 5–36; William Bartram, *Travels of William Bartram* (New Haven, 1958); Thomas P. Abernethy, "The West Florida Rebellion," in *The South in the New Nation* (Baton Rouge, 1961), 330–66; J. J. Albert, "Report from the Secretary of War . . . in relation to the nature of the obstructions in the Bayou Manchac," 27th Cong., 3rd sess., Ex. Doc. 21, December 30, 1842, 1–3; A. A. Humphreys, "Letter of the Secretary of War communicating . . . in relation to the cost of opening, for first class steamboat navigation, Bayou Manchac, Amite River, Lakes Maurepas and Pontchartrain," 40th Cong., 2nd sess., Ex. Doc. 31, March 11, 1867, 1–12; "Bayou Manchac," *De Bow's Review* 5, no. 11 (1868): 983–85; Department of the Army, New Orleans District, Corps of Engineers, "Announcement of Public Meeting to Initiate a Study of Bayou Manchac and Amite River, Louisiana" (6 July 1977), and Colonel Early J. Rush III, "A Study on a Navigable Channel between Lake Maurepas and the Mississippi River at Bayou Manchac," public speech typescript (4 August 1977), 1–5, in Joe Minton Collection, Center for Southeast Louisiana Studies, Archives and Special Collections.

2

BOOM IN THE BAYOUS

Land Speculation and Town Planning in the Florida Parishes under British Rule

ROBIN F. A. FABEL

WHAT ARE NOW THE FLORIDA PARISHES OF LOUISIANA ONCE FLEW the flag of Great Britain. Victory over the Bourbon monarchies of France and Spain in the Seven Years' (French and Indian) War brought vast territories into the British Empire. The Union Jack then raised in Canada, one of those vast territories, was destined to keep flying there for a very long time. By contrast Britain's postwar acquisitions in the most southerly region of North America, which were also vast, would stay British for less than twenty years; but they are not without interest, nor do they lack some permanent importance.

By the Treaty of Paris of 10 February 1763, Spain ceded its Florida colony to the British Crown; France ceded to the king of England all French holdings on the Gulf of Mexico, including, most notably, the port of Mobile. The only land east of the Mississippi not surrendered to Britain was the "island" of New Orleans. Allegedly to make the loss of Florida more acceptable to Spain's king, the French monarch transferred to him all his claims to New Orleans and to territories west of the Mississippi.[1]

The British government decided that its southern acquisitions were too big for management by a single colonial establishment. It therefore created two new colonies from them. The province of East Florida extended as far west as the Apalachicola River. The colony of West Florida covered the area from the Apalachicola to the Mississippi. Its northern boundary, as defined in the royal proclamation of 7 October 1763, was 31 degrees of latitude.[2] To this day that parallel is also the northern boundary of the Florida Parishes of the state of Louisiana.

This essay is about a speculative boom in those parishes: why it occurred and who was involved. A surprisingly high percentage of the population of the British colony of West Florida took part in it. By the dozen they applied for tens of thousands of acres in what was the province's Wild

West: the Mississippi region and, for particular consideration here, what became the Florida Parishes.

This scramble for land could be called, to borrow a phrase, "irrational exuberance." It was not rational because it took place at a particularly turbulent time and in particularly hazardous circumstances.

Four conditions then prevailing would seem to have made acquiring land in a Crown colony, with all its attendant trouble and expense, unusually risky in 1772, the year that the land boom began.

The first of these conditions was the unstable political situation. The authority of the king of England in North America had never been more in question.

The second was the risk of death and destruction. Some Native Americans, the francophile *petites nations* of the lower Mississippi region, were traditionally hostile to the British.

The third deterrent was the possibility of Spanish conquest. His Most Catholic Majesty King Carlos III had never reconciled himself to his reluctant transfer of Florida to Britain. There was a well-founded expectation that, given a favorable chance, he would order the invasion of British West Florida, probably from his neighboring province of Louisiana.

The fourth danger, well-known to inhabitants from experience and to outsiders from press reports, was the high mortality rate in West Florida. Tropical diseases, yellow fever and malaria in particular, had taken a heavy toll of immigrants and soldiers in the 1760s.

It was in the 1760s that one of the four hazards, Indian hostility, had indeed delayed expansion to the west. Major Arthur Loftus left New Orleans in February 1764 with four hundred redcoats in ten large barges. His purpose was to assert Britain's new presence on the Mississippi. Long before even reaching Natchez an ambush halted his progress. The first volley killed five soldiers. Fire came from both sides of the river. Loftus consulted his officers and decided the price of pushing on upstream would be too high. His expedition turned tail and went back to New Orleans. Loftus believed his assailants were Choctaws, close comrades of the French in the recently ended French and Indian War, but they turned out to be all from the *petites nations:* Tunicas, Ofogoulas, Chetimachas, and Houmas.[3]

This skirmish showed that even a small scratch force of Native Americans, only thirty by some accounts, could thwart a major military enterprise in the region. It and other events suggesting small-tribe hostility did not deter George Johnstone, British West Florida's first governor, from nurturing high hopes for his province. He foresaw that West Florida would be, in his words, "the Emporium of the New World" and that the hub of its commercial glory would be Manchac. What is meant here is not today's Manchac at the eastern end of Lake Maurepas, but a Manchac unmarked on current maps, at the junction of the Mississippi River and Bayou Manchac. Since that bayou (at the time also called the Iberville River) connected with the lakes, and since the lakes connected with the Gulf of Mexico, he anticipated the development of a new trade route. The growing produce of the Illinois country would go by this route to the sea, which was much shorter in miles and in time than the traditional one. Manchac would replace New Orleans as an entrepôt. This fancy of Johnstone's was based on the belief that Bayou Manchac was navigable for nine months of the year. In fact it was navigable, not nine, but only three months annually.[4]

Such disappointing news did not blunt Johnstone's optimism. He sent Captain Lieutenant James Campbell to hire laborers to deepen the bayou and to clear the stumps, logs, and other debris clogging it. Campbell did not complete the task, which was Sisyphean in nature. Not finishing in one dry season would mean starting from the beginning the next year—every year. There is no doubt that if the Iberville had been thoroughly dredged, creating a navigable canal, and that if it had also been found possible to keep it clear year-long, trade would have been diverted from New Orleans and, in consequence, the region around Manchac would have been much more attractive to immigrants than in fact it was. Belief in its feasibility persisted, but the bayou was never properly cleared throughout the years of British rule. In addition to the so-called Iberville Canal, Johnstone also wanted a fort at Manchac.

Fulfillment of the governor's plans depended on amicable relations with the Native Americans in the Manchac area. Charles-Philippe Aubry, French governor of Louisiana, remained in office for a time even after his king ceded the province to his Spanish cousin. While he awaited replacement by a Spanish counterpart, Aubry cooperated with Johnstone's schemes. He allowed Campbell to hire laborers in New Orleans and advised traditionally pro-French Indians of the lower Mississippi to befriend British newcomers. His advice was particularly necessary because, strictly for selfish reasons, unlicensed traders of several nations, French *coureurs de bois*, and very occasionally a Spaniard predicted a dire future for the Indians wherever the British settled. Aubry's prestige enabled him largely, though not completely, to nullify such menacing rumors. They lingered in reduced strength for some years. As late as 1771 a Spanish subject, John Terrasco, warned Biloxis and Pascagoulas that the purpose of the Britons' stationing of a deputy Indian agent at Manchac was to enslave them and to sell them abroad.[5]

A bigger potential threat than the *petites nations* were the Alabamas, a branch of the mighty Creek nation. After the French built Fort Toulouse on the Talapoosa River in the country of the Alabamas in 1717, they developed strong trade and kinship ties with them. In August 1765 fifty Alabamas and Houmas attacked the nascent British fort at Manchac. Engineer Lieutenant Archibald Robertson and a handful of men under his command spent two frightening days locked in a room. Outside they could hear the sounds of rampage. The Indians had combined to loot what they could take away, to kill the little garrison's supply of livestock, and to throw its artillery pieces into the Mississippi River.[6]

Better relations with Indians was one prerequisite for an interest in buying western lands. Stable and suitable government was another. The energetic Johnstone left West Florida in 1767. Three chaotic years under three different governors or acting governors followed. Two of them were army officers; the other was from the navy.[7] None of the three was able to give what Peter Chester, another army officer and the last and longest-ruling governor of the province, could offer.

A talented administrator and publicist, Chester had large ambitions for his colony, and during his tenure he approved, with an intelligently applied generosity unmatched by his predecessors, abundant land grants in the west. His optimism was a major driving force behind the demand by speculators and settlers for land.

For the best protection and convenience of residents he advocated their settlement in townships.[8] Since many otherwise suitable spots for townships on the Mississippi below Natchez had already been allocated to absentee or otherwise unfit owners, he wanted a new township, Harwich, at Manchac. Chester assured the earl of Hillsborough, the secretary of state responsible for the American colonies, that the Manchac region was full of promise. He sent the earl five maps detailing the lands bordering the Iberville, Comite, and Amite Rivers. Provided immigrants settled there, he argued, Harwich, protected by the nearby Manchac fort, would surely prosper.[9] The merchants doing business there would supply British manufactures to inhabitants of the upper Mississippi and would buy the produce of their plantations. They would also supply the needs of itinerant Indian traders and handle all the furs and peltry they brought in. Giving many specifics about navigability and river soundings, Chester urged the desirability of resuming the dredging of the Iberville. He commended the lands north of the Iberville as exceptionally fertile, good for indigo, hemp, and cotton. Rice would suit the poorer, lower-lying land near Lake Maurepas.

Chester might well have amplified his sensible proviso that Harwich would thrive only if immigrants continued to swell his province's population. Not just Harwich, but the whole of the unexploited vastness of the western districts, Natchez and Manchac in particular, would stagnate without more people. In this knowledge, Chester encouraged newcomers to his province, interpreting regulations liberally for their benefit.[10]

By September 1771, when Chester wrote so enthusiastically to the earl of Hillsborough, the prospects for a large immigration had improved with the fading of war talk. The rumor-fueled fears of Indian conspiracies on the Mississippi had died down. So too had the crisis with Spain over the Falkland (Malvinas) Islands that could have brought, and nearly did bring, resumption of an Anglo-Spanish conflict. In fact a township such as Harwich could be strategically valuable, wrote Chester, if war with Spain should break out again: A British force voyaging down the Ohio and Mississippi Rivers could resupply itself at Manchac in readiness for an assault on Spanish New Orleans.[11]

Seconding Chester in his enthusiasm for Manchac was Jacob Blackwell, the collector of customs at Mobile. While visiting London, Blackwell wrote a "Memorial on Customs and Trade" for governmental perusal. He wrote of lost revenue, of how smugglers were trading on the Mississippi, paying no export duties on the British produce (mostly furs and skins) that were coming down from the Illinois country. They were supplying new immigrants, whose numbers, insisted Blackwell, were "certain" to swell rapidly, with duty-free imports. Meanwhile, he wrote, trade at Mobile languished. It gave employment to no more than one ship a year and naturally produced minimal customs revenues. Blackwell advocated the establishment of two new customs houses. They should both be located in what are now the Florida Parishes of Louisiana. One should be at the end of Lake Pontchartrain and the other should be built at Manchac. West Florida was simply too large and its economic activities too dispersed for customs houses on the Gulf of Mexico to suffice.[12]

Because the Mississippi region of West Florida, weeks away in travel time from the provincial capital, could not be administered efficiently from Pensacola, a strong case could be, and was, made for a new colony on the Mississippi. The ambitious and well-connected former lieutenant governor of West Florida, Montfort Browne, had returned to England in 1770. He publicized the desirability of the Mississippi lands, why there should be a separate colony created there, and why he should be its governor.[13]

Probably in part because of Browne's activities, Mississippi received a spate of favorable publicity at this time in both British and American newspapers. The *Scots* magazine for July 1771 printed two items about the Mississippi region. One reported, "Many principal merchants in the city are soliciting grants on the borders of the Mississippi, which is universally reckoned one of the finest climates in the world, and produces, besides, an infinite variety of other valuable commodities, and much better tobacco than the best Virginia." The other stated that "several boards of trade have been held in which the propriety of establishing a government there has, we hear, been absolutely determined upon."[14]

The new colony never materialized, but Chester's province apparently benefitted from the publicity that Browne had generated. In 1772 a rush for land followed. Farm land and town lots, if one had the right qualifications, could be had in abundance and free of cost but for surveying and governmental fees. The British government had from 1763 used two methods to attract immigrants to Florida. The family right system entitled the head of a household to one hundred acres, and fifty acres each for a spouse, indentured servants, and slaves. The other method awarded bounty on a sliding scale to veterans of the French and Indian War. They ranged from fifty acres for a private soldier to five thousand acres for an officer of field rank.[15]

The potential of Manchac as a trading post made settlement on the bayous and rivers in its vicinity unusually attractive. Since the region had no roads except the rough tracks used by the packhorses and mules of traders with Native Americans, settling on waterways was vital for the transportation of crops. Fortunately rivers were plentiful, although they varied in quality as thoroughfares. The Comite, a tributary of the Amite, was navigable only intermittently during the year. The western arm of the Iberville, as noted before, connected with the Mississippi during only three months of the year. The Amite was thought the best, it seems, of the rivers near Manchac. More petitioners sought land on or near it than on any of the other rivers in the vicinity.[16] Its great advantage was that year-round the Amite connected via the eastern branch of the Iberville River with Lakes Maurepas and Pontchartrain. They in turn gave access to the Gulf of Mexico, Pensacola, and Mobile and finally to the markets of Europe and the West Indies. Those markets could absorb the products—rice, cotton, hemp—for which the area's soil and climate seemed fit; conditions also seemed right for the production of indigo, which was particularly prized because of potential profitability. Although colonial growers were forbidden to export indigo to any country except Britain, the English Crown paid a bounty on every pound of indigo imported from its colonies in order to supply the dye needs of the ever-growing British textile industry.[17]

Thompson's Creek, which like the Iberville, Amite, and Comite Rivers ran in what became known as the Florida Parishes of Louisiana, falls into a different category from them. Its attraction lay less in its proximity to Manchac and more that it disgorged into the Mississippi opposite Pointe Coupée in Spanish Louisiana. For its time and place Pointe Coupée was well settled.[18] Stretched out, as one commentator worded it, "eight leagues [24 miles] in length . . . all cleared and cultivated with houses regularly built about a gunshot distance from one another,"[19] it was a place of social and commercial contact for new arrivals. It was also, it seems, a source of good indigo and inferior tobacco. Either could be exchanged for sundry British manufactured goods or for slaves. An arrangement, necessarily informal because contrary to Spanish regulations, seems to have existed whereby a British planter would legally import a cargo of more slaves than he needed to employ on the Mississippi's eastern (that is, British) shore, and then sell, illegally, those he did not use in Spanish Pointe Coupée.[20]

For these riverine lands there were two bursts of frenzied buying, beginning in 1772. The first came to an end in October 1773, when the Crown declared a moratorium on land grants. The second round of land-grabbing began on 11 November 1775, when the king not only lifted the ban on sales but also allowed, at the discretion of the governor in council, bounty acreage for subjects who could claim they had been forced to leave older colonies for refusing to abandon their allegiance to him.

In each of these periods Governor Chester supported the establishment of planned towns. The first, Harwich, was laid out at Manchac, north of the fort and of the handful of trading houses, residences, and taverns that then existed. A second, Dartmouth, was planned for location at the fork of the Amite and Iberville Rivers. By no coincidence both towns bore names that were among the titles of secretaries of state for the American colonies in office in the 1770s.[21] Flattering establishment bigwigs was by no means confined to the British Floridas. To take but one of several possible examples, a township named Dartmouth was laid out in the early 1770s near Fort James at the fork of the Broad and Savannah Rivers in nearby Georgia.[22]

Forty petitioners applied for eighty-two lots in Harwich.[23] It is hard to believe that those who applied for many more lots than they could possibly have occupied would have done so for any reason other than the expectation of reselling surplus lots at a profit. The biggest spenders were members of West Florida's ruling elite. They stood to lose heavily under the law of the province, unless they could resell their extra lots quickly. A buyer had two years to build on his or her lot a house of at least 30 by 15 feet with a brick chimney; failure to do so meant he or she was liable to pay an annual fee of one pound sterling. If nothing was built within ten years, the lot was forfeit.[24]

Philip Livingston Jr., a leader of West Florida's establishment, bought sixteen lots. Private secretary to Governor Chester was only one of the many income-producing posts he obtained in the province. He was also acting provincial secretary, deputy clerk of the council, clerk of the ordinary court, chancery clerk of patents, clerk of the legislature, collector of customs at Mobile, notary public, and acting receiver general, according to his critics.[25] Alexander Macullagh, who bought ten Harwich lots, was the colony's deputy secretary, while Elihu Bay Hall, who bought nine lots, was the judge presiding over Pensacola's vice-admiralty court. Their official duties meant that none of the three intended to live in Harwich. They were certainly buying speculatively in the hope of capital appreciation, but their commitment to Harwich shows that Governor Chester had company in his optimism for Manchac's future, and certainly a start was made there.

In August 1772 a deputy superintendent of Indians at Manchac wrote that "the township [of Harwich] is now fix'd and laid out."[26] Purchase money came into the provincial treasury, but as applications for lots slowed, the provincial council extended the deadline for accepting them. Harwich did not flourish, but hope for it survived, and in January 1777 a committee formed to revive the project. The money collected until that time from the sale of Harwich lots, between £500 and £600, was to be used to clear the levee on the Mississippi and the two rows of lots nearest to it.[27]

In spite of much optimism and some effort most of the permanent residents of the Manchac district preferred not to move to Harwich. They either lived a mile or so south of it, near the fort, or on nearby plantations.

None of the twelve peace commissioners appointed for the Manchac District in 1777 owned a lot in Harwich. In the following year a jury of the general sessions convened at Harwich (presumably in a building but possibly in the open air). Of the twenty-three jurymen present who were described as "the principal merchants, planters, and inhabitants of Manchac District," only four owned Harwich lots.[28]

The poor response to the creation of Harwich did not deter Governor Chester from planning another township nearby. If he thought that distaste for involvement in the war in the north that began with the shots fired at Lexington, combined with royal offers of land bounty in the Floridas to Loyalists, would stimulate a fresh burst of southward emigration, he was right. Unfortunately for him most royalists fleeing the Revolution preferred, largely for geographical reasons, to relocate in East, not West, Florida. During the Revolutionary War, East Florida received 17,000 loyal refugees. Petitioners for land citing loyalty to the crown in West Florida numbered only 1,369.[29]

Naturally unaware of future immigration and in the belief that the lukewarm response to the offer of Harwich lots resulted from overpricing, the optimistic Chester urged that lots in the new township of Dartmouth should cost as little as £10, and certainly no more than £30.[30]

Chester succeeded in persuading the council that creating Dartmouth was a viable project, but their confidence was misplaced. The township proved even less attractive than Harwich.

The countryside in the vicinity of both had more appeal than Harwich and Dartmouth themselves. Chester had rightly foreseen that Loyalist refugees fleeing scenes of revolution would want property. Many of them could qualify on more than one count for abundant acreage, and they besieged the provincial council with petitions for it. They saw themselves as estate owners. As such, they could be fairly sure of supporting themselves, even if the apparently endless Revolutionary War and the cessation of imports from Britain that went with it continued. By contrast the war made dubious the survival of the urban businesses that in locations at the nexus of water routes, like Harwich and Dartmouth, might have prospered in time of peace.

The prewar rush for land between November 1772 and October 1773 was different in kind and motivation from the boom that followed the royal offer of bounty land to Loyalists of 11 November 1775. Some examples from the earlier applications may throw light on motivations.

The previously mentioned Philip Livingston would have been a gold medallist if awards had been given for land acquisition in West Florida. His multiple offices enabled him to know how and when to lay claim to the most promising land. His biographer, Ruth Connor Nichols, estimated that, exclusive of town lots, he amassed a total of at least 40,500 acres.[31] His enemies estimated that he had cornered more than twice as much, 100,000 acres.[32] In the Manchac region, however, exclusive of his sixteen Harwich lots, Livingston had, on the Amite, a holding that by reputation was the best-improved plantation on the river. Apart from housing for his overseer and, separately, for his slaves, Livingston had two buildings for his own use. If typical of the region, his main dwelling would have been of modest dimensions, perhaps as little as 16 by 20 feet. The primary structure would likely be of trimmed logs, plastered on the inside and clapboarded outside. It would have been roofed with wooden shingles and almost certainly had a veranda, in eighteenth-century usage a piazza, on one or more sides. Next to his house was a fenced three-acre garden and orchard.

The contents of Livingston's cellar throw light on the taste for drinks of either himself, or his social peers or, most likely, both. Livingston kept bottles on hand of each kind in dozens. In descending order of volume the cellar stocked rum, Madeira, claret, porter, port, gin, and brandy.

The flesh of the pig dominated his food store: Livingston had eight barrels of pork to one of beef. Delicacies included white sugar, cheese, vinegar, oil, spices, and tea, but no coffee.

Livingston had more land plowed to grow corn—one hundred acres—than any other single crop. Probably rice, which he grew on thirty acres, and corn were the basis of his slaves' rations. Like many planters of his kind, Livingston hoped to profit from indigo, and he devoted seventy acres to it. Deerskins apart, timber products proved West Florida's best export. The Amite region was well suited to their production, and Livingston's work force made staves for barrels by the tens of thousands.[33]

Livingston was part owner of the largest plantation in the region. Chesterfield, punningly named after its prime owner, Governor Peter Chester, embraced 6,550 acres. James Bruce, Pensacola's customs collector and a very senior member of the West Florida council, also had title to large acreage. Bruce must have delegated his official duties, for he spent months on end at his plantation on the Amite, which he worked with ten slaves.[34]

Bruce grew no indigo. Concentrating more on corn, he even built a mill house to convert his crop into flour.[35] It is less clear that Bruce actually cultivated his extensive holding on Thompson's Creek, where he owned 4,000 acres in addition to his 2,600 acres on the Amite.

Another prominent West Floridian was a Scot, Adam Chrystie.[36] After qualifying as a lawyer in England, Chrystie emigrated to West Florida and was one of the four assemblymen elected to represent Manchac. He talked with confidence to the provincial council of persuading one hundred Scottish families to immigrate to the province. Would the council please reserve 40,000 acres of western land for him to settle them? The only thing in fact reserved was the council response to his request.[37]

Chrystie's grandiose scheme came to nothing, but he did buy 1,000 acres on the Amite for £1,092.[38] This price was comparatively high, probably because his tract was conveniently located for the transportation of crops near the fork of the Amite and the Iberville. Before the coming of the Revolution halted further development of his land, Chrystie had cleared 264 acres of it. Chrystie worked this and other holdings elsewhere with a considerable force of slaves. During the Revolution, as an active Loyalist, he clothed and armed twenty-two of them.[39] The seller of this choice acreage was William Johnstone, a captain in the Royal Artillery who had no connection, as far as I have been able to discover, with George Johnstone, West Florida's first British governor.[40] Like Chrystie, William Johnstone worked his land with some dozens of slaves.[41] William Marshall, another bigwig of the Manchac region, owned 1,500 acres on the Comite, 500 on the Amite, and between twenty and thirty slaves.[42]

Not every petitioner for land intended to work it. Doubtless many petitioners invested exclusively and seriously for capital appreciation. There is, however, something mysterious, even frivolous, perhaps, about six applications made on 28 July 1772. All were for land on Thompson's Creek. All were for exactly 1,000 acres. All were from women. Each was married to a man of substance in the colony,[43] so certainly they did not want the land merely to survive. Motives are difficult to guess. None of the land would be free; it would have to be paid for, since none of the women was a head of household. The episode has the feel of a gamble, the spirit in which people in the late 1990s bought Internet stocks.

If speculation was prominent in prewar land grants, compensation was more noticeable in land awarded during the Revolutionary War. Chester, always eager to encourage immigrants, rewarded applicants beyond what they could claim on family right for proven loyalty to the Crown. Acting with his council, he rejected outright very few of the 248 petitions from self-professed Loyalists.[44] Most petitioners of this type looked beyond the Manchac region to Natchez, but 40, about 1 in 6 of them Loyalists or self-styled Loyalists, did want land on the rivers and bayous near Manchac. More than half of them, 21, sought land on or near the Amite, 11 looked to Thompson's Creek, while only 8 asked for grants on the more remote Comite.

In general it seems that the size of Loyalist bounty land granted had less to do with zeal in fighting rebels and more with the amount of property abandoned in emigrating to Florida. Several immigrants from the West Indies had seen no fighting, but the war had blighted their traditional trade with New England.[45] William Walker had been a major landowner and a member of the governing council of the island of St. Vincent. He fled to West Florida in 1776 and received two thousand acres on the Comite on family right and an additional one thousand acres for proven loyalism.[46] Many new arrivals came without family or slaves. On family right they could claim only one hundred acres. In every case they were granted an additional one hundred acres, and in some instances an extra two hundred acres.

Concerning this topic questions remain that would merit attention. There has been no consideration here of the effects on the local Indians of the granting to white men and women massive tracts of land that Indians had traditionally used for farming and hunting. Such consequences were equally unconsidered by the West Florida council when it was distributing territorial largesse. It is a complex topic. One knows that Indian headmen complained of interlopers, but there is no need for an automatic assumption of hostility to the British in the relevant years. It would be particularly mistaken in connection with the *petites nations*. By the time the first phase of the land boom began in 1772–1773, the small tribes of the lower Mississippi had become much reduced in size. They were terrified of being drawn into the prolonged war then being waged by two much larger Indian groups, the Creeks and the Choctaws. They looked for protection to the nearest imperial nations. At Manchac they curried favor with both the commandant of Fort San Gabriel, the little post on the Spanish side of Bayou Manchac, and also with John Thomas, the British assistant superintendent of Indians a few hundred yards away on the British side of the bayou. The Tunicas seem not to have been simply practicing miniature realpolitik with Thomas, but to have been genuinely fond of him. In 1775, the year in which the Creek-Choctaw war came to an end, the Tunicas gave him land west of Thompson's Creek north of their village. Twelve of the leading Tunicas, including at least two women, deeded him a square tract on the Mississippi three miles in length. It was reward, they said, "for the many services done and performed by him ... for these last ten years past." In return Thomas had to pay a token: a handful of earth with a willow twig growing in it.[47]

Naturally, happy Tunicas did not necessarily mean complacency among other Indian peoples about white plantations in the region. It is a question to be pursued. It is beyond dispute that those Britons who sank money into what became the Florida Parishes of Louisiana gained nothing from their speculation if they quit the area after the British surrender, but another question for examination is whether such investment could have yielded profit. Unswayable devotion to the king of England was by no means universal in British West Florida,[48] and study of the fortunes of those who transferred their allegiance from George III to Carlos III and stayed on might help answer that question. Another might be, What happened to the potential for trade with the Illinois country that was so confidently anticipated, once the devoutly believed-in Iberville Canal was shown to be a castle in the air? These and related questions remain for further research and assessment.

What in conclusion can be said about the boom on the bayous? First, it was an exclusively Anglo phenomenon. The French in West Florida, who had stayed on, mostly in Mobile, after the French king abandoned his claims to the North American mainland following the French and Indian War, took no part in it. Second, the several ambitious plans for townships all proved premature. Third, the speculation in land was dominated by the social and governing elite of West Florida. Although many settlers of limited means petitioned for comparatively small plots of free land, the riffraff of West Florida—what Johnstone called the overflowing scum of the empire—mostly squatted on land. They did not seek title to it. That elite who did go to the expense of obtaining title to substantial tracts did not come from the ranks of the British aristocracy: No titled names are to be found among the residents. They came from the respected bourgeoisie. Its members could be Britons like Governors Johnstone and Chester from the commissioned officer class, or Americans like Philip Livingston, who was from one of the politically influential families of New York. Merchants too were of West Florida's elite. They seem to have had little interest in speculating in bayou land, although a few chose to live there. John Fitzpatrick was a merchant. He is the best-remembered resident of Manchac where he traded profitably under British rule, but that the area did have at least some economic potential for plantation owners too is suggested by the example of Adam Chrystie, who was one of that minority of investors in the Florida Parishes who actually worked the land. In the British period the most lucrative product for planters was timber and timber products but potentially more promising was indigo. The end of British rule also meant the end of the bounty that made it attractive.

The market in Britain for indigo and other crops associated with British industry was one of the gusts helping to inflate the bayou bubble. The expected development of a network of water routes by which to carry those crops, in addition to skins and hides, to the markets of the world was another. A more important third was that immigrants would come continuously and in sizable numbers to the bayou country. It did not happen. People did not come, and without them, even if the British had retained West Florida, the bubble would have subsided.

NOTES

1. J. Leitch Wright Jr., *Anglo-Spanish Rivalry in North America* (Athens: University of Georgia Press, 1971), 112.

2. The Royal Proclamation of October 7, 1763, in *Speeches and Documents on Colonial Policy*, ed. Arthur Berriedale Keith (London: Oxford University Press, 1918), 1:4.

3. *New York Mercury*, 11 June 1764.

4. Johnstone to Sir John Lindsay, 10 December 1764, Colonial Office, Class 5 (America and West Indies), 582:499, Public Record Office, Kew (referred to hereinafter as CO5); *New York Mercury*, 17 July 1765; *Massachusetts Gazette*, 25 July 1765.

5. Deposition of Wills Escott and Alexander McIntosh concerning a meeting on 25 October 1771, British Library Add., MSS 21672:26.

6. Harry Miller Lydenberg, ed., *Archibald Robertson: His Diaries and Sketches in America, 1762–1780* (New York: New York Publishing Library, 1930), 12–15.

7. They were Montfort Browne, Elias Durnford, and John Elliot.

8. Chester to the earl of Hillsborough, 23 June 1771, in CO5/588:291.

9. Chester to Hillsborough, 28 September 1771, in CO5/588:499.

10. Robin Fabel, *The Economy of British West Florida, 1763–1783* (Tuscaloosa: University of Alabama Press, 1988), 181.

11. Chester to Hillsborough, 28 September 1771, in CO5/588:498.

12. Jacob Blackwell, "Memorial on Customs and Trade on the Mississippi," London, 22 July 1772, PRO Treasury 1/496:146.

13. Robin Fabel, "An Eighteenth Colony: Dreams for Mississippi on the Eve of the American Revolution," *Journal of Southern History* 59 (1993): 647–72.

14. For similar reports on this side of the Atlantic, see *Massachusetts Gazette,* 2 and 9 November 1772.

15. Clinton N. Howard, *The British Development of West Florida, 1763–1769* (Berkeley: University of California Press, 1947), 8–9.

16. British petitioners for land on the main rivers of what became Louisiana's Florida Parishes numbered as follows: Amite River, 121; Thompson's Creek, 62; Comite River, 33; Iberville River (Bayou Manchac), 1.

17. Up to 1771 the bounty was sixpence sterling and thereafter fourpence a pound.

18. Philip Pittman, *The Present State of the European Settlements on the Mississippi,* ed. Robert R. Rea (Gainesville: University Presses of Florida, 1973), 34.

19. Robin Fabel, ed., "The Letters of R: The Lower Mississippi in the Early 1770s," *Louisiana History* 24 (fall 1983): 416.

20. John Fitzpatrick to Arthur Strother, 7 November 1769, to Isaac Johnson, 27 December 1774, to Oliver Pollock, 17 October 1776, and to Thomas O'Keefe, 18 June 1768, in Margaret Fisher Dalrymple, *The Merchant of Manchac: The Letterbooks of John Fitzpatrick, 1768–1790* (Baton Rouge: Louisiana State University Press, 1978), 77, 181, 213, 295.

21. A secondary title of Wills Hill, earl of Hillsborough, secretary from January 1768 to August 1772, was Baron Harwich, while his successor in office, from August 1772 to November 1775, was William Legge, earl of Dartmouth.

22. Edward J. Cashin, *William Bartram and the American Revolution on the Southern Frontier* (Columbia: University of South Carolina Press, 2000), 135.

23. Cecil Johnson, *British West Florida, 1763–1783* (New York: Anchor Press, 1971), 146, has numbers that differ slightly from mine.

24. CO5/610:2.

25. CO5/580:159.

26. John Thomas to Thomas Gage, 13 August 1772, in Gage Papers, William Clements Library, University of Michigan, Ann Arbor.

27. Council Minutes for 14 January 1777, CO5/634:454.

28. They were William Marshall, who owned two lots, and James Elliot, Daniel Hickey, and Daniel Lewis, all of whom owned one lot apiece.

29. Robin Fabel, "Loyalist West Florida: An Ambiguous Community," in *Loyalists and Community in North America,* ed. Robert M. Calhoon, Timothy M. Barnes, and George A. Rawlyk (Westport, Conn.: Greenwood Press, 1994), 136.

30. Council Minutes for 18 November 1777, CO5/631.

31. Ruth Corinne Connor, "Gentleman Phil, Eighteenth-Century Opportunist, 1740–1810" (Master's thesis, Auburn University, 1982).

32. "Petition of Gentlemen, Freeholders, and Principal Inhabitants of West Florida," read 14 August 1779, CO5/580:156.

33. Robert R. Rea, "Planters and Plantations in British West Florida," *Alabama Review* 29 (1976): 223–25.

34. From February to December he was absent from the council. CO5/592:231.

35. Rea, "Planters and Plantations," 224–25.

36. Chrystie was eminent but was not of Chester's coterie. On the petition demanding Chester's recall in 1779 his was the first of 132 signatures. CO5/580:149.

37. Council Minutes for 13 June 1764, CO5/634:208.

38. Chrystie's agent said he cleared between two hundred and three hundred acres and, but for the revolution, would have made £1,500 a year from them. Deposition of James Amoss, 17 October 1786, Chalmers Papers, Force Collection 8A #41, Manuscript Division, Library of Congress.

39. Rea, "Planters and Plantations," 226.

40. Johnstone had retired from full-time participation in the Royal Artillery. He performed no military duties in West Florida in its peacetime years.

41. During the siege of Pensacola in 1781 he supplied thirty slaves to help fortify the town. "Agreement between Capt. William Johnstone and Officers of the Ordinance Board," 16 March 1781, CO5/616:133.

42. CO5/609:45, 76.

43. Jane Chester, the governor's wife; Elizabeth Chadwick, Chester's daughter; Rebecca Durnford, wife of the surveyor general; Rebecca Blackwell, wife of Mobile's collector of customs; Anne Raincock, married to a councillor; and Isabella Bruce, whose husband James was also of the council.

44. Many grants did not become immediately effective. If a petitioner claimed acreage on the basis of absent family or slaves, he could not patent it until they had arrived in West Florida.

45. Andrew J. O. Shaughnessy, *An Empire Divided: The American Revolution and the British Caribbean* (Philadelphia: University of Pennsylvania Press, 2000), 144.

46. Council Minutes for 26 December 1776, CO5/634, and for 22 January 1778, CO5/631.

47. Indenture of 29 April 1775 between "the several chiefs, headmen, warriors and women of the nation of Indians called Tonicas and John Thomas," CO5/617:136–37. Thomas died the following year.

48. F. deBorja Medina Rojas, *Jose de Ezpeleta, Gobernador de la Mobila* (Seville: Escuela de Estudias Hispano Americanos de Sevilla, 1980), 38, 40.

3

SLAVERY IN LOUISIANA'S FLORIDA PARISHES UNDER THE SPANISH REGIME, 1779–1803

GILBERT C. DIN

*A*LTHOUGH SPAIN ACQUIRED THE FLORIDA PARISHES—THAT territory north from Bayou Manchac and the Amite River to the thirty-first parallel (the present Louisiana-Mississippi boundary)—by conquest from Great Britain in 1779, settlement in this region had started earlier. The French were the first Europeans to begin colonization successfully in the lower Mississippi Valley in the early eighteenth century. Nevertheless, over a span of more than a half century, they provided few colonists or slaves to the area known today as the Florida Parishes.[1] In 1766, shortly after the French period in Louisiana ended, a census showed that the portion of the colony the Spaniards assumed had 11,476 inhabitants, of whom 5,940 were slaves. While this census of west Louisiana and the New Orleans district omitted the Florida Parishes because they were now British territory, it illustrates that France had scarcely populated its gigantic former colony.[2]

Shortly after the French arrived in the Mississippi Valley, they introduced the dismal institution of black slavery. Although slaves were scant at first, between 1719 and 1731 several thousand more arrived, who quickly surpassed the white population. For the twenty years following 1731, however, few slaves entered the colony, since merchants found it more profitable to sell them in the sugar-rich French West Indies than in debt-ridden Louisiana.[3] Because of the sudden influx of slaves, in 1724 the French drew up regulations for their control in Louisiana called the Code Noir, which was modeled on the 1685 slave laws of the same name for the West Indies. While the 1724 Code Noir had provisions that afforded Louisiana slaves some protection, officials and masters generally employed only its worst features and ignored regulations that benefitted slaves. Furthermore, the Catholic Church in the colony did little more than baptize slaves. Under both the French and the Spaniards, priests deferred to masters; the few priests in colonial Louisiana ministered overwhelmingly to whites, not blacks. For example, they denied blacks extreme unction (the last rites) and usually did not marry slaves, since masters refused to sanction legal, i.e., church, marriages. That ceremony would have compelled owners to sell husbands and wives together, which most preferred not to do. One priest in the 1770s admitted that clerics in Louisiana had traditionally treated whites differentially to draw a distinction between them and blacks.[4]

The British, who succeeded the French on the Mississippi's east bank except for the Isle of Orleans (the region that extended below Bayou Manchac to the Gulf of Mexico) by the 1763 Treaty of Paris, contributed the first substantial settlers to the Florida Parishes.[5] British official Elias Durnford estimated in 1774 that 3,700 whites and 1,200 slaves resided in British West Florida, an area that extended along the Gulf Coast from East Florida to the Mississippi. He neglected to specify how many of them lived on the Mississippi. By the time the American Revolutionary War arrived in the lower Mississippi Valley a few years later, most of the estimated 2,500 British and their 600 slaves on the Mississippi lived around Natchez, while relatively few inhabited the Florida Parishes.[6] After the Spanish conquest of the Mississippi's east bank in 1779, many British settlers remained on their lands, as only a portion of them and their slaves departed. This was true at Natchez, and it seems to have been true for the Florida Parishes settlements of Manchac, Baton Rouge, and Feliciana, too.[7]

Because the French generally neglected the area that contains the Florida Parishes, their slave code had little meaning there. In contrast the British sent both settlers and bonds people and introduced their own slave system within four years of their arrival. Despite the meagerness of blacks, the Britons decreed a stringent code for the few present; more typically, harsh laws flourished only where slaves outnumbered whites and threatened their safety. The West Florida law made manumission for Africans difficult to obtain; consequently, few free blacks resided in the colony. Slaves lived with numerous other restrictions imposed upon them. Among them, they could not keep farm animals, sell anything, purchase alcoholic beverages legally, or use firearms unless their owners consented. Furthermore, British law afforded slaves little protection, and punishment for infractions was severe. Two justices of the peace and three freeholders, who, of course, were all white, tried slaves accused of misconduct. Trials needed to take place within eight days of the crime, with punishment, including executions, imposed immediately following the trial. Appeals to a higher tribunal to review the case and sentence did not exist. Although British law considered bonds people as property (chattel), owners faced a £100 fine for killing a slave and death for repeating the crime—if authorities enforced it. Finally, the West Florida slave regulation imposed on all whites, regardless of class, responsibility for implementing the slave laws that benefitted only masters.[8]

These laws illustrate how whites expected blacks to behave but reveal nothing about them. In reality, slaves at all times lived grudgingly under white ownership. That they aspired to freedom can be seen in the plot that formed in the Baton Rouge area in July 1776. Among the conspirators were several slaves belonging to the planter William Dunbar, sometimes regarded in retrospect as an eighteenth-century savant. He became enraged on learning that the rebellious slaves included two of his own upon whom he had never laid a whip, an oversight he, no doubt, soon corrected. Africans, however, regarded any form of slavery, no matter how mild, intolerable, and some would risk everything to escape its wicked grasp. Dunbar showed that despite his learning, his primary concern was economics, not the benign treatment of blacks.[9]

During the British period, merchants introduced slaves, for sale both to their own planters on the Mississippi, which had the colony's best agricultural lands, and to Louisiana farmers. British merchants found the black trade profitable. Because Spanish governor Luis de Unzaga of Louisiana (1770–1776) realized that the mercantile restrictions his predecessor, Lieutenant General Alejandro O'Reilly (1769–1770),[10] had imposed on the province's commerce were destructive, he tolerated illicit trade so as not to bankrupt planters and drive them from the colony. Illegal commerce with Louisiana at Bayou Manchac turned that tiny British settlement into a thriving trade emporium in the 1770s.[11] British merchants not only sold goods and slaves, often on credit, to Louisiana planters, but purchased agricultural crops from them. In 1777, when Bernardo de Gálvez (1777–1782) succeeded Unzaga as governor, conditions that accommodated smuggling began to decline, and it was a harbinger of things to come. The first sign of a change occurred in April 1777, when Gálvez seized British boats that commerced unlawfully on the Mississippi, although he soon allowed British vendors to open shops in New Orleans, where he exercised some control over them. More devastating to British West Florida than Gálvez's actions, however, was the 1778 raid by American rebel James Willing that plundered Loyalist plantations and settlements around Baton Rouge and Manchac.[12]

Nevertheless, during the British regime a debut was made in the settlement of West Florida. As Robert R. Rea has written, "By the 1770s the richer western lands of the Mississippi River valley were attracting both speculators and settlers. From Natchez to Baton Rouge, on the Mississippi, English planters were beginning to clear the woods and erect their homes, and on the Amite River, between Lake Maurepas and the Iberville River (Bayou Manchac), a most promising start had been made."[13] Upon Spain's entry into the American Revolutionary War the next year, Governor Gálvez quickly conquered Great Britain's army posts on the Mississippi and seized control of the British-occupied lands.[14] In the Spanish era that followed, the population continued to grow in both whites and black slaves, most of whom entered from the United States.

Although censuses then as now are approximations of the total number of inhabitants, they provide the only available figures. The first Spanish census of Baton Rouge in 1782, the sole area in the Florida Parishes counted, revealed the presence of 68 whites, 2 free blacks, 101 black slaves, and 5 mulatto slaves, for 176 inhabitants in all. Most, if not all of them, were holdovers from the British era. Governor Esteban Miró of Louisiana (1782–1791) produced two province-wide censuses in 1785 and 1788. The first listed Baton Rouge as having 270 inhabitants. Before Miró's second provincial census appeared, a local tally at Baton Rouge the next year reported that whites numbered 70, which was a significant decline in white inhabitants unless the figure is an error; free blacks who were really mulattos had doubled over the 1782 figure to 4, but slaves had nearly tripled to 278, for a total population of 352. The 1788 census, which revealed a larger population of 682, probably counted the inhabitants more carefully.[15]

In 1795, a comprehensive census was taken at Baton Rouge. It placed the number of slaves at 375, whites at 319, and free blacks at 12, for a total population of 706. The Baton Rouge district then held 108 landholdings, which were mainly farms, because most of their 69 owners had no slaves. Many owners of Africans possessed only a scant number, one to five. John Turnbull, the district's most affluent resident, owned 75 slaves, followed by Armand Duplantier with 69, Samuel Steer with 46, William Marshall with 22, and Madam Smith with 20. Ranking sixth in the ownership of slaves was the mulatto Juan Baptista Bienville, who had 16. He was one of two free people of color who owned both land and slaves in the district. These six masters alone possessed two-thirds of the slaves in the Baton Rouge district.[16]

Neighboring Manchac, at the junction of the Mississippi and Bayou Manchac, in 1785 had only 77 inhabitants, who increased to 284 by 1788. Perhaps it reflects an undercounting of the district's population in 1785. Manchac, in a 1795 census, had a white population of 222, who lived on 67 farms but cultivated only 479 arpents of land. The small area farmed indicates that most landholdings had not yet been fully cleared; the inhabitants owned only 110 slaves, who made up the principal work force. Manchac had increased its total inhabitants to 332, but this represented only a modest increment.[17]

Little is known about the first inhabitants at Feliciana, or New Feliciana as it was also called, an area north of Baton Rouge and today adjacent to Mississippi.[18] Some settled there before the Spanish conquest in 1779, and others entered afterward. While Spain defrayed the costs for the transport and settlement of the Canary Islanders and many Acadians who immigrated to Louisiana, the arriving Americans generally paid all their own expenses. Besides these hardy settlers, however, were some destitute Americans who took up residence in Feliciana. They received free passage from Philadelphia to Louisiana on two ships, the *Lydia* and the *Concepción*. Governor Miró had dispatched the vessels to Philadelphia to purchase flour in March 1788, after a devastating fire destroyed most of New Orleans. Among these immigrants, 209 of a total 303 received government assistance consisting of free land in Feliciana, rations, and tools.[19] Possibly they comprised the only American settlers helped in this way during Louisiana's colonial period.

Feliciana first appeared in the 1788 census as holding 730 inhabitants, a figure larger than Baton Rouge's 682 residents for the same year. Census takers doubtlessly expended greater energy in counting people in 1788, since earlier censuses appear to have ignored Feliciana's settlers, and 1,696 inhabitants for all the Florida Parishes was perhaps a reasonably accurate enumeration. The 1788 census, however, clashes with another made at Feliciana in 1793. It counted only 232 whites, 132 slaves, and no free people of color, for a total 364 persons. They resided on 57 landholdings. Slave owners among whites numbered 29, not one of whom owned many slaves.[20] Possibly the census tallied only one or two districts within Feliciana. In comparison with Feliciana, more is known about Baton Rouge and, for a time, about Manchac because of the regular army officers posted at their forts.[21]

In July 1801, Commandant Carlos de Grand-Pré at Baton Rouge, speaking for all the Florida Parishes, placed its population at 3,564. Possibly he derived his figure from a census that has since vanished. At the time, Grand-Pré was commenting on oath-taking by the foreign (non-Spanish and French) inhabitants, who comprised the bulk of the residents. He had recently expelled several of them for fomenting disturbances.[22] While most settlers caused no problems and demonstrated their loyalty to the Spanish regime, a handful of them were inveterate troublemakers who would have exacerbated tensions anywhere they lived.

All commandants assigned to the most important districts in Spanish Louisiana and West Florida were regular army officers, and they dealt with slavery, since they possessed both civil and military authority. Among the commandants between 1779 and 1796 who served at Baton Rouge, which was the Florida Parishes' notable military post, were Pierre Joseph Favrot (1779–1781), Ignacio Delinó Chalmette (1781–1784), Francisco de Vergés (1784–1787), and José Vázquez Vahamonde (1787–1796).[23] About late 1797, Colonel Carlos de Grand-Pré took over as the commandant of Baton Rouge and the Florida Parishes, a post he retained beyond 1803.[24] He was originally designated to succeed Manuel Gayoso de Lemos as governor of the Natchez district, but that situation changed in 1798. Early that year, the United States took possession of the Mississippi's east bank down to the thirty-first parallel because of the 1795 Spanish-American Treaty of San Lorenzo (Pinckney's Treaty). Grand-Pré then received the consolation post of Baton Rouge, although for years afterward he continued to label himself the governor of the Natchez district.[25] From about 1787, the Spaniards had endeavored to build up the population around Natchez in a counter-colonization scheme and had encouraged American settlement with free lands and benevolent rule. With the United States takeover in 1798, Spain evacuated its forts at Nogales (today, Vicksburg) and Natchez and shifted its withering military defenses on the Mississippi's east bank to Baton Rouge.[26]

Earlier in 1769, upon taking charge of Louisiana in all respects, the Spaniards introduced their slave laws. Older histories of Louisiana often assert that in the Spanish period the French 1724 Code Noir, the first comprehensive slave law in the Mississippi Valley, remained in effect. This is not true, although for several years after the start of the Spanish era many masters behaved as if it were.[27] Spanish slave laws differed significantly from the French Code Noir and the British West Florida slave regulations.

Among differences, the Spaniards allowed slaves who had their purchase price to buy their freedom, and masters could not refuse them.

Moreover, owners could not demand an arbitrary price that overvalued their slaves. Spanish law insisted on a fair market value and decreed that if slave and master disputed the purchase price, a judge would appoint an unbiased person to appraise the slave, which often resulted in a compromise. Furthermore, the Spaniards permitted masters to emancipate slaves for whatever reason and do so before a notary; masters did not have to post a sum of money for freeing a slave as had occurred earlier. In the French era, only the Superior Council, which originally was a law court before also becoming the colony's governing body, could free slaves, and it infrequently consented. In contrast, no Spanish governmental authority at any level had to grant permission for the emancipation of slaves. If a master objected to manumitting a slave, the latter could ask the governor's court to intervene, and it usually favored the slave. Spanish jurisprudence did not regard slavery as a necessarily permanent condition. Spanish law also decreed that slaves have counsel when accused of crimes, and sentences imposed by either the governor or an *alcalde ordinario* (a municipal magistrate) could be appealed first to a body of three persons, consisting of the judge who initially tried the case and two councilors (*regidores*) of the New Orleans municipal council (city government or *cabildo*), and second to the captain general in Cuba. Governors routinely routed death sentences to the captain general's appellate court for review, for anyone who received such a penalty—white, Native American, or black.[28]

Spanish law permitted slaves to complain to the authorities about abuse by their masters. Earlier, the French government had not tolerated their slaves doing so, and French planters protested repeatedly throughout the Spanish era that this abominable practice empowered slaves to malinger and humiliate masters. During the governorship of Francisco Luis Hector, barón de Carondelet (1792–1797), slave complaints abounded, since the governor endeavored to regulate slavery in a more benevolent fashion.[29]

Persons living in the Florida Parishes in the late eighteenth century generally did not write about the life of slaves on their plantations. Some generalizations, however, can be made based on the many documents generated throughout Louisiana at that time. Needless to say, life for slaves was often not easy and sometimes was filled with violence because of the vicious character of some owners and overseers. Masters expected work from their blacks, but many at the same time disliked spending any money on them. That led to the introduction of the "slave economy," which had started in the Caribbean and entered the Mississippi Valley in the French era; it allowed slaves to produce much of their own food in gardens and raise a few animals. Slaves worked their gardens on Sundays and religious holidays, days that were theirs to use any way they wished; after their daily dawn-to-dusk chores ended; during their two-hour lunch breaks; and at whatever other spare time they found. They sold some of the food raised, corn in particular, to the master or to other slaves. Men sometimes used their free days to work off the plantation for farmers or planters who required extra help, earning a half-peso (fifty cents) if they were unskilled and more if they were artisans. Masters who required the labor of their slaves on Sundays, especially at harvest, had to pay for it or grant them compensatory time. Another practice sometimes employed let artisan slaves hire themselves, and their free time enabled them to earn the rent money to pay their masters, funds to live on, and, if they were lucky, money with which to purchase themselves. Usually, however, most plantation slaves spent their limited earnings on foodstuffs, nicer apparel than the work garments owners provided, and alcoholic beverages. Some few slaves even acquired guns, which they used to hunt, since game in that age was plentiful, and the hunters either ate or sold what they shot.[30]

On large plantations, men sometimes found women to marry, but ceremonies were commonly informal arrangements because masters seldom permitted Catholic Church marriages for their slaves. At other times slave men found women on neighboring plantations, which limited visitation to Sundays and nocturnal rendezvous that eluded white scrutiny. Children born to a slave couple or woman could not be sold until age fourteen, although masters often fudged on the children's age. Owners sometimes allowed dances and social gatherings of neighborhood slaves at one plantation, although fearful governors and planters occasionally prohibited assemblies of large numbers of blacks. Musicians were usually self-taught and played homemade instruments. These gatherings gave slaves opportunities to fraternize, buy and sell the numerous items they produced, and engage in revelry. Masters relied on trustworthy slaves to keep order, since the latter realized that such congregations could be stopped. Men sometimes used alcohol at these gatherings, which they made or bought from enterprising poor whites. In many respects, socializing by slaves paralleled white assemblies and celebrations in the countryside, but on a far more modest scale.[31]

Some slave activities are brought to light in a case of alleged master abuse that involved Carondelet and the Florida Parishes in May 1792. At that time, four slaves from the Baton Rouge district appeared in New Orleans to protest about Samuel Steer[32] (master of Jery, César, and Mayor) and William Marshall (master of Ned). The slaves accused their owners of working them on holidays, prohibiting them from raising poultry and pigs, giving them rotten food, and punishing them arbitrarily. Ned further demanded to be sold to another master, which Spanish law permitted if the current master was abusive. After listening to the complainants, Governor Carondelet instructed the Baton Rouge commandant, José Vázquez Vahamonde, to investigate the validity of their charges.

Upon receiving his instructions, Vázquez questioned Steer's and Marshall's neighbors, who all testified approvingly about the two. Rejecting the slaves' allegations, the neighbors asserted that Steer treated his slaves fairly; never worked them on Sundays, holidays, or after hours; gave them plots for gardens; allowed each slave to keep chickens and one pig; and never deprived them of the moneys they earned from selling the produce and animals they raised. Steer, however, was a strict master who permitted visits only from slaves with permission slips and, similarly, required them for his slaves who left the plantation. In his deposition, Steer stated that he had lived quietly and enjoyably in the district for fifteen years (since 1777), followed carefully Governor Miró's slave instructions of May 1, 1784,[33] punished his blacks only when they misbehaved, and provided them with medical attention, food, clothes, and garden plots. Nevertheless, Steer admitted that he had recently thrown away two pigs his slaves were cooking for a feast one Sunday because they had not solicited his permission; the next Sunday, however, he allowed them to hold their dance and supplied them with food, a cook, and their other needs. The other planter, Marshall, similarly denied Ned's accusations of treating his slaves severely, although he had punished Ned twice, once for a nocturnal visit to the plantation of William Dunbar who complained about it, and again for the slave's quarrelsome demeanor that resulted in clashes with virtually everyone with whom he came into contact.[34]

When Governor Carondelet received the testimonials, he quickly dismissed as invalid the slaves' charges against Steer and Marshall. He then ordered the Baton Rouge commandant to punish the four slaves for their deception. Carondelet decreed that the leader of the group, Jery, receive fifty lashes and the others twenty-five, after which they were to be returned to their owners.[35]

Whether this incident had any effect on other slaves in the district is unknown. But in January 1793, eleven slaves belonging to Daniel Hickey of Manchac fled. Upon discovering their flight, Hickey surmised they had gone to New Orleans to lodge grievances against him with the governor. Anticipating that he would have to answer complaints about his treatment of slaves, Hickey solicited and obtained favorable reports about his conduct. Among those providing testimonials was the Manchac post commandant Captain Francisco Rivas, who described Hickey's treatment of slaves positively. Rivas claimed that the planter had always deported himself well and kept his storehouse open to the slaves to take corn, beans, and squash as they saw fit. He let them use his mill to grind their corn, often supplied them with meat, and dressed them well. Rivas explained that the year before Hickey had lost most of his harvest, and he now needed his laborers to plant indigo. The Manchac commandant provided the governor with several other testimonials that supported his contention of Hickey's upright character.[36]

Father Charles Burke, an Irish priest in Spanish service who ministered in Baton Rouge and Manchac, gave one of the testimonials. He described Hickey as a Catholic and asserted that many neighbors testified that the slaves had no legitimate reason to complain. According to the cleric, Hickey treated them with "much indulgence" and nowhere else were blacks better dressed or punished less. Even Baton Rouge commandant Vahamonde, who had visited Hickey's plantation in the Manchac district several times, confirmed these testimonials. He added that when the slaves labored assiduously, Hickey rewarded them with meat, and when rain drenched them while at work he indulged them with *aguardiente* (raw brandy) to relieve their chills and ward off illness. These testimonials, including those of two commandants, produced the desired effect. When Hickey went down to New Orleans to claim his slaves, the governor returned them. What complaints the slaves lodged against their master, and whether they were authentic or contrived, remain unknown.[37]

In April 1796, another case of a slave complaining about his master arose that involved the Baton Rouge commandant. Philibert, who belonged to Alejandro Patin of Pointe Coupée and Baton Rouge, had lodged grievances against his owner at Baton Rouge. Philibert fled to the Baton Rouge commandant because the head of his own district of Pointe Coupée, Guillermo Duparc, seems to have dismissed slave complaints; several blacks from that district had recently taken their protests to Baton Rouge. Vahamonde, the commandant there, sent the slave down to the governor in New Orleans. Once in the city, Governor Carondelet ordered the slave returned to Pointe Coupée and Commandant Duparc to investigate Philibert's charges to determine their validity. Meanwhile, the commandant was to hold the slave if the accusations were legitimate or return him to the owner if they were not.[38] During this time, Philibert was held in irons, and Patin could not retrieve him until the owner satisfied the expenses for the slave's arrest and incarceration.[39]

After issuing these orders, the governor rescinded them, probably because he now doubted Duparc's ability to act impartially. Consequently, Francisco Allain, who took Philibert upriver, turned him over to Vázquez in Baton Rouge on April 27. Vázquez then investigated the circumstances surrounding the case, which provided more details about the slave's flight. His owner Patin had given Philibert fourteen lashes because he had allowed crows to feed on two corn patches. After the punishment, the slave stole a pirogue and crossed the Mississippi to denounce his master. Philibert regarded the beating as unjust, but it seems that he told neither Vázquez in Baton Rouge nor Carondelet in New Orleans the real reason for the lashing. On concluding his investigation, Vázquez defended Patin, declaring that he treated his slaves well. Although Carondelet had sent Vázquez the slave to hear his complaint and render justice, on this occasion the outcome was not what Philibert expected. Instead, the commandant gave the slave twenty-four lashes, as decreed in article 23 of the regulation on the police of slaves. Only then did Vázquez restore the slave to his master, who put Philibert to work.[40]

Three days later, however, Vázquez ordered another fifteen lashes for Philibert because of the many accusations he had made. Immediately following the second lashing, the slave purloined another pirogue and absconded again. Patin, meanwhile, crossed the river to consult with Vázquez. The owner declared that the slave, who had belonged to his now-deceased mother, was an incorrigible maroon. In the past, only Alexandre DeClouet, longtime commandant at Attakapas (also now deceased), had been able to make Philibert behave through punishment. Patin recommended that if the slave were apprehended, he be locked up in irons until the owner could arrange for Philibert's sale. In New Orleans, the governor approved the measures taken by Vázquez and the wishes of Patin.[41]

In 1793, another incident involving the treatment of blacks occurred in the Manchac district. Santiago (James) Alston, who owned a plantation approximately twenty-two miles from Manchac, shot and killed Antonio, a runaway black slave who belonged to Lorenzo Sigu. Alston reported the death and turned himself in at Fort Bute, where Commandant Rivas took him into custody. On receiving this information and being advised by the government attorney Nicolás María Vidal, Governor Carondelet instructed Rivas to release Alston under a bond until final disposition of the case. Three friends of Alston soon pledged their property to ensure he would appear when the law required his presence. Unfortunately, nothing more is known about this case or if the government pursued it, although shooting at unarmed runaway slaves at that time was banned.[42]

The French had accepted the nefarious convention of pursuers firing their guns at defenseless fugitives, and the Spaniards tolerated it for years. This policy had permitted the killing of numerous runaways in the 1770s and early 1780s, particularly during the hunt for the maroon slave leader Juan San Malo in 1783–1784. At that time, protests against the slayings escalated. Small slave owners, in particular, abhorred the practice, especially when their runaways who still possessed a monetary value were killed. In the mid-1770s, led by the more affluent larger planters of the New Orleans district, the New Orleans Cabildo began taxing slave owners throughout lower Louisiana for a fund that compensated proprietors two hundred pesos for their blacks killed as fugitives. Possibly the larger masters of the New Orleans district willingly consented to the loss of some slaves of dubious value to teach others that they would not countenance flight, but slave owners farther removed from the city often resisted contributing to the fund, some alleging that it benefitted the New Orleans planters whose slaves absconded more often. When in 1778 the king accepted the tax but made participation voluntary, the dissident slave owners stopped contributing to the fund. Their refusal to participate doomed the fund, although several governors attempted in vain to revive it.[43]

Shooting at runaways, however, continued until an incident in 1787 proved how vicious and reckless the policy was. A slave from the Florida Parishes, who lived on the northern edge of Lake Pontchartrain, had been in New Orleans selling vegetables. As he returned home by boat across the lake, a militia patrol headed by a Captain Eduardo mistook him for a fugitive and shot him to death. The patrol fired their weapons without provocation or warning and without learning whether the black was a fugitive or not. The murder of the innocent slave finally persuaded the governor to ban the custom, and the prohibition lasted until 1795. At that time in the wake of the Pointe Coupée slave conspiracy, Governor Carondelet issued new instructions on slaves and runaways that resumed the often lethal practice.[44]

The slave conspiracy at Pointe Coupée in April 1795, the most serious sign of black agitation during the Spanish period, seems not to have gained a following in the neighboring Florida Parishes. The plotting in the Pointe Coupée district was limited to several plantations. Upon learning of the conspiracy, Commandant Vázquez at Baton Rouge notified Governor Carondelet that everything in his area appeared quiet. Nevertheless, the commandant instructed his syndics, who were assistants to district commandants, to be ready with their arms and, at the first sign of trouble, to kill all the dogs belonging to slaves. Vázquez also initiated various night patrols while awaiting Carondelet's orders. He requested reinforcements because he described the local fort as "open on all sides." Conditions in the area remained tranquil, with the exception of a free black laborer who came from the Pointe Coupée district.[45]

Lexime, the itinerant black artisan, arrived with a passport from the Pointe Coupée commandant, who requested emphatically not to allow him to return. Lexime seems to have been guilty of unspecified misconduct. Vázquez soon grumbled darkly that the artisan took two days to reach Baton Rouge, time spent in unknown but suspicious activity in the countryside. The commandant felt inclined to arrest the African; nevertheless, he desisted because a local inhabitant, Antonio Desautel, had hired Lexime to help repair houses.[46]

On April 18, after discovery of the Pointe Coupée slave conspiracy, Carondelet issued instructions to all district commandants of lower Louisiana. At five o'clock on the morning of April 30, masters, whom their district commandants had previously notified, were to inspect the slave cabins and seize firearms, ammunition, and anything of a suspicious nature. Vázquez did so and reported the next day. He found nothing irregular in the slave quarters of his district. Masters temporarily confiscated the hunting weapons they found, which they were to keep until the governor notified them.[47]

Contrary to Governor Carondelet's great concern, the Pointe Coupée conspiracy did not kindle further unrest throughout lower Louisiana. Nor did the Spaniards follow up the conspiracy with an era of widespread repression of slaves and free blacks. Ferment unleashed by the French and Haitian revolutions in the early 1790s worried the Spaniards, particularly Governor Carondelet, who penned numerous high-strung letters that exaggerated the turmoil to higher authorities in Cuba and Spain. Despite these letters, he initiated neither an oppressive slave regime nor experienced continued slave agitation during the remainder of his governorship.[48]

Everywhere slavery flourished, masters faced the nagging problem of fugitive slaves.[49] As early as 1782, the governor inquired about runaways in the Baton Rouge district. The American Revolutionary War had diverted some attention from slaves, and the number of fugitives had increased sharply. In answer to the governor, the commandant claimed not to have runaways in his district, but that might have been wrong, as elsewhere throughout the province they were abundant. Often black fugitives and military deserters fled up the Mississippi toward foreign territory. On March 9, 1786, Governor Miró instructed Baton Rouge commandant Francisco de Vergés to arrest runaway slaves who tried to cross his district. Moreover, he was to send them down to New Orleans as quickly as possible in order to minimize costs to owners.[50]

Governor Manuel Gayoso de Lemos (1797–1799) sent another such advisory on maroons many years later. On February 25, 1799, he informed Commandant Grand-Pré of Baton Rouge that more than fifty fugitive slaves from New Orleans were either heading upriver toward Natchez, which was now an American possession, or already there. He alerted Grand-Pré that some of the slaves had doubtlessly fled through his district. Gayoso advised his local officials, especially the syndics, to arrest all blacks and whites traveling without passports. He added, "If [the flight of slaves] is not prevented at the start, the consequences will be fatal to the [slave] owners and to agriculture. You must well know the harm, and I do not have to encourage this order further, inasmuch as I am persuaded of your zeal and interest in the prosperity and tranquillity of your District and of the Province."[51] Gayoso's statement clearly reflected the dependence of planters on Africans for the development of agriculture, most of which could not have been accomplished without their labor.

On receiving the governor's warning, Grand-Pré immediately notified the commanders and syndics under his authority to take action. They quickly apprehended more than twenty fugitive blacks and sent them to Grand-Pré. He believed that if these slaves were from New Orleans, districts on the river below his should have assisted in their capture. Nevertheless, he promised to work to reduce the number of maroons. No doubt many of the runaways Grand-Pré's subordinates arrested were not from New Orleans; instead, they probably were blacks who had momentarily de-

serted their owners in the Florida Parishes and had not wandered far.⁵²
Most fugitive slaves remained near their master's plantation because their
kith and kin lived either there or nearby, and while masters frequently and
callously separated them in sales, slaves preferred not to be parted.

Several months later, on May 11, 1799, Gayoso informed Grand-Pré that
the slave Juan Bautista, whom he believed belonged to Joseph Cabo, had
been apprehended and delivered to the royal jail in New Orleans. If, indeed, it was Cabo's slave, the governor allowed the owner to reclaim the
black upon paying the costs for his arrest, conduct to New Orleans, and
maintenance while in jail.⁵³ Years earlier slave owners who contributed to
the fugitive slave fund did not have to pay for these services.

Only two weeks later, Governor Gayoso issued new instructions to
Grand-Pré about the purchase of slaves in neighboring American Natchez.
Gayoso had learned from the American governor at Natchez that an inhabitant of his district named Aistord (?) had sold a black, who had murdered
a local person, to a resident of Spanish Bayou Sara (near today's St. Francisville). Gayoso instructed Grand-Pré to arrest the slave quietly and return
him to the Natchez governor. He further decreed that the buyer of the slave
should lose the money he paid as a penalty for his crime; it was possible,
however, that the purchaser had not known about the slave's offense. The
real culprit was the American owner, who sold the criminal slave across
the international boundary to avoid suffering a financial loss. Gayoso ordered the Baton Rouge commandant, "As a general rule, do not permit the
purchase of any black from Natchez, unless the seller presents an authentic
document [proof of ownership] and a certificate from our consul [Captain
José Vidal of Concordia—modern-day Vidalia, Louisiana]. Furthermore,
always send the *cimarrones* [fugitive slaves] to New Orleans as quickly as
possible and notify me."⁵⁴

Some Spanish runaway slaves believed that freedom could be attained
simply by crossing the international border into the United States, but that
was not true at this time on the Mississippi. In May 1799, Governor Gayoso
advised Grand-Pré that he had ordered the construction of a strong house
(small fort) and jail at Concordia, opposite American Natchez, for locking
up runaway slaves and army deserters who fled to American soil and were
returned. Gayoso sent the Spanish consul at Concordia, who was a regular
army captain, a corporal and six soldiers to operate the new facilities.⁵⁵

The next month, Grand-Pré reported to Gayoso the killing of a slave in
the Natchez territory, whose American bill of sale neither specified the

slave by name nor provided a description of him. The sale prompted Grand-Pré to question the value of issuing such ambiguous documents. He observed that since the beginning of Spanish control of Louisiana, the vending of slaves required formal paperwork: It needed to be done before a notary or district commandant so a record would be preserved, proof of ownership had to be supplied to validate the sale, and the slave had to be present so as to include a description in the bill of sale. Grand-Pré averred that he had never tolerated an exception to these rules. Meanwhile, the Americans in Natchez continued apathetically at best in recording slave sales.[56]

Slave mistreatment by masters in the Florida Parishes is not well-known, although it no doubt occurred. Slavery, based on violence and force, was by its very nature an abusive institution, and masters frequently treated slaves solely as property, not as human beings. Nevertheless, slave owners differed in their management of blacks; the former were not a homogeneous group. While not all masters purposely mistreated Africans, it must be recognized that merely holding slaves in bondage was both dehumanizing and cruel. Among owners who abused slaves, the best-known example comes not from the Florida Parishes but from neighboring Pointe Coupée.

In that district, several owners had behaved wretchedly toward their blacks, and Madame LeBlond (Marie Bara *dit* LeBlond), her husband, and son appear to have conducted themselves most viciously. In 1792 Post Commandant Valentin Le Blanc accused her of beating, chaining, inadequately clothing, and starving her bonds people. One of the LeBlond slaves, Saya, ran away to New Orleans to protest to the government the LeBlonds' depravity. Horrified by her story, Governor Carondelet sold Saya to a benevolent planter to prevent her further mistreatment.[57] Nevertheless, aside from the forced sale of Saya and several other slaves, the LeBlond family seems to have evaded both physical and financial punishment. They probably received the money from the forced sales since they appear not to have been fined.

In April 1800, the infamous LeBlond family surfaced again in the documentation because of continued abuse of their slaves. The commandant of the Pointe Coupée district appears not to have been overly concerned about this problem. His inattention prompted the slaves of his district to cross the river to Baton Rouge to complain there. Commandant Grand-Pré reported that many slaves from the west bank had appeared before him to protest their ill-use. Although he took the slaves into custody, he both listened to their grievances and investigated to learn if their accusations were well founded. Some slaves, he observed, had arrived in Baton Rouge "extremely mistreated." While he reprimanded their masters, he nevertheless returned the slaves to them. Grand-Pré then received two slaves, a male and a female, who belonged to the notorious Madame LeBlond. Aware of her unsavory reputation, Grand-Pré grimly noted that "the wide recognition of that woman's inhumanity toward her slaves [is] without equal." He commented that in the early 1790s, Governor Carondelet had compelled her to sell several slaves because of her continued abuse and failure to heed his orders. Because of her earlier misconduct, Grand-Pré now sent the two injured slaves to the interim military governor, Sebastián Nicolás Calvo de la Puerta y O'Farrill, Marqués de Casa-Calvo (1799–1801), who replaced the deceased Gayoso. In the Pointe Coupée district, however, several more masters remained whose slaves had repeatedly complained about mistreatment. Grand-Pré worried that the cruelties of these owners might provoke the slaves to attempt a second revolt.[58] Grand-Pré's reference was to the 1795 Pointe Coupée conspiracy, and he implied that brutal treatment of the slaves was behind the conspiracy. While perhaps that was true, the plotters also aspired to freedom.

When the two LeBlond slaves whom Grand-Pré sent to New Orleans in 1800 arrived there, Governor Casa-Calvo locked them up. Almost immediately, Madame LeBlond's son-in-law, Pierre Bertonière, appeared before him demanding their return. Instead, the governor admonished Bertonière that his mother-in-law's inhumane treatment of slaves could result in severe consequences for her. Nonetheless, Casa-Calvo refrained from either punishing or fining LeBlond, and he limited himself to issuing a written warning. Only if her abuse of slaves persisted was the Baton Rouge commandant to initiate legal proceedings (gather proof of mistreatment) against LeBlond. The governor added to the commandant, "As you will not ignore, and as everyone knows, the brutality with which she punishes those whom she should treat as children, there will be no lack of reasons for her not to repent her harsh behavior."[59]

Two weeks later, Grand-Pré acknowledged receipt of the governor's written admonition that he was to present to Madame LeBlond. But rather than deliver the message personally, Grand-Pré entrusted it, as well as her two abused slaves, to the Pointe Coupée commandant. Petrified at the possibility of new punishment on their arrival at LeBlond's, the slaves fled from the boat carrying them. They again sought out Baton Rouge commandant Grand-Pré as a protector, since they trembled at the thought of being restored to the custody of the dreaded LeBlond family. Grand-Pré, however, confidently believed that the governor's warning would suffice to alter the family's conduct. He again assigned delivery of the slaves to the Pointe Coupée commandant, who in the past had not worried about the mistreatment of blacks.[60] Unfortunately, our knowledge of what happened to the hapless LeBlond slaves ends here. Whether the family improved its deplorable behavior is highly questionable.

A problem that concerned the development of Louisiana at the dawn of the nineteenth century was the importation of slaves to labor at clearing lands, building levees to shield fields from annual inundations, and performing numerous agricultural chores. On May 3, 1801, the inhabitants of New Feliciana sent a petition to Grand-Pré about recent discussions on the importation of slaves. In the 1780s and early 1790s, slaves for sale had poured into Louisiana to expand agriculture and perform other economic tasks. During this time, the 1789 French Revolution erupted and preached liberty, equality, fraternity, and the brotherhood of men, concepts that slaves found exceedingly appealing. Two years later, the Haitian slave revolution exploded, and it set a disconcerting example to masters everywhere. After the execution of the French king and queen in 1793, conservative Spain joined the first coalition of monarchies and declared war on republican France, an act that resulted in some disquiet in Louisiana among the French still loyal to France, regardless of its form of government. Moreover, by the mid-1790s, the need for slaves in Louisiana fell with the decline of the province's two principal crops, tobacco and indigo. At the same time, the 1795 Pointe Coupée conspiracy frightened whites into opposing the further importation of slaves for sale; blacks throughout Louisiana and West Florida's Mississippi districts already exceeded the white population by several thousand. Consequently, in February 1796, Governor Carondelet retroactively terminated their introduction as of January 1.[61]

Within a short time, however, political and economic conditions in Louisiana reversed themselves dramatically. The 1793–1795 war that raged between France and Spain ended, France resumed the practice of slavery, and Louisiana's two new labor-intensive crops, cotton and sugarcane, gained in popularity. To expand production of cotton and cane fields, many planters now endorsed the resumption of slave imports. In 1800 New Orleans planters sought Governor Casa-Calvo's permission to readmit slaves, and both the governor and intendant supported their entry. In a similar vein, in May 1801, a large contingent of planters and farmers of New Feliciana gathered to sign a petition, advocating the reintroduction of slaves.[62]

The 140 agriculturalists who met to petition the government represented the four districts of the Feliciana jurisdiction. They stressed that many of them faced imminent ruin for a variety of reasons. They had purchased their slaves in the United States and claimed that, if they were now forced to return the Africans to American soil, it would expose them to the possibility of the slaves' confiscation, emancipation, or fines of three hundred pesos per black. Even worse, according to the petitioners, some slaves arrogantly demanded their freedom and many more believed that a general emancipation was at hand. But still other problems confronted would-be colonists in the Florida Parishes. The petitioners related that for the last three years Spanish authorities had ceased granting land and halted the importation of slaves belonging to settlers. They alleged that newcomers, ignorant of the new rules, had sent money to the United States for the purchase of "young and innocent slaves" (nonviolent blacks who had neither been involved in a conspiracy nor a revolt). The Feliciana planters petitioned that settlers ignorant of the laws on the introduction of slaves or who had sent money to purchase them in the United States be allowed to bring them in legally, all under the conditions and precautions that the Spanish government deemed necessary to avoid illegal commerce, fraud, and contraband. But if that were not possible, they begged permission to petition the king and suspend temporarily the execution of the new order.[63]

On June 9, after receiving the petition and making a copy for his records, Commandant Grand-Pré forwarded their request to the governor. He explained that the Feliciana planters wanted to lift the ban on the introduction of slaves that former governor Carondelet had imposed. While Casa-Calvo defended the prohibition on slaves coming from the United States because of the recent turmoil in Virginia caused by Gabriel's rebellion,[64] Grand-Pré doubted that the threat from that quarter extended down to Louisiana, especially in the introduction of slaves of a "tender age." He requested that the petition be brought to the attention of the king so that he could resolve it according to his pleasure.[65]

On June 8, the day before Grand-Pré wrote, Governor Casa-Calvo granted Samuel Flowers, a prominent Baton Rouge planter, and his son

Henry permission to bring in slaves for their plantation because of Flowers's honorable conduct. However, the governor established parameters that they needed to respect. They could not introduce slaves from the French West Indies or those who either spoke French or had their heads filled with "seditious maxims." Casa-Calvo, scion of a wealthy Cuban planter family, endorsed the entry of slaves to promote agriculture and industry in Louisiana, including the Florida Parishes. He charged Grand-Pré with scrupulously observing the regulations and inspecting the slaves when they arrived.[66]

The following month, Grand-Pré noted that Flowers and his son had just returned from the United States (presumably the Mississippi territory). They brought sixteen slaves with them, consisting of two men, five women, two boys, and seven girls. Grand-Pré personally examined the slaves and declared them free of the prohibitions that the governor had dictated. All of them were born and raised in the United States and spoke only English. Grand-Pré added, "The blacks were admitted in conformance with your disposition of the 8th of last month."[67]

In one of the last statements issued by Commandant Grand-Pré on the slaves of his district, on October 7, 1802, he commented on their behavior. He complained about the insolence and drunkenness of some Africans and the libertinism of others, all of which he attributed to the indolence of their owners. He added, however, that this deplorable condition had been corrected and good order imposed on all slaves.[68] In describing this situation, however, Grand-Pré neglected to explain in detail the slaves' misbehavior; if, in fact, the disorders reached the proportions he claimed; and how owners had disciplined their slaves. Unfortunately, little more is known about slavery in the Florida Parishes.

In examining how this institution functioned under the Spaniards in the Florida Parishes, several observations can be made. First, the region constituted only one district of West Florida on the Mississippi and neighboring Louisiana and, consequently, enjoyed no distinctive policy for the regulation of slaves. Instead, it followed the general laws for these two colonies at large. What distinguished the Florida Parishes from much of the rest of Louisiana at that time was the presence of Americans and Britons, who constituted the bulk of the inhabitants.[69] Despite the makeup of these settlers, no major unresolved problems flourished between them and the Spanish authorities between 1779 and 1803.

Second, and as already explained, Spanish law was generally milder than

French or British slave practices, especially in punishment and manumission, particularly in allowing bonds people to purchase their freedom.[70] Among governors, Carondelet tried diligently to make slavery more humane, and one act was to limit the number of lashes that could be inflicted on slaves. Overall, the inhabitants of the Florida Parishes seemed to have adjusted to Spanish slave law, and the Spaniards tried not to upset them. Nevertheless, questions remain about the number of slaves who achieved their freedom in the Florida Parishes during the Spanish era and if masters placed obstacles in their way. Surviving censuses, unfortunately, do not answer these thorny questions. It is known that in most rural areas some slaves became free, either through buying their freedom or through the generosity of masters and others, who freed their slave children, mistresses, and faithful retainers. Nevertheless, possibly fewer slaves were manumitted in the Florida Parishes than elsewhere in Louisiana. *Coartación*, the practice by which slaves bought their own freedom, occurred mainly in the city, and far more slaves became free in New Orleans than elsewhere in the colony. Rural blacks, especially those lacking the skills white employers sought, earned lower pay and, not surprisingly, found it difficult to amass the money needed to purchase their liberty. Urban slaves, in contrast, generally possessed greater know-how and opportunities to garner the necessary funds.[71] While Spanish law permitted slaves to complain about abusive masters and allowed the vending of mistreated slaves to new and perhaps gentler owners, it did not always bring the results slaves desired inasmuch as some post commandants failed to perform their duty and some slaves attempted to subvert the law to their own advantage. More distressing, however, was the lack of genuine punishment for cruel masters, such as the notorious LeBlond family, since governors seemed content to issue only warnings. Possibly this was motivated by the Spaniards' desire neither to distress nor alienate the important planter class.

    Finally, Spanish policy strove to avoid antagonizing any faction in the population in an effort to minimize conflict in the colony. This attitude extended even to slaves: The Spaniards aspired to avert a repressive slave regime that might provoke an African insurrection. This policy originated well before the French and Haitian revolutions erupted, since Minister of the Indies José de Gálvez declared as much in 1776, when he devised regulations for the treatment of slaves in Louisiana.[72] Later, in the early 1790s and prior to the Pointe Coupée slave conspiracy in 1795, Governor Carondelet repeatedly enunciated this attitude. He realized only too well that treating Africans rigorously could elicit a desperate response by them.[73]

The Spanish government fervently sought cooperation, not opposition, from its inhabitants. The Crown did not want to pour out soldiers and money—which were in short supply—to keep its subjects submissive. More important was using the colonials to defend Spanish territory against hostile outside forces. Within Louisiana and West Florida, Spain sought reconciliation with the different factions in society, and this policy extended all the way from masters at the top down to slaves at the bottom.[74]

NOTES

1. Stanley Clisby Arthur, *The Story of the West Florida Rebellion* (St. Francisville, La.: *St. Francisville Democrat*, 1935), 7–12, contains some early information on the area that later became known as the Florida Parishes. Early works, such as Arthur's, must be used carefully, however, because they are often riddled with errors and biased interpretations. Although the term *Florida Parishes* arose in the nineteenth century, it is used here for convenience.

2. "Resumen General," New Orleans, Census of 1766, ms. 569, folio 107, Museo Naval, Madrid.

3. Thomas N. Ingersoll, "Old New Orleans: Race, Class, Sex, and Order in the Early Deep South, 1718–1819" (Ph.D. diss., University of California, Los Angeles, 1990), 47–48; John G. Clark, *New Orleans, 1718–1812* (Baton Rouge: Louisiana State University Press, 1970), 21–157; N. M. Miller Surrey, *The Commerce of Louisiana during the French Regime, 1699–1763* (New York: Columbia University Studies in History, Economics, and Public Law, 1916).

4. On the 1685 slave code for the French islands see Louis Sala-Molins, *Le Code noir, ou le calvaire de Canaan* (Paris: Presses universitaires de France, 1987); for the Louisiana 1724 Code Noir see Hans W. Baade, "The Law of Slavery in Spanish *Luisiana*, 1769–1803," in *Louisiana's Legal Heritage*, ed. Edward F. Haas (Pensacola: Perdido Bay Press, 1983), 43–86. See also Carl A. Brasseaux, "The Administration of Slave Regulations in French Louisiana, 1724–1766," *Louisiana History* 21 (spring 1980): 139–58, and Mathé Allain, "Slave Policies in French Louisiana," *Louisiana History* 21 (spring 1980): 127–38. Gilbert C. Din, *Spaniards, Planters, and Slaves: The Spanish Regulation of Slavery in Louisiana, 1763–1803* (College Station: Texas A&M University Press, 1999), 54–56.

5. Robert L. Gold, *Borderland Empires in Transition: The Triple-Nation Transfer of Florida* (Carbondale, Ill.: Southern Illinois University Press, 1969); Andrew C. Albrecht, "The Origin and Settlement of Baton Rouge, Louisiana," *Louisiana Historical Quarterly* 28 (January 1945): 5–68; Louise Butler, "West Feliciana: A Glimpse of Its History," *Louisiana Historical Quarterly* 7 (January 1924): 90–120.

6. Robin Fabel, *The Economy of British West Florida, 1763–1783* (Tuscaloosa: University of Alabama Press, 1988), 47; Cecil Johnson, *British West Florida, 1763–1783* (New York: Anchor Press, 1971); Clinton N. Howard, *The British Development of West Florida, 1763–1769* (Berkeley: University of California Press, 1947); Rose Meyers, *A History of Baton Rouge, 1699–1812* (Baton

Rouge: Centennial Corporation of Baton Rouge, 1976), 41, erroneously writes that around Baton Rouge the British had developed "a thriving plantation economy."

7. Fabel, *Economy of British West Florida,* 207; Clinton N. Howard, "Early Settlers in British West Florida," *Florida Historical Quarterly* 24 (July 1945): 46; memorial of Harris Alexander and many others to the Conde de Gálvez (Bernardo de Gálvez), Natchez, March 1, 1783, Archivo General de Indias, Papeles Procedentes de Cuba, legajo (hereinafter abbreviated as AGI, PC, leg.) 2352; Bernardo de Gálvez to Esteban Miró, Mexico City, October 20, 1785, in AGI, PC, leg. 2352. Minister of the Indies José de Gálvez granted permission for the British residents to remain in 1785; a copy of this letter, but with erroneous dates, is in *The Favrot Family Papers: A Documentary Chronicle of Early Louisiana,* ed. Guillermo Náñez Falcón, 3 vols. (Tulane: Howard-Tilton Memorial Library, 1988), 2:40–41.

8. Fabel, *Economy of British West Florida,* 22–25, 38, 42. For purposes of comparison see the British system for handling both slaves and free blacks in East Florida as discussed in Wilbur H. Siebert, "Slavery in East Florida, 1776 to 1785," *Florida Historical Quarterly* 10 (January 1932): 139–61; and J. Leitch Wright Jr., "Blacks in British East Florida," *Florida Historical Quarterly* 54 (April 1976): 425–42.

9. Meyers, *History of Baton Rouge,* 58. See also Eron Rowland (Mrs. Dunbar), ed., *Life, Letters, and Papers of William Dunbar* (Jackson, Miss.: Press of the Mississippi Historical Society, 1930); and Arthur H. DeRosier Jr., "William Dunbar: A Product of the Eighteenth Century Renaissance," *Journal of Mississippi History* 28 (August 1966): 185–227. Fabel, *Economy of British West Florida,* 29.

10. On O'Reilly see Vicente Rodríguez Casado, *Primeros años de dominación española en la Luisiana* (Madrid: Diana Artes Gráficas, 1942), 293–350; Bibiano Torres Ramírez, *Alejandro O'Reilly en las Indias* (Seville: Escuela de Estudios Hispano-Americanos, 1969); and John Preston Moore, *Revolt in Louisiana: The Spanish Occupation, 1766–1770* (Baton Rouge: Louisiana State University Press, 1976), 185–215.

11. Margaret Fisher Dalrymple, ed., *The Merchant of Manchac: The Letterbooks of John Fitzpatrick, 1768–1790* (Baton Rouge: Louisiana State University Press, 1978), 14–18, 21. On Unzaga, see Light Townsend Cummins, "Luis de Unzaga y Amezaga, Colonial Governor, 1770–1777," in *The Louisiana Governors: From Iberville to Edwards,* ed. Joseph G. Dawson III (Baton Rouge: Louisiana State University Press, 1990), 52–56; and Din, *Spaniards, Planters, and Slaves,* 48–65.

12. John Walton Caughey, "Bernardo de Gálvez and the English Smugglers on the Mississippi, 1777," *Hispanic American Historical Review* 12, no. 1 (1932): 46–58, and "Willing's Expedition down the Mississippi, 1778," *Louisiana Historical Quarterly* 15 (January 1932): 5–36. Henry O. Robertson, "Tories or Patriots? The Mississippi River Planters during the American Revolution," *Louisiana History* 40 (fall 1999): 445–62.

13. Robert R. Rea, "Planters and Plantations in British West Florida," *Alabama Review* 29 (July 1976): 22.

14. Bernardo de Gálvez's conquest of the British posts on the Mississippi east bank has been told many times. The standard work is John Walton Caughey, *Bernardo de Gálvez in Louisiana, 1776–1783* (Berkeley: University of California Press, 1934), 149–70. Gilbert C. Din, in "Lieutenant Raimundo DuBreüil, Commandant of San Gabriel de Manchac, and Bernardo de Gálvez's 1779 Campaign on the Mississippi River," *Military History of the West* 29 (spring

1999): 1–30, corrects a number of Caughey's errors. See also Albert W. Haarmann, "The Spanish Conquest of British West Florida, 1779–1781," *Florida Historical Quarterly* 50 (October 1960): 107–34; Eric Beerman, *España y la independencia de los Estados Unidos* (Madrid: Editorial Mapfre, 1992); and Bettie Jones Conover, "British West Florida's Mississippi Frontier Posts, 1763–1779," *Alabama Review* 29 (July 1976): 177–207.

15. Census of Baton Rouge, 1782, AGI, PC, leg. 192; "Etat de Habitants," Baton Rouge, November 15, 1786, ibid.; Charles Gayarré, *History of Louisiana*, 4 vols., 3rd ed. (New Orleans: Armand Hawkins, 1885), 3:170, 215. In 1795, Gov. Francisco Luis Héctor, Barón de Carondelet, composed a list of slaves in the colony that placed Baton Rouge's slave population at 420, an increase of 142 in nine years. Similar to other censuses, it probably undercounted slaves ("Esclavos de la Luisiana," Carondelet, [c. 1795], [New Orleans], AGI, PC, leg. 211A).

16. Census of Baton Rouge, December 31, 1795, Joseph Vázquez Vahamonde, AGI, PC, leg. 34. Fabel, *Economy of British West Florida*, 47.

17. Gayarré, *History of Louisiana*, 3:170, 215; 1795 Census of Manchac, December 31, 1795, AGI, PC, leg. 33. Possibly the Manchac planters were unwilling to divulge the true number of slaves they owned because the governor planned to tax them.

18. *Feliciana* comes from the name of Governor Gálvez's wife, Felicitas in Spanish and Felicité in French.

19. On the influx of immigrants to Louisiana, see Gilbert C. Din's articles, "Proposals and Plans for Settlement in Spanish Louisiana, 1787–1790," *Louisiana History* 11 (summer 1970): 205–6; "The Immigration Policy of Governor Esteban Miró in Spanish Louisiana," *Southwestern Historical Quarterly* 73 (October 1969): 155–75; and "Spain's Immigration Policy in Louisiana and the American Penetration, 1792–1803," *Southwestern Historical Quarterly* 76 (January 1973): 255–76. On the arrival of Canary Islanders and Acadians in Louisiana, see Gilbert C. Din, *The Canary Islanders of Louisiana* (Baton Rouge: Louisiana State University Press, 1988), and Carl A. Brasseaux, *The Founding of New Acadia: The Beginning of Acadian Life in Louisiana, 1765–1803* (Baton Rouge: Louisiana State University Press, 1987).

20. Gayarré, *History of Louisiana*, 3:215; 1793 census of Feliciana, AGI, PC, leg. 208A; Antonio Acosta Rodríguez, in *La población de Luisiana española, 1763–1803* (Madrid: Gráficas Condor, 1979), 465–66; Governor Miró to Luis de Las Casas, no. 161, New Orleans, April 30, 1791, in AGI, PC, leg. 1440A.

21. Francisco Rivas to Carondelet, nos. 93, 96, 98, Fort Bute de Manchac, September 1, October 11, 17, 1794, respectively, all in AGI, PC, leg. 30. While the Spaniards evacuated the cannons at the Manchac fort to Baton Rouge, Rivas became commandant of the nearby Galveztown district and fort (Pedro Rousseau to Carondelet, no. 1, on the royal galley *La Venganza* before the Baton Rouge fort, November 15, 1794, ibid.).

22. Carlos de Grand-Pré to the Marqués de Casa-Calvo, no. 275, Baton Rouge, July 6, 1801, in AGI, PC, leg. 106A; Acosta, in *Población de Luisiana española*, 245.

23. Wilbert James Miller, "The Spanish Commandant of Baton Rouge, 1779–1795" (M.A. thesis, Louisiana State University, 1965), 16. A sketch of Francisco de Vergés or François-Xavier-Dagobert de Vergés, is in Carl A. Brasseaux, *France's Forgotten Legion: Service Records of French Military and Administrative Personnel Stationed in the Mississippi Valley and Gulf Coast Region, 1699–1769* (Baton Rouge: Louisiana State University Press, 2000).

24. Manuel Gayoso de Lemos to the Conde de Santa Clara, no. 99, New Orleans, January

23, 1798, in AGI, PC, leg. 1500; I. J. Cox, *The West Florida Controversy, 1798–1813* (Baltimore: Johns Hopkins Press, 1918).

25. Grand-Pré to Manuel Gayoso, New Orleans, January 15, 1798, in AGI, PC, leg. 49; Junta de Guerra, New Orleans, July 6, 1798, ibid., leg. 1501A. On the Treaty of San Lorenzo, or Pinckney's Treaty, see Samuel Flagg Bemis, *Pinckney's Treaty: America's Advantage from Europe's Distress, 1783–1800*, rev. ed. (New Haven: Yale University Press, 1960); and on Grand-Pré, see Lawrence Kinnaird and Lucia B. Kinnaird, "The Red River Valley in 1796," *Louisiana History* 24 (spring 1983): 184–94.

26. Din, "Immigration Policy of Governor Esteban Miró," 155–75, and "Proposals and Plans for Colonization in Spanish Louisiana," 197–213; Perchet to Carondelet, Baton Rouge, December 19, 1796, in AGI, PC, leg. 1501B.

27. Older histories of Louisiana, particularly those of François-Xavier Martin, *The History of Louisiana, from the Earliest Period* (1882; reprint Gretna, La.: Pelican, 1975), 214; Alcée Fortier, *A History of Louisiana*, ed. Jo Ann Carrigan, 2 vols. (Baton Rouge: Claitor's, 1966–72), 2:7; and Henry E. Chambers, *A History of Louisiana: Wilderness, Colony, Province, State, People* (Chicago: American Historical Society, 1925), 301, have claimed that the French Code Noir continued under the Spaniards. Baade, "The Law of Slavery in Spanish *Luisiana*," 43–86.

28. Din, *Spaniards, Planters, and Slaves*, 42–44, 75–79, 101–10, 159–67. On the evolution of the French Superior Council in Louisiana see Jerry Micelle, "From Law Court to Local Government: Metamorphosis of the Superior Council of French Louisiana," *Louisiana History* 9 (1968): 85–107.

29. Din, *Spaniards, Planters, and Slaves*, 133–53; Javier Malagón Barceló, *Código negro carolino (1784)* (Santo Domingo: Ediciones de Taller, 1974).

30. Din, *Spaniards, Planters, and Slaves*, and Roderick A. McDonald, *The Economy and Material Culture of Slaves: Goods and Chattels on the Sugar Plantations of Jamaica and Louisiana* (Baton Rouge: Louisiana State University Press, 1993); Ira Berlin and Philip D. Morgan, eds., *Cultivation and Culture: Labor and the Shaping of Slave Life in the Americas* (Charlottesville: University Press of Virginia, 1993).

31. Din, *Spaniards, Planters, and Slaves*; McDonald, *Economy and Material Culture of Slaves*; Berlin and Morgan, eds., *Cultivation and Culture*. See also Roger Abrahams, *Singing the Master: The Emergence of African American Culture in the Plantation South* (New York: Pantheon Books, 1992); and Ann Patton Malone, *Sweet Chariot: Slave Family and Household Structure in Nineteenth-Century Louisiana* (Chapel Hill: University of North Carolina Press, 1992). Slaves living in the vicinity of New Orleans went there for social and economic activities, and their assemblies were often large. See Jerah Johnson, "New Orleans's Congo Square: An Urban Setting for Early Afro-American Culture Formation," *Louisiana History* 32 (spring 1991): 117–57.

32. Fabel, *Economy of British West Florida*, 33, 105, 207–8; Census of Baton Rouge, December 31, 1795, AGI, PC, leg. 33; Manuel Juan de Salcedo to Grand-Pré, New Orleans, May 13, 1802, in AGI, PC, leg. 106B.

33. Miró's *bando* of May 1, 1784, is in AGI, PC, leg. 3A; Din, *Spaniards, Planters, and Slaves*, 93–94.

34. Testimonies of Santiago (James) Burch, Juan Fridge, Francisco Pousset, Gabriel Armand Duplantier, Thomas Lilly, Samuel Steer, and William Marshall, all in AGI, PC, leg. 25A;

Din, *Spaniards, Planters, and Slaves*, 138–39. According to the 1795 census, William Marshall then had twenty-two slaves (Census of Baton Rouge, December 31, 1795, AGI, PC, leg. 33).

35. Vázquez to Carondelet, no. 30, Baton Rouge, July 23, 1792, in AGI, PC, leg. 25A; Din, *Spaniards, Planters, and Slaves*, 139–40.

36. Francisco Rivas to Carondelet, no. 34, Manchac, January 12, 1793, in AGI, PC, leg. 26. Early the next month, Rivas appointed Hickey as one of the three syndics for the Manchac district (Rivas to Carondelet, no. 38, Fort Bute de Manchac, February 3, 1793, ibid.). Vázquez to Carondelet, no. 110, Baton Rouge, September 25, 1793, in AGI, PC, leg. 27A; Fabel, *Economy of British West Florida*, 124–25.

37. Testimonial of Carlos Burke, priest of Baton Rouge and Manchac, January 11, 1793, testimonial of Hubert Rowell and J. W. Butler, Manchac, January 12, 1793, testimonial of Vázquez, Baton Rouge, January 13, 1793, all attached to Rivas to Carondelet, no. 34, Manchac, January 12, 1793, in AGI, PC, leg. 26. On Irish priests serving the Spaniards in West Florida see Gilbert C. Din, "The Irish Mission to West Florida," *Louisiana History* 12 (summer 1971): 315–34; Michael J. Curley, *Church and State in the Spanish Floridas* (Washington, D.C.: Catholic University of America Press, 1940); and two articles by Jack D. L. Holmes, "Irish Priests in Spanish Natchez," *Journal of Mississippi History* 29 (August 1967): 169–80, and "Father Francis Lennan and His Activities in Spanish Louisiana and West Florida," *Louisiana Studies* 5 (1966): 255–65.

38. Carondelet to Guillermo Duparc, New Orleans, April 18, 1796, in AGI, PC, leg. 130. In the 1795 census of Baton Rouge, Alejandro Patin is listed as heading a household of four whites, two free female blacks, and six male and three female slaves (Census of Baton Rouge, December 31, 1795, ibid., leg. 33).

39. [Carondelet] to Vázquez, New Orleans, May 31, 1796, ibid., leg. 129.

40. Vázquez to Carondelet, no. 272, Baton Rouge, June 3, 1796, ibid., leg. 33.

41. Ibid.

42. Rivas to Carondelet, no. 9, Manchac, April 10, 1793, and attached [Carondelet] to Rivas, New Orleans, April 20, 179(3), both ibid., leg. 26; Guillermo Duparc to Carondelet, no. 28, Pointe Coupée, May 18, 1793, and enclosure, both ibid., leg. 208B.

43. Gilbert C. Din and John E. Harkins, *The New Orleans Cabildo: Colonial Louisiana's First Municipal Government, 1769–1803* (Baton Rouge: Louisiana State University Press, 1996), 153–82.

44. Din, *Spaniards, Planters, and Slaves*, 120–21; "A Regulation Concerning the General Police; the Keeping of Bridges, Roads, and Bridges and Causeways in Repair, and the Government of Slaves" can be found in James A. Padgett, ed., "A Decree for Louisiana Issued by the Baron of Carondelet, June 1, 1795," *Louisiana Historical Quarterly* 20 (July 1937): 600–605. The June 15, 1795, fugitive slave regulations are published in the New Orleans newspaper *Le Moniteur de la Louisiane*, a copy of which is in the Archivo Histórico Nacional (Madrid), Estado, leg. 3902, expediente 6, and published in Jack D. L. Holmes, ed., "The Earliest Extant Issue of *Moniteur de la Louisiane*," *Louisiana History* 7 (spring 1966): 133–55.

45. Vázquez to Carondelet, nos. 214, 217, Baton Rouge, April 21, 27, 1795, respectively, both in AGI, PC, leg. 31.

46. Vázquez to Carondelet, no. 216 and unnumbered letter, Baton Rouge, April 26 and May 1, 1795 respectively, both in AGI, PC, leg. 31.

47. Vázquez to Carondelet, no. 218, Baton Rouge, May 1, 1795, ibid., leg. 31; Din, *Spaniards, Planters, and Slaves*, 158–59.

48. Din, *Spaniards, Planters, and Slaves*, 154–93; Gilbert C. Din, "Carondelet, the Cabildo, and Slaves: Louisiana in 1795," *Louisiana History* 38 (winter 1997): 5–28; and Jack D. L. Holmes, "The Abortive Pointe Coupée Conspiracy," *Louisiana History* 11 (fall 1970): 342–62. A personal and, in my opinion, inaccurate account in many places about the conspiracy and its aftermath is Gwendolyn Midlo Hall, *Africans in Colonial Louisiana: The Making of a Creole Culture* (Baton Rouge: Louisiana State University Press, 1992). Ernest R. Liljegren, "Jacobinism in Spanish Louisiana, 1792–1797," *Louisiana Historical Quarterly* 22 (January 1939): 47–97; Gilbert C. Din, "Father Jean Delvaux and the Natchitoches Revolt of 1795," *Louisiana History* 40 (winter 1999): 5–33.

49. On fugitive slaves, see John Hope Franklin and Loren Schweninger, *Runaway Slaves: Rebels on the Plantation, 1790–1860* (New York: Oxford University Press, 1999); Gerald W. Mullin, *Flight and Rebellion: Slave Resistance in Eighteenth-Century Virginia* (New York: Oxford University Press, 1972); and Richard Price, ed., *Maroon Societies: Rebel Slave Communities in the Americas*, 2d ed. (Baltimore: Johns Hopkins University Press, 1979). On Louisiana's fugitive slaves, see Gilbert C. Din, "*Cimarrones* and the San Malo Band in Spanish Louisiana," *Louisiana History* 21 (summer 1980): 237–62, and *Spaniards, Planters, and Slaves*.

50. [Pedro Piernas] to Ignacio Delinó, New Orleans, July 22, 1782, in AGI, PC, leg. 195; [Miró] to Francisco de Vergés, New Orleans, March 9, 1786, ibid., leg. 117A.

51. [Gayoso] to Grand-Pré, New Orleans, February 25, 1799, ibid., leg. 106A.

52. Grand-Pré to Gayoso, no. 230, Baton Rouge, March 14, 1799, ibid.

53. [Gayoso] to Grand-Pré, New Orleans, May 11, 1799, ibid., leg. 106B. On costs to masters for the recovery of their runaway slaves, see Din, *Spaniards, Planters, and Slaves*. Grand-Pré to the Marqués de Casa-Calvo, no. 318, Baton Rouge, May 28, 1800, in AGI, PC, leg. 106A; [Casa-Calvo] to Grand-Pré, New Orleans, June 28, 1800, in AGI, PC, leg. 106A.

54. [Gayoso] to Grand-Pré, [New Orleans], May 26, 1799, in AGI, PC, leg. 106B.

55. [Gayoso] to Grand-Pré, New Orleans, May 7, 1799, ibid., leg. 33.

56. Grand-Pré to Gayoso, no. 273, Baton Rouge, June 5, 1799, ibid.

57. Le Blanc to Carondelet, Pointe Coupée, August 2, 4, 1792, both ibid., leg. 25A; Carondelet to Le Blanc, New Orleans, August 8, 10, 1792, both ibid., leg. 18; Din, *Spaniards, Planters, and Slaves*, 137; Petition of Jorge, Felipe, Sara, Beca, and Coyo, slaves of Luis Tournoir, to the governor, New Orleans, August 7, 1794, AGI, PC, leg. 30; Duparc to Carondelet, no. 59, Pointe Coupée, September 2, 1794, in AGI, PC, leg. 30.

58. Grand-Pré to Casa-Calvo, no. 306, Baton Rouge, April 19, 1800, in AGI, PC, leg. 106A.

59. [Casa-Calvo] to Grand-Pré, New Orleans, April 24, 1800, ibid.

60. Grand-Pré to Casa-Calvo, no. 311, Baton Rouge, May 11, 1800, ibid.

61. Actas del Cabildo, 1769–1803, 10 vols. (Microfilm of WPA transcripts in Spanish), vol. 4, bk. 1, pp. 40–42 (June 20, 1795), of the Cabildo minutes; Clark, *New Orleans*, 217–19; Din, *Spaniards, Planters, and Slaves*, 185–86. See also Thomas N. Ingersoll, "The Slave Trade and Ethnic Diversity of Louisiana's Slave Community," *Louisiana History* 37 (spring 1995): 133–61.

62. Petition of the inhabitants of New Feliciana to Grand-Pré, May 3, 1801, AGI, PC, leg. 106A. On the development of Louisiana's economy, see Clark, *New Orleans*, 158–274.

63. Petition of the inhabitants of New Feliciana to Grand-Pré, May 3, 1801, AGI, PC, leg.

106A; Gov. Manuel de Salcedo to Martín Duralde, New Orleans, August 19, 1802, ibid., leg. 76; Gov. Salcedo to Vicente Fernández Teixeiro, New Orleans, May 4, 1802, ibid., leg. 76, and others in the same legajo.

64. On Gabriel's rebellion in Virginia in 1800, see Douglas R. Egerton, *Gabriel's Rebellion: The Virginia Slave Conspiracies of 1800 and 1802* (Chapel Hill: University of North Carolina Press, 1993).

65. Grand-Pré to Casa-Calvo, Baton Rouge, June 9, 1801, in AGI, PC, leg. 106A.

66. [Casa-Calvo] to Grand-Pré, New Orleans, June 8, 1801, ibid.

67. Grand-Pré to Casa-Calvo, Baton Rouge, July 8, 1801, ibid.

68. Grand-Pré to Salcedo, no. 297, Baton Rouge, October 7, 1802, ibid.

69. The area under Grand-Pré's control had criminals, who assaulted roads and were mostly or entirely Americans, as well as scores of American army deserters. Grand-Pré to Casa-Calvo, no. 260, Baton Rouge, March 14, 1801, ibid.

70. On free people of color in the colonial era and on the ways they became free see Kimberly S. Hanger, *Bounded Lives, Bounded Places: Free Black Society in Colonial New Orleans, 1769–1803* (Durham, N.C.: Duke University Press, 1997), which supercedes in most respects older works on the same subject, such as Donald E. Everett, "Free People of Color in Colonial Louisiana," *Louisiana History* 7 (winter 1966): 21–50; H. E. Sterkx, "The Free Negro in Ante-Bellum Louisiana" (Ph.D. diss., University of Alabama, 1954); and Ira Berlin, *Slaves without Masters: The Free Negro in the Antebellum South* (New York: Pantheon Books, 1974).

71. On slaves becoming free in New Orleans, see Hanger, *Bounded Lives*. Hanger, "Avenues to Freedom Open to New Orleans' Black Population, 1769–1779," *Louisiana History* 31 (summer 1990): 237–64; Gwendolyn Midlo Hall, "Raza y libertad: La manumisión de los esclavos rurales de la Luisiana bajo la jurisdicción del capitán general de Cuba," *Anuario de estudios americanos* (Escuela de Estudios Hispano-Americanos, Seville, Spain) 43 (1986): 365–76; Hubert H. S. Aimes, "Coartación: A Spanish Institution for the Advancement of Slaves into Freedmen," *Yale Review* 17 (1908–1909): 412–31.

72. Royal instructions to the governor of Louisiana, San Lorenzo, November 25, 1776, AGI, PC, leg. 174B; Din, *Spaniards, Planters, and Slaves*, 67–69.

73. On Carondelet's policy toward slaves, see Din, *Spaniards, Planters, and Slaves*, 133–93.

74. Alexander De Conde, *This Affair of Louisiana* (New York: Charles Scribner's Sons, 1976); and E. Wilson Lyon, *Louisiana in French Diplomacy, 1759–1804* (Norman, Okla.: University of Oklahoma Press, 1934).

Pierre LeMoyne, sieur d'Iberville, the first European explorer
of the Florida Parishes
*La Verna R. and Edwin A. Davis Collection, picture 1064, Center for Southeast
Louisiana Studies, Southeastern Louisiana University*

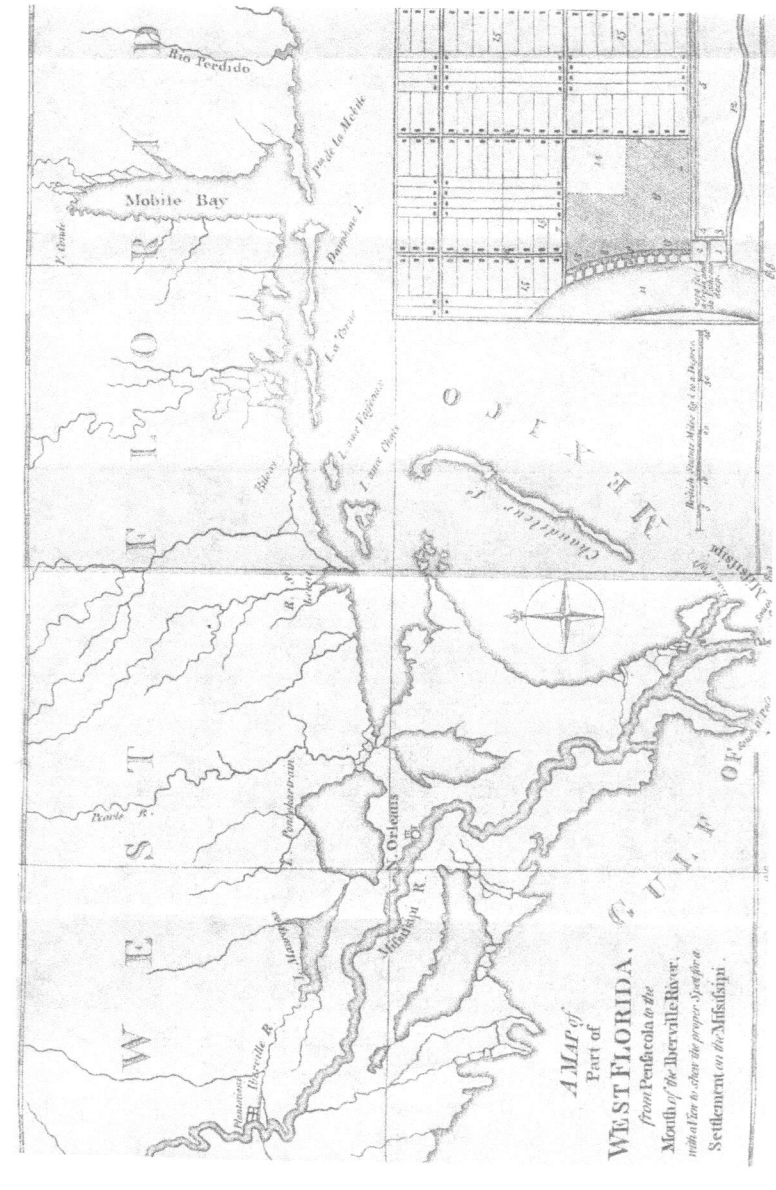

Map revealing the plans for the English settlement at Bayou Manchac, 1772
Oversize Map Collection, Center for Southeast Louisiana Studies, Southeastern Louisiana University

Native American family on the north shore of Lake Pontchartrain, ca. 1700
Painting by Alfred Boisseau, 1847, courtesy New Orleans Museum of Art

Slaves harvesting sugarcane, ca. 1840
La Verna R. and Edwin A. Davis Collection, picture 1150, Center for Southeast Louisiana Studies, Southeastern Louisiana University

Naval battle on Lake Borgne, December 1814
Painting by Thomas L. Hornbrook, courtesy U.S. Naval Academy Museum

Irregular forces raiding a farm to secure horses, ca. 1864
Sketched by W. D. Mathews; La Verna R. and Edwin A. Davis Collection, picture 246, Center for Southeast Louisiana Studies, Southeastern Louisiana University

Slaves ginning cotton
La Verna R. and Edwin A. Davis Collection, picture 1177, Center for Southeast Louisiana Studies, Southeastern Louisiana University

Timber cutting among a stand of pines in the Florida Parishes, ca. 1890
Fajoni-Lanier Collection, picture 111, Center for Southeast Louisiana Studies, Southeastern Louisiana University

Black timber cutters clearing land in southern Tangipahoa Parish, ca. 1910
Hammond, Louisiana, Collection, picture 108, Center for Southeast Louisiana Studies, Southeastern Louisiana University

Black family in Washington Parish, ca. 1920
Fajoni-Lanier Collection, picture 35, Center for Southeast Louisiana Studies, Southeastern Louisiana University

Frolicking along a stream in the Florida Parishes, a popular summer pastime now threatened by demands placed on the regional environment
La Verna R. and Edwin A. Davis Collection, picture 1601, Center for Southeast Louisiana Studies, Southeastern Louisiana University

II | CONFRONTING THE CHALLENGE OF AMERICA

4

GIVING JACKSON VICTORY

Thomas ap Catesby Jones, the Battle of Lake Borgne, and British Frustration along the Gulf

GENE A. SMITH

*I*N MID-MAY 1815, SEVERAL MONTHS AFTER THE IMMEDIATE THREAT of a British invasion had passed, Daniel Todd Patterson, commander of the U.S. Navy's New Orleans station, called a court of inquiry to investigate the British capture of Thomas ap Catesby Jones's gunboat flotilla on Lake Borgne. During the previous December 1814 battle Lieutenant Jones had put up a spirited fight, sacrificing himself, his men, and his boats to a numerically superior British invasion force. The British had quickly overpowered Jones's tiny flotilla during the brief engagement, and the victory had given them easy control over Lake Borgne as well as permitted them to choose their point of attack against the city of New Orleans. The gunboats had been the first line of the American defense, and Jones's defeat off the coast of St. Tammany Parish had left General Andrew Jackson's force in New Orleans exposed and at the mercy of the British invasion. Jones's setback had also left Louisiana—including the Florida Parishes, the Gulf Coast, and even the future of the United States—in question.[1]

When Jones appeared before the May 1815 court of inquiry he had to answer for his capture, or what many authors have subsequently called "an American disaster" that could have brought defeat to a commander with less fortitude than Andrew Jackson. The court questioned why Jones had positioned his vessels as he did, why he had not continued his retreat to Fort Petites Coquilles on the Rigolets, and why he had not sent a messenger to warn Jackson of the British advance. Jones unflinchingly answered every question, explained every decision, and corroborated it all with official reports and witnesses who confirmed that he had made the correct decisions. He sat before his judges, knowing full well that he had done all within his power to sustain the honor of his country and the reputation of the navy. He had followed his orders explicitly, and given the circumstances he faced, he had done everything within his power to forestall the British advance. Nevertheless, in December 1814 his defeat seemed to have been a foregone conclusion that gave the enemy an immediate advantage in their Louisiana campaign. Not surprisingly, the British expected it to be wholly successful.[2]

During the battle Jones had relied on instincts that he had sharpened during seven years of experience along the Gulf Coast. He had arrived on the New Orleans station in the spring of 1808, and during his first four years he had scoured the swamps and bayous of the lower Delta, the coastal inlets of the Florida Parishes, as well as most of the lower Mississippi River. He had sailed the waters of the Gulf, curtailing smuggling, privateering, piracy, and slave trading before the United States declared war on Great Britain in the summer of 1812. His service on what had been called an "inactive, forlorn station" had been onerous and had offered him few chances for professional recognition. But with the beginning of the war with Britain, Jones and other naval officers along the Gulf believed that they would have opportunities for transfers and promotions. Ships would be sent to sea to prevent the British from blockading the Atlantic coastline and harassing American trade. Experienced junior officers, such as Jones, would also be needed aboard seagoing vessels and at important naval stations along the East Coast. Even so, Jones did not secure the transfer he wanted. He was forced to remain along the Gulf Coast, where it seemed as if the war, and with it his chance for recognition, was passing him by.[3]

The war had not bypassed Jones, Louisiana, or the Gulf Coast. British policy-makers had instead chosen to concentrate on other objectives. British concerns focused on defeating Napoleon in Europe and protecting Canada from American imperialistic expansion—virtually every British military operation in North America considered first and foremost the safety of the threatened Canadian provinces. Despite the Canadian focus, Louisiana still figured prominently in British North American operations. During the 1790s British military plans had called for seizing the land between New Orleans and Pensacola, including Mobile and the Florida Parishes, to protect the Canadian territories to the north. If successful, this plan would have permitted the British to create a series of western North American colonies that would have linked Canada to the Gulf Coast while also frustrating Napoleon's ambitions for a New World empire. Although the American purchase of Louisiana in 1803 ultimately removed the immediate French threat to Britain's plans for the Gulf Coast, it did not assuage

English concerns that Louisiana, and its control over the Mississippi River, still remained the key to British possession of Canada.[4]

Once the war with the United States began, British policy-makers and military officers were quickly reminded that the fate of Canada ultimately lay along the Gulf Coast. In November 1812, some five months after the United States had declared war, Sir John Borlase Warren, British commander of the North American Squadron, proposed a diversion against New Orleans to relieve the American siege against Canada. He insisted that such an operation would close the Mississippi River as well as "cut off the resources of the American Southern States, . . . who are now actively employed against the Canadas." A year later Warren called again for his country to "strike some decisive stroke against the enemy," preferably "a vigorous attack to the southward in taking possession of New Orleans and bringing forward the Indians and Spanyards [sic] . . . and a division of black troops to cut off the resources of the Mississippi."[5]

During 1813 other officers made similar suggestions for a British victory. Naval captain James Stirling, concluding that Louisiana was "very open to attack," sent to the First Lord of the Admiralty, Viscount Melville, a detailed memorandum on the geography of the region. The conquest of Louisiana by British forces supported by Indians, blacks, and "displeased" Spaniards would, according to Stirling, place "the interior states of Kentucky, Ohio, Tenesee [sic] and part of Virginia at the mercy of Great Britain." Likewise Admiral Henry Hotham, the commanding officer at Bermuda, suggested to the government that "the place where Americans [were] most vulnerable is New Orleans and . . . [its capture] will be the severest blow America can meet with." Hotham also implied that an attack against Louisiana would, more importantly, "check [the Americans'] operations against Canada."[6]

In 1813 the fortunes of war in North America had worsened for Britain as army and naval forces suffered losses to Oliver Hazard Perry on Lake Erie and to William Henry Harrison at the Battle of the Thames. Moreover, British naval supremacy on Lake Ontario seemed to be threatened, and if those setbacks had not been reversed, it could have resulted in the total loss of Canada. Fortunately, Napoleon's empire was also beginning to disintegrate, and this freed seasoned, battle-trained British troops for North American service and permitted the government to refocus on offensive operations against the United States. But until the revised strategy could be put into effect, the Royal Navy had instructions "to institute a strict and rigorous blockade of [American] ports and harbours . . . and of the River Mississippi."⁷

In the spring of 1814, when Vice-Admiral Alexander Forrester Inglis Cochrane replaced Warren as commander of the much-reduced North American station, he acknowledged that a successful blockade had already been enacted. More important, Cochrane recommended to the admiralty that a small force—of regulars, Indians, black slaves, Baratarian pirates, and disaffected citizens—could "take possession of N. Orleans by which we should have considerably weakened the [American] efforts against Canada." Cochrane's plan, virtually the same as Warren's from a year earlier, apparently resonated strongly with the lords of the admiralty at this time, for in late July, Viscount Melville requested a confidential opinion from Admiral Sir William Domett about a possible Louisiana campaign. Domett recommended an offensive operation with troops assembling during the fall at Negril Point in Jamaica and departing no later than December. With that endorsement the government in early August approved Cochrane's plan for an attack, allotted him five thousand men as well as twenty shallow-draft vessels and additional arms for the Indians, and appointed General Robert Ross as the army commander.⁸

During the September 1814 operations against Baltimore, General Ross suffered a fatal wound, which left the army without an officer in North America the equivalent of Cochrane, his naval counterpart. Ross and Cochrane had worked well together during the Chesapeake operations, each contributing his expertise to a successful campaign. The British government had expected that the officers would triumph along the Gulf as well. Yet Ross's replacement—the able and qualified General Sir Edward Michael Pakenham—had done little to shape or plan the Louisiana campaign. He had not offered his expertise nor challenged Cochrane's decisions. As such, Pakenham had to accept the strategic decisions that Cochrane had already made, decisions that had been built upon questionable information. Ross's death signaled the beginning of a series of disappointments that frustrated the British and resulted in a humiliating defeat at the climactic Battle of New Orleans in early January 1815.

When Cochrane took command in the spring of 1814, he had learned that the southern Indians were also fighting against the United States. But Cochrane did not know that one tribe, the Creeks, were also fighting a civil war in which one faction remained loyal to the United States and the other suffered a devastating defeat against Andrew Jackson at the March 1814

Battle of Horseshoe Bend. Nor did Cochrane realize that the other major southern tribes—the Cherokees and Choctaws—had completely sided with the United States. Knowing only that a sizable number of Indians were still fighting a common foe, Cochrane had sent Captain Hugh Pigot and a small complement of men to the Gulf with arms and supplies for the Indians. Brevet Captain George Woodbine stayed among the southern Indians throughout the summer and fall of 1814, training and drilling, supplying and feeding, as well as trying to recruit additional warriors. Throughout Woodbine convinced himself and reported to Cochrane that the Indians were potentially powerful allies who could be counted on during the Louisiana campaign. However, Cochrane learned by early December that the southern Indians hostile to the United States could contribute very little to British operations; Cochrane was thus prevented in his attempt to supplement his force with Indian warriors.[9]

During his campaign in the Chesapeake Cochrane had also encouraged slaves to run away and had enlisted those willing to take up arms against their former masters. He believed that outfitting and arming blacks would alter the course of the war because it would demoralize the Americans, forcing them to defend themselves simultaneously against a British attack and armed slave uprisings before they could send troops to the Canadian frontier. Cochrane had also insisted that "thousands [of slaves] will join upon their masters['] horses" simply because of "their hatred to the citizens of the United States." Cochrane had found so little difficulty recruiting slaves and employing them during his successful Chesapeake campaign that he anticipated similar results during his expedition along the slaveholding Gulf. Besides, reports from Florida and Louisiana already indicated that there was "a strong and irresistible party in the free people of colour, and the slaves who to a man will join" the British cause. True, runaway slaves fled from Georgia and the Mississippi Territory to the British base on the Apalachicola River in Spanish Florida, but they did not participate in or alter the outcome of the Louisiana campaign. More important, very few of the Louisiana slaves Cochrane anticipated would don red coats actually assisted the British, and fewer still participated in the Louisiana campaign. Instead, Jackson persuaded slaves and free blacks from south Louisiana and the Florida Parishes to join the American cause. He guaranteed "a full and entire pardon" to slaves who helped defend the city and promised a monetary and land bounty to those "sons of freedom"—or free blacks—who joined his cause. Jackson's proclamations ultimately denied to Cochrane and the British a second important source of much-needed manpower.[10]

Jean Lafitte and his Baratarian associates represented a third potential source of soldiers that Cochrane wanted to employ in his Louisiana campaign. Based on the Island of Barataria to the south and west of New Orleans, this lawless group operated a prosperous smuggling ring that supplied slaves and other contraband goods to the settlers of Louisiana. The Baratarians blatantly plundered foreign merchant ships, disregarded international neutrality laws, and violated American revenue laws—and the U.S. government could do little to suppress their activities. Cochrane seized on the idea that the Baratarians could provide assistance by either joining the British expedition or by remaining neutral, and in early September 1814 he sent Captain Nicholas Lockyer to meet with Jean Lafitte. For two days the two men discussed the prospects of an alliance in which the Baratarians would provide their assistance and knowledge, and in return the British would offer to protect and aid the pirates in their struggle against the United States. Ironically, Lafitte refused the British offer and instead chose to join the American cause just as Commodore Patterson and Colonel George T. Ross finalized plans for a campaign against the Baratarian stronghold. Two weeks later, 16 September 1814, American army and naval forces destroyed Lafitte's base at Grand Terre. Despite the American attack Lafitte and his associates remained loyal to the United States, depriving Cochrane not only of an important source of manpower and equipment, but also of a source of vital information regarding the geography of the region.[11]

Finding himself disappointed in his attempt to recruit the Baratarians, Indians, or runaway slaves, Cochrane turned to the disaffected populations of Louisiana and Spanish Florida, who he mistakenly thought were "very anxious to get rid of the Americans." Cochrane had been led to believe that the disposition of the region's inhabitants toward Britain and America was "as various and as motley as" the population itself; he had been told that the Spaniards supported their country and the French theirs, but both groups worked primarily against the Americans. This prompted Cochrane and the British Ministry to project that the expeditionary force might "find in the inhabitants a general and decided disposition to withdraw from their recent connexion with the United States." If he found this attitude, Cochrane was instructed to secure both "their favour and co-operation." If Cochrane did so, he believed that the British would "receive the whole Province of Louisiana from the United States."[12]

Cochrane did not find a population eager to assist his force. The British and Indian invasion of Pensacola, Florida, in September 1814 should have offered a more realistic indication of what the British might find in Louisiana. British commanders had thought that the Spanish in Florida would appreciate and readily accept military support. They instead found that Spanish officials and citizens refused to cooperate or assist with preparations to defend the town. British forces responded by dealing harshly with merchants, citizens, and officials, threatening to destroy the city, and taking with them slaves and the Spanish garrison without permission as they evacuated the city. This angered and alienated the people of Pensacola even more. When the Americans drove the British out of the city in November 1814, Andrew Jackson made sure that Spanish citizens were treated fairly, which both surprised and pleased them. Not surprisingly, news of the American and British occupations, and of the treatment of Spanish citizens, found its way across the Florida Parishes to New Orleans and helped create enmity and suspicion that drove Louisianians firmly into the American fold, again depriving Cochrane of another important source of support.[13]

Cochrane did not gain the support he had anticipated from the Indians, slaves, Baratarians, or from the discontented population, and without their help he had to modify his original operational plans. Initially, he had wanted to land troops at Pensacola or Mobile and march overland through the Florida Parishes toward New Orleans. Yet the British attempt to take Mobile in September 1814 had failed miserably. The inability to hold Pensacola, combined with the failed Mobile attack and the lack of local support, should have warned Cochrane that the Louisiana expedition had gotten off to a dangerous start. Cochrane's inability to secure the necessary small boats that he needed for the shallow waters of the Gulf created another problem. He had known for some time that he "never [could] reduce New Orleans without" shallow-draft vessels, and throughout the summer he had instructed his officers to collect all the small craft that they could; the admiralty had also ordered twenty shallow-draft boats be made available for the Louisiana expedition. But by December 1814 Cochrane admitted that he was still "deficient in Flat Boats or the means of transporting Troops into shallow water." Regardless, Cochrane continued with his plans, and by early December the British invasion fleet was assembling along the Gulf Coast.[14]

Cochrane and his superiors had thoroughly studied the possible invasion routes. His first plan had been to proceed overland through the Florida Parishes toward New Orleans. The British army would secure the northern shore of Lake Pontchartrain, cutting off all land approaches to the Isle of Orleans, while the navy would blockade the water approaches to the city; but the British failure to capture Mobile or to hold Pensacola forced Cochrane to rely on a seaborne attack. Given his limited options, Cochrane concluded that Lake Borgne was the most feasible route toward New Orleans, as the saltwater estuary offered three approaches to New Orleans. The first was through the Rigolets from Lake Borgne into Lake Pontchartrain. Although this avenue, combined with the Bayou St. John, would have permitted the British to move by water within two miles of New Orleans, it required many light, shallow-draft vessels, which the British obviously had problems securing. There were also other problems facing the British along this route, including Fort Petites Coquilles—which the British believed had more than five hundred men and forty guns—and a sizable blockship that had reportedly been under construction at Madisonville since 1813. The unfinished blockship supposedly carried twenty-six 32-pound cannon and had only a 6½-foot draft, making it by far the most formidable weapon in those shallow waters. Cochrane's second alternative was through Lake Borgne to the Plain of Gentilly, from which British troops could march to the city along the Chef Menteur Road. But because of the road's accessibility, Jackson had defended it with both men and artillery, and a pitched battle there would have allowed the Americans to fall back and construct other lines of defense well away from the city.[15]

The last route, and ultimately the one Cochrane chose, called for using Bayou Bienvenu, which drained the area east of New Orleans and stretched from Lake Borgne to within a mile of the Mississippi River. From there British forces could proceed north nine miles along the river levee, a narrow strip of land through the region's sugar plantations, toward New Orleans. While this approach appeared to be the path of least resistance, it too was fraught with obstacles. The bayou was shallower than expected, preventing British ships from entering the estuary or providing gunfire support to cover their barges' advance. Furthermore, the distance from Cat Island, at the mouth of Lake Borgne, to Bayou Bienvenu was sixty-two miles, and it took thirty-six hours of hard rowing to reach it. But the most serious obstacle, according to British midshipman Robert Aitchison who was present during the operation, was Thomas ap Catesby Jones's "insolent little flotilla" of "five American gunboats, of great strength," that commanded the shoal waters. Jones's craft had to be destroyed or they would wreak havoc for the British invasion force.[16]

Jones had arrived on Lake Borgne in early December with five gunboats and the tender *Alligator;* his flotilla numbered in all just twenty-six guns and 204 men. Even though it was a paltry force with which to meet Cochrane's sizable expedition, Jones had been given very simple instructions: Wait for the enemy outside the Rigolets between Ship and Cat Islands; confront British barges and small boats unless assaulted by a superior force; and if attacked, withdraw to the Rigolets and the protection of land batteries at Fort Petites Coquilles. The Rigolets were to be Jones's last line of defense, where he should "sink the enemy, or be sunk." In accordance with his orders, Jones sent two gunboats to Dauphine Island while the others remained off St. Mary's Island anticipating the impending arrival of the British fleet.[17]

On 8 December gunboats *Nos. 23* and *163* spied the British frigates *Armide* and *Seahorse* and the brig-sloop *Sophia* as they sailed westward along the chain of islands off the Florida Parishes. This was the advance force of Cochrane's fleet. The gunboats followed until the British ships anchored at dusk, then they proceeded to St. Mary's Island to inform Jones of their discovery. Over the next four days Jones observed "from 20 to 30 sails," including four British ships-of-the-line, several brigs, schooners, sloops, and barges concentrating in the channel between Cat and Ship Islands. This proved to Jones that Lake Borgne was to be their approach and that it was "no longer safe or prudent" to remain in his present position. Jones began retreating to the west.[18]

On the morning of 13 December 1814, Cochrane ordered his barges to move against the American gunboats. Jones responded to the British activity by sending Sailing Master William Johnson and the *Seahorse* to destroy channel markers and supplies onshore at Bay St. Louis. By 2:00 P.M. the British barges had secured Pass Christian as they slowly continued westward toward Jones's becalmed gunboats. A strong westerly wind, blowing for several days prior to the assault, had reduced the lake's depth, leaving the American gunboats grounded. Jones could therefore only watch as the British inched closer. Finally, Jones ordered his men to throw overboard "all articles of weight that could be dispensed with," and at 3:30 P.M. the tide "commenced," permitting the gunboats to withdraw toward the Rigolets.[19]

As Jones retreated westward, he saw that the British had sent three barges against the *Seahorse* as it destroyed the supplies at Bay St. Louis. William Johnson's schooner, armed with its one six-pounder and supported by two six-pounders mounted onshore, fought off the initial British attack, but four other British barges soon joined in. Johnson held off the seven barges for more than thirty minutes before realizing his situation was hopeless. With no other options, Johnson burned the storehouse and supplies onshore, ignited the *Seahorse* to prevent its capture, and retreated overland. Johnson climbed a tree and watched from shore as the War of 1812 came in full fury to Lake Borgne and the Florida Parishes.[20]

Jones continued retreating westward until one o'clock on the morning of 14 December 1814, when the winds died, the tide changed, and the gunboats ran aground near the Malheureux Island passage. At dawn's light Jones saw that the British were steadily advancing; he estimated their distance as nine miles away, rowing hard, and closing fast. A lack of wind, combined with a strong eastward ebb tide, forced Jones to anchor his craft in a defensive position to "give the enemy as warm a reception as possible." Although Jones wanted to concentrate his craft in a battle line formation, a strong current drove his flagship, *No. 156*, and *No. 163* about one hundred yards east of the other three gunboats, leaving them exposed in the center of the American line.[21]

At 9:30 A.M. British barges overwhelmed the *Alligator*, which had been forced to anchor some distance to the southeast of Jones's gunboats. Thirty minutes later Captain Nicholas Lockyer, who commanded the British assault, anchored his barges just beyond the range of Jones's guns and gave his men a much-needed rest and the opportunity for breakfast. After thirty minutes Lockyer resumed his advance toward Jones, who was still unable to restore his defensive line because of the tide. Jones's *No. 156* became the first gunboat to face the full force of the British attack.[22]

As the British approached, Jones counted three light gigs and forty-two barges armed with light carronades and estimated that the craft carried upward of 1,000 men and officers. In reality the British force numbered more than 1,200 men, whereas Jones had but 183 men, and only 36 in his gunboat. Jones reported that at 10:39 A.M. the British barges came within cannon range of his vessel, and he ordered his ships to fire their heavy guns. For more than ten minutes the American boats fired their long guns with little effect on the approaching enemy. By 10:50 the smaller British guns, now within range, began firing, and Jones noted that the "action became general and destructive on both sides."[23]

Jones had previously instructed his sailors to mount their boarding nets, and shortly before noon the soldiers on three of the British barges tried to board. Jones's sailors fired their cannon and small arms at the British, inflicting heavy casualties as they sunk two enemy barges and killed or wounded nearly every enemy officer aboard them. Jones recalled that the "unfortunate enemy" barely escaped drowning by clinging to the capsized barges until other vessels came to their aid. Soon four more British barges came forward, and after a spirited fight they, too, were driven back with heavy casualties. During this second assault Jones used his pistol to shoot a soldier trying to board his gunboat and then also mortally wounded Lieutenant George Pratt, the officer who reportedly had defaced the naval monument at the Capitol during the British occupation of Washington, D.C., in August 1814. As Pratt fell backward into his barge, a soldier behind him fired his musket. The shot penetrated Jones's left shoulder, and as he fell to the deck several other balls passed through his clothes and cap. Nonetheless, Jones continued screaming orders as he lay on the deck of his gunboat, covered with blood. A few minutes later he fainted because of the blood loss, and Master's Mate George Parker assumed command until he, too, was severely wounded. Some fifteen minutes later, when the smoke of the battle had cleared, it was apparent that the British were in control of Jones's gunboat; the victors counted eighteen killed or wounded Americans aboard *No. 156*, the latter including both Jones and Parker.[24]

After capturing Jones's vessel, the British turned the flagship's cannon on the other American gunboats, and, one by one, they too succumbed to the numerically superior force. The British victory over Jones's *No. 156* had been the turning point of the Battle of Lake Borgne and had given them control over that crucial water approach. While the British had secured the lake and an approach to New Orleans, it had not been without great loss to their own forces. When Jones wrote his action report some months later, he claimed that British casualties had been staggering, yet the British officially reported only seventeen killed and seventy-seven wounded. American casualties for the entirety of Jones's flotilla had amounted to only six killed, thirty-five wounded, and the remainder captured. Despite the trifling number of casualties, the Battle of Lake Borgne had been a costly defeat for the United States and Andrew Jackson.[25]

While the British easily overwhelmed Jones's flotilla, their conquest was but a hollow and meaningless victory that over-inflated British expectations. Throughout the fall of 1814 Cochrane had gotten very little encouraging news about his planned Gulf expedition. The Indians were not the fighting force Cochrane had anticipated. Black slave soldiers had not swelled British ranks as Cochrane expected, nor had their flight created a hardship for the United States. The Baratarian pirates had not chosen to join with the British against the Americans. The Spanish and French populations along the Gulf had not embraced the British as liberators, but viewed and treated them as conquerors. The British attempt to take Mobile and to hold Pensacola had failed miserably, which ultimately meant that the assault against New Orleans would have to be a waterborne operation rather than land attack through the Florida Parishes. Last, the British invasion flotilla had serious problems securing enough small craft for their naval operation. These British setbacks should have prompted Cochrane to reconsider his plans. Instead, Cochrane secured ten thousand peninsular veterans rather than five thousand regulars originally promised by the admiralty, and the additional soldiers emboldened him about British prospects. The enlarged force also gave Cochrane new confidence that a direct assault, even without local support, would be an easy victory; Washington, after all, had been easily captured a few months earlier with far fewer men. The battle against Jones's small flotilla on Lake Borgne only reconfirmed Cochrane's expectations of an easy victory and falsely restored lost British confidence. In fact, one high-ranking British officer prematurely proclaimed that the victory on Lake Borgne was "a most brilliant affair, and brilliant consequences may attach to this success."[26]

Arguably, the Battle of Lake Borgne was one of the most important catalysts of the British disaster on the Plains of Chalmette. Certainly other factors contributed to the British defeat, but none of them resulted from months of information or planning; they were happenstance or accidental. The victory on Lake Borgne somehow erased all the other setbacks that Cochrane had suffered during the fall of 1814, reinvigorating and boosting British expectations and morale. Cochrane held the Americans in contempt, and the easy victory on Lake Borgne reconfirmed his beliefs. He proudly reported after the battle that Captain Lockyer had "attacked with such judgment and determined bravery, that notwithstanding [the Americans'] formidable force, their advantage of a chosen position, and their studied and deliberate preparation, he succeeded in capturing the whole of these vessels, in so serviceable a state as to afford at once the most essential aid to the expedition." As such, the battle on Lake Borgne prompted Cochrane and other British officers to believe that the New Orleans expedition would be boldly successful.[27]

When "Jones sacrificed his small flotilla" along the shores of St. Tammany Parish, little did anyone realize that he was helping to determine the final outcome of the Gulf campaign. Jones's defense gained much-needed time for Jackson to increase his complement of troops and to bolster his defenses and resolve south of New Orleans. Moreover, as prisoners, Jones and his fellow Americans fed their captors faulty information about the locations and strength of Jackson's troops, forcing the British to exercise greater caution as they advanced. Ultimately Jones's defense bought for Jackson nine days, which was vital, if not decisive, in determining the final outcome.[28]

Although Jones and his fellow seamen had done all they could—as warriors and then as prisoners—to forestall the British assault, the defeat on Lake Borgne had not been Jones's fault alone. Had Jones and the New Orleans station had twenty operable gunboats on Lake Borgne as had been called for by the Navy Department, the British might never have been able to cross the lake at all, which would have postponed or perhaps even eliminated altogether any climactic battle at Chalmette. But because of hurricanes, tornadoes, and decay, the flotilla only had six vessels on the station, five of which were in service with Jones on the lake when Cochrane's barges began their assault. Furthermore, had Jones's craft been equipped with oars, as had been ordered by the secretary of the navy, the British barges probably would not have caught the gunboats. But such was not the case. Jones's gunboats could neither retreat nor withstand a determined attack by such an overwhelming British force. Although the results of the battle seemed predetermined in favor of the British, Jones's stubborn defense helped provide a different result for the Louisiana campaign and the fate of the United States.[29]

British policy-makers had expected the southern campaign to be overwhelmingly successful. Even the Duke of Wellington, who had refused to accept a command in North America, anticipated that his brother-in-law General Pakenham would capture New Orleans. Once it had been secured, Wellington even insisted that it should be held for the future. The British ministry unquestionably wanted to occupy New Orleans, the Florida Parishes, and the entire Gulf Coast, perhaps as a permanent possession; they did not believe that Spain could withstand future American expansion.

British ministers also thought that retaining possessions along the Gulf would give them continued influence with the Indians and runaway slaves, permit them to promote western disunion from the United States, and, more important, provide a link with and greater protection for Canada. The failed attack against New Orleans all but shattered British plans for the Gulf Coast.

In early February 1815, before news of the Treaty of Ghent arrived in the Gulf, British forces captured Fort Bowyer, which guarded the entrance to Mobile Bay. This easy victory provided the British with a renewed foothold along the Gulf Coast, from which they could plan to march again through the Florida Parishes and cut off New Orleans. Yet before British forces could secure the city of Mobile, news arrived indicating that the war had ended. The restoration of peace between the United States and Britain in late February 1815 completely dismantled and finally ended all British plans for securing Louisiana, the Gulf Coast, and the Mississippi Valley, and linking them to their Canadian provinces.[30]

When Lieutenant Thomas ap Catesby Jones appeared before the naval board of inquiry in the spring of 1815, the fate of New Orleans and the Florida Parishes, the Gulf Coast, and even the United States had long since been determined. Nonetheless, from Monday, May 15, until Friday, May 19, Jones described what had happened during his battle on Lake Borgne, as well as explained why his defeat had left the entire coast of Louisiana exposed to a British attack. During the proceedings the court probed every facet of the battle before unanimously concluding that Lieutenant Jones had "evinced . . . a judgment highly creditable to his character." Even though a numerically superior force had easily overwhelmed the young officer and his flotilla, the court concurred that Jones had done all within his power to "gain the best position for his squadron." He had also demonstrated "a firmness and intrepidity worthy the emulation of his countrymen, and reflecting the highest honour on the service to which he belongs." Finally the court concluded that Jones and his men had "performed their duty on this occasion in the most able and gallant manner, and that the action has added another and distinguished honour to the naval character of the country."[31]

The overlooked Battle of Lake Borgne that defined Jones's life was the naval prelude to the climactic Louisiana campaign—an event that inextricably fused the destinies of New Orleans and the Florida Parishes, Louisiana and the territories of the Purchase, as well as the Gulf Coast and the

United States. The battle also linked Jones's gallant defeat to Andrew Jackson's monumental victory on the Plains of Chalmette. When Daniel Todd Patterson reviewed the ruling of the court of inquiry in May of 1815, he acknowledged that in Jones's "unequal contest, . . . the national and naval character has been nobly sustained." Moreover, Patterson indicated that the battle was one of the most significant naval episodes of the War of 1812, one that "contributed, in no small degree, to the eventual safety of" New Orleans, Louisiana, and the Gulf Coast.

While the battle on Lake Borgne helped unquestionably to define the Louisiana campaign, it also helped to explain Jones's long naval career. Throughout his life he was always proud to refer to his tour of duty at New Orleans and his sacrifice at Lake Borgne. Some twenty-plus years after his defeat, in February 1841, the State of Virginia awarded Jones a beautiful sword for his valiant and distinguished service during the War of 1812. During the ceremony Jones admitted, "Unlike my compatriots in war . . . my efforts were not crowned with victory." Nonetheless, Jones knew full well that the sword being awarded to him was a symbol of his pledge "for renewed and increasing devotion to [his] country and to her cause." Although Jones steadfastly demonstrated that devotion and loyalty throughout his almost fifty years of naval service, it was that fateful day in December 1814 along the shores of the Florida Parishes that became the crowning moment of his career. It was also that same December 1814 day that introduced the Florida Parishes into the mainstream of America as attentions focused on a seemingly insignificant battle that ultimately determined the future and development of the United States. Jones's defeat on Lake Borgne, combined with British frustrations during the Louisiana campaign, gave Andrew Jackson and the United States the victory they needed for the future.[32]

Notes

1. "A Court of Inquiry assembled in the Naval Arsenal, at New Orleans . . . ," 15–19 May 1815, and Andrew Jackson to the Secretary of War, 27 December 1814, both cited in Arsène Lacarrière Latour, *Historical Memoir of the War in West Florida and Louisiana in 1814–15, with an Atlas,* ed. Gene A. Smith (1816; reprint Gainesville: Historic New Orleans Collection and the University Press of Florida, 1999), 300–302, 229–30, respectively. A narrative of Jones's life can be found in Gene A. Smith, *Thomas ap Catesby Jones: Commodore of Manifest Destiny* (Annapolis, Md.: Naval Institute Press, 2000).

2. Wilburt S. Brown, *The Amphibious Campaign for West Florida and Louisiana* (Tuscaloosa: University of Alabama Press, 1969), 81.

3. Christopher A. McKee, *A Gentlemanly and Honorable Profession: The Creation of the U.S. Naval Officer Corps, 1794–1815* (Annapolis: Naval Institute Press, 1991), 306; Thomas ap Catesby Jones to the Secretary of the Navy, 25 September 1812, 22 January 1813, in Letters Received by the Secretary of the Navy from Officers below the Rank of Commander, 1802–1884, National Archives, RG 45, M148; Jones's service along the Gulf is chronicled in Smith, *Thomas ap Catesby Jones*, 13–32.

4. Keith S. Dent, "The British Navy and the Anglo-American War of 1812 to 1815" (M.A. thesis, University of Leeds, 1949), 352; J. Leitch Wright, *Britain and the American Frontier, 1783–1815* (Athens: University of Georgia Press, 1975), 122–25, 135–36.

5. John Borlase Warren to Lord Melville, 18 November 1812, 16 November 1813, in Warren Papers, National Maritime Museum, Greenwich, England (hereinafter cited as NMM).

6. James Stirling to Viscount Melville, 17 March 1813, in James Stirling Memorandum, Historic New Orleans Collection, New Orleans (hereinafter cited as HNOC); Henry Hotham Book of Remarks, 1813, Hotham Collection, DDHO 7/99, Brynmor Jones Library, University of Hull, Hull, England.

7. Brian Jenkins, *Henry Goulburn, 1784–1856: A Political Biography* (Montreal: McGill-Queen's University Press, 1996), 79–80; James Pack, *The Man Who Burned the White House: Admiral Sir George Cockburn, 1772–1853* (Annapolis, Md.: Naval Institute Press, 1987), 171; Lord Bathurst to Lords Commissioners of the Admiralty, 25 March 1813, in British Public Records Office, Admiralty Office Papers, 1/4223, Kew, England (hereinafter cited as PRO, ADM); Viscount Melville to Admiral Hope, 13 November 1812, in Robert Saunders-Dundas Papers, NMM.

8. Alexander F. I. Cochrane's Observations to Lord Melville Relative to America, 1814, War of 1812 MSS, Lilly Library, Indiana University, Bloomington, Ind.; Lord Melville to William Domett, 23 July 1814, and Domett to Melville, 26 July 1814, both in Melville Castle Muniments, GD 51/2/523/1–2, National Archives of Scotland, Edinburgh; John Wilson Croker to Alexander Cochrane, 10 August 1814, in PRO, War Office 1/141, 15–24 (hereinafter cited as WO); Earl Bathurst to Robert Ross, 10 August 1814, in PRO, WO 6/2, 6–8.

9. John K. Mahon, "British Strategy and Southern Indians: War of 1812," *Florida Historical Quarterly* 44 (April 1966): 287–98; George Woodbine to Alexander F. I. Cochrane, 25 July 1814, in Alexander Cochrane Papers, MSS 2328, National Library of Scotland, Edinburgh (hereinafter cited as NLS).

10. Alexander F. I. Cochrane to Earl Bathurst, 14 July 1814, in PRO, WO 1/141; Hugh Pigot to Cochrane, in Cochrane Papers, MS 2326, NLS; George Woodbine to Hugh Pigot, 25, 28 May 1814, and Edward Nicolls to Cochrane, 12 August 1814, in Cochrane Papers, MS 2328, NLS; Latour, *Historical Memoir*, 149, 205–6.

11. Jane Lucas DeGrummond, *The Baratarians and the Battle of New Orleans* (Baton Rouge: Louisiana State University Press, 1961), 37–48; Edward Nicolls to Alexander F. I. Cochrane, 27 July 1814, in Cochrane Papers, MS 2328, NLS; Arthur P. Hayne to Inspector General Office, Seventh Military District, 17 September 1814, in Butler Family Papers, HNOC; Frank L. Owsley Jr., *Struggle for the Gulf Borderlands: The Creek War and the Battle of New Orleans, 1812–1815* (Gainesville: University Presses of Florida, 1981), 109–12; Edward Nicolls to Mon-

sieur Lafitte, 31 August 1814, and William H. Percy to Monsieur Lafitte, 1 September 1814, both in the Edward Nicolls and William H. Percy Letters, HNOC; Latour, *Historical Memoir,* 25–29.

12. Edward Nicolls to Alexander F. I. Cochrane, 27 July, 12 August 1814, in Cochrane Papers, MS 2328, NLS; Earl Bathurst to Robert Ross, 6 September 1814, in PRO, WO 6/2, 9–13; Benson J. Lossing, *Pictorial Field-Book of the War of 1812* (New York: Harper and Brothers, 1869), 1026.

13. John Innerarity to James Innerarity, 7 November 1814, in "Letters of John Innerarity," *Florida Historical Quarterly* 9 (1931): 127–30; Vincente de Ordozgoitti to Juan Ruiz Apodaca, 21 September 1814, in Archivo General de India, Papeles Procedentes de Cuba, legajo 1856; James Gordon to Alexander F. I. Cochrane, 18 November 1814, in PRO, ADM 1/505; Frank L. Owsley Jr., "British and Indian Activities in Spanish West Florida during the War of 1812," *Florida Historical Quarterly* 46 (1967): 119–20.

14. Edward Nicolls to Alexander Cochrane, 12 August 1814, in Cochrane Papers, MS 2328, NLS; Alexander Cochrane to Hugh Pigot, 9 June 1814, ibid., MS 2346; Edward Codrington to Mrs. Edward Codrington, 7 June 1814, in Sir Edward Codrington Papers, COD/7/1, NMM.

15. James Stirling to Lord Viscount Melville, 17 March 1813, in James Stirling Memorandum, 1813, HNOC; John Shaw to the Secretary of the Navy, in Miscellaneous Letters, 1801–1884, RG 45, M124; William C. C. Claiborne to James Madison, 9 July 1813, in *Official Letter Books of W. C. C. Claiborne, 1801–1816,* ed. Dunbar Rowland, 6 vols. (Jackson, Miss.: State Department of Archives and History, 1917), 6:238; John Shaw to Daniel Patterson, 21 December 1813, in Letters Received by the Secretary of the Navy, Captains' Letters, 1805–1861, 1866–1885, NA, RG 45, M125; Owsley, *Struggle for the Gulf,* 126–27; Brown, *Amphibious Campaign,* 83.

16. Brown, *Amphibious Campaign,* 48; Alexander Cochrane to John Wilson Coker, 9 March 1815, in *Naval Chronicle* 23 (1815): 337; Hugh F. Rankin, ed., *The Battle of New Orleans: A British View; The Journal of Major C. R. Forrest* (New Orleans: Hauser Press, 1961), 5; Robert Aitchison, "Autobiography of Admiral R. Aitchison," 64, HNOC; "Letter from a British Soldier at New Orleans," *Naval Chronicle* 33 (January–June 1815): 485–86; C. J. Forbes to James Cobb, 28 January 1815, in "Unpublished Letter Relative to the Battle of New Orleans," *Louisiana Historical Society Proceedings* 9 (1916): 80.

17. A. Lacarrière Latour, *Historical Memoir of the War in West Florida and Louisiana in 1814–15, with an Atlas,* ed. Jane Lucas DeGrummond (1816; reprint Gainesville: University of Florida Press, 1964), 57–59; Jones to Patterson, 9 December 1814, in Letters Received by the Secretary of the Navy from Officers below the Rank of Commander, 1802–1884, NA, RG 45, M148.

18. "Statement of Lieutenant Thomas ap Catesby Jones to Daniel T. Patterson, 12 March 1815," NA, RG 45, HJ Box 181, 1814–1815 (hereinafter cited as "Jones Statement"); Dudley Avery to Mary Ann, 14 December 1814, in Avery Family Papers, Southern Historical Collection–University of North Carolina, Chapel Hill (hereinafter cited as SHC–UNC); Alexander Cochrane to John Wilson Coker, 9 March 1815, in *Naval Chronicle* 23 (1815): 337–38; Jones to Patterson, 11 December 1814, in *Journal of the House of Representatives during the First Session of the Second Legislature of the State of Louisiana* (New Orleans: P. K. Wagner, 1814), 40–41.

19. "Jones Statement."

20. Memorial of Thomas Shield, Congressional Report no. 66, 4 January 1819, copy in the Andrew Hynes Papers, HNOC; "Jones Statement"; Lieut. Moore to John, 13 December 1814, in Kean-Prescott Papers, SHC–UNC.

21. "Jones Statement."

22. Ibid.

23. Ibid.

24. Ibid.; Clericus, "Biographical Sketch of Thomas ap Catesby Jones," *Military and Naval Magazine* (1834): 130–31; Alexander Walker, *Jackson and New Orleans* (New York: J. C. Derby, 1856), 104; Spencer C. Tucker, *The Jeffersonian Gunboat Navy* (Columbia: University of South Carolina Press, 1993), 169.

25. John Henry Cooke, *A Narrative of Events in the South of France and of the Attack on New Orleans, in 1814 and 1815* (London: T. & W. Boone, 1835), 162–63; Nathaniel Herbert Claiborne, *Notes on the War in the South* (Richmond: William Ramsay, 1819), 56–57; Andrew Jackson to James Monroe, 27 December 1814, in *Niles' Weekly Register*, 4 February 1815, 7:357.

26. Bathurst to Robert Ross, 28 September 1814, in PRO, WO 6/2, 19–24; Brown, *Amphibious Campaign*, 81; Edward Codrington to his wife, 23 November–31 December 1814, in Codrington Papers, COD/7/1, NMM.

27. Alexander Cochrane to John Wilson Croker, 16 December 1814, in *Naval Chronicle* 33 (January–June 1815): 337; Alexander Cochrane to Viscount Melville, 10 November 1814, in War of 1812 MSS, Lilly Library, Indiana University.

28. W. L. Ainsworth, "An Amphibious Operation that Failed: The Battle of New Orleans," *Naval Institute Proceedings* 71 (February 1945): 197; Edwin N. McClellan, "The Navy at the Battle of New Orleans," *Naval Institute Proceedings* 5 (December 1924): 2046–47.

29. Owsley, *Struggle for the Gulf*, 139–40; Daniel Patterson to William Jones, 22 November 1813, 7 December 1813, 21, 31 January 1814, in Letters Received by the Secretary of the Navy from Commanders, 1804–1886, NA, RG 45, M147; Paul Hamilton to John Shaw, 25 September 1812, and William Jones to Daniel Patterson, 18 October 1813, in Letters Sent by the Secretary of the Navy to Officers, 1798–1868, NA, RG 45, M149; "Letter from a British Soldier at New Orleans," *Naval Chronicle* 33 (January–June 1815): 485.

30. Wright, *Britain and the American Frontier*, 179–81.

31. "A Court of Inquiry," 300–302.

32. *Richmond Enquirer*, 25 February 1841; *Southern Literary Messenger* 7 (April 1841): 316–20.

5

A THRESHOLD OF UNOBTAINABLE COMMITMENT

Irregular Operations in Louisiana's Florida Parishes, 1862–1865

SAMUEL C. HYDE JR.

THE CHECK ON AMERICAN MILITARY POWER DURING THE VIETNAM conflict revitalized a persistent debate in Civil War historiography. The success enjoyed by a poorly equipped yet determined guerrilla force against elements of the world's finest army provided reason to question the certainty of a Union victory. History abounds with examples of the success attainable through irregular operations. From the triumphs of Spanish guerrillas during the Napoleonic wars to the legendary exploits of Francis Marion, the "Swamp Fox" of the American Revolution, the late eighteenth and early nineteenth centuries provided multiple examples of the effectiveness of irregular operations. Yet guerrilla campaigns require an enormous level of commitment both from those seeking to sustain the irregulars and from their opponents. The success or failure of guerrilla operations during the American Civil War accordingly centered on which of the antagonists proved willing to pay the higher price of commitment.

Most significant, irregular operations raised the level of human suffering. Guerrilla wars seldom extend only to combatants but almost always include the civilian population. The residents of regions subject to guerrilla campaigns typically find it impossible to remain neutral and frequently find themselves the victims of both sides in the conflict. But despite the suffering they produce, guerrilla campaigns also often prove to be very effective. The most aggressive critics of irregular operations are frequently those who remain least effective in suppressing them or those most frustrated by their inability to direct their actions.

Historians have long debated the possibilities for success that may have accompanied a Confederate decision to resort to irregular operations in the aftermath of Appomattox. This study examines events in one specific area of the southern interior where circumstances motivated the residents to resort to nonconventional warfare in a desperate effort to counter the actions of the enemy. The outcome of that effort suggests that similar results likely would have accompanied the reliance on irregular forces in wider regions of the South.

With the outbreak of hostilities between North and South in early 1861, the dilemma of irregular operations became apparent almost immediately. The wisdom of employing irregulars against the Federal army provoked intensive debate across the South for the duration of the war, particularly in seemingly isolated areas of the southern interior where the vast advantages in men and material enjoyed by the North proved especially apparent. The South's policy of "Cordon Defense" left large areas of the southern heartland virtually undefended by regular Confederate forces. Highly publicized guerrilla wars raged along certain poorly defended regions of the border states, such as Missouri; but though less studied, many regions of the southern interior also experienced the catastrophe of irregular warfare. By examining these less analyzed yet equally ferocious guerrilla campaigns, a more accurate discernment of their potential for success may emerge.

A comprehensive Union policy for addressing irregular operations was formulated in the office of General Henry W. Halleck. His experiences in Missouri during the winter of 1861–1862 left Halleck frustrated by the effectiveness of certain guerrilla groups and, even more so, by the absence of Federal directives governing their suppression. General Orders Number 100 was designed not only to provide a uniform national policy for anti-guerrilla operations but also to explain the distinction between partisans and guerrillas. The order identified partisan rangers as "distinctly authorized" uniformed raiders, such as the detached Confederate cavalry units operating in northwestern Virginia under the command of John Singleton Mosby. Guerrillas, by contrast, were defined as those country people who are often engaged in peaceful pursuits but occasionally fight and resort to brigandage. The order further directed that, when captured, partisans should be treated as prisoners of war, while guerrillas were to be treated as "highway robbers or pirates" not entitled to the privileges of prisoners of war. Moreover, civilians who provided military information or served as guides for the enemy were to be regarded as "war-traitors" subject to immediate execution. The intention of General Orders Number 100 seemed designed to establish clear guidelines for distinguishing between the two types of irregular forces. But the broad terminology concerning citizen involvement provided ample room for the discretion of individual commanders.[1]

One region that witnessed the emergence of a less publicized guerrilla war of substantial consequence was the Florida Parishes of Louisiana. The Florida Parishes constitute that territory within the "toe" of eastern Louisiana between the Pearl and Mississippi Rivers. Home to the state capital, the largest Confederate training base in the western theater of the war at Camp Moore, and the staging point for any move against the South's largest city, New Orleans, the territory remained at the forefront of Union planning for the subjugation of the lower Mississippi Valley.

Containing Union forces and protecting the residents and resources of the Florida Parishes would prove to be an overwhelming challenge for Confederate troops. Part of the difficulty involved defending—without a navy—a region surrounded by water and penetrated by numerous navigable streams. The effort to secure the region against an enemy possessing irresistible naval power and seemingly limitless assets eventually strained Confederate resources to the breaking point. But in their hour of despair the residents would prove resourceful, learning to rely on themselves rather than government.

The celebration of independence and the excitement over the war prevailed unabated in the Florida Parishes until the spring of 1862, when the consequences of their bold endeavor first became apparent. In April 1862, a two-pronged catastrophe befell the western Confederacy. The feared invasion from the north necessitated the removal of all available manpower from the lower Mississippi region in an effort to check the Union advance. The ensuing Battle of Shiloh resulted in heavy losses and particularly severe casualties for units recruited in the Florida Parishes, which for the first time brought the bloody cost home. Despite the heavy casualties, the Federal army remained unbroken and continued to menace the lower Mississippi Valley from the north, giving the residents no relief from the burdensome fear of invasion by a hostile army.[2]

Unlike the northern threat, the menace from the south came unexpectedly. In late April 1862, a powerful Federal fleet passed the forts on the lower Mississippi and forced the capitulation of New Orleans. The fall of New Orleans deprived Louisiana and southwestern Mississippi of their principal market and effectively sealed the region off from contact with the outside world. Suddenly the residents of the Florida Parishes faced the threat of imminent invasion on two fronts and, for the first time, starvation. As remnants of Mansfield Lovell's tiny force streamed north from New Orleans to Camp Moore they brought despair and apprehension with them. Watching the trains unload their melancholy cargoes near her home in Tangipahoa, Louisiana, Abigail Amacker described the depression prevailing in the area: "The Federals have taken New Orleans, the hour seems very dark for us, God grant we may have peace shortly. A great many soldiers have come and are coming into this neighborhood, we fear starvation just now more than the Lincolnites."[3]

As outlined by Major General George B. McClellan, overall commander of Union forces, the plan for the subjugation of eastern Louisiana and the lower Mississippi Valley began with the capture of New Orleans. After seizing New Orleans, Federal forces were instructed to secure the avenues of approach to the city and, particularly, to gain control of Pass Manchac and the surrounding lakeshore area in lower Livingston Parish. The plan also called for the capture of Baton Rouge as soon as possible following the fall of New Orleans. To fulfill this mission Washington dispatched a land force eighteen thousand strong augmented by a powerful naval flotilla, certain to outgun and outnumber anything the southerners could gather in opposition.[4]

Whether the Yankees realized that eastern Louisiana and southwestern Mississippi sat virtually devoid of Confederate troops remains unclear. In response to Richmond's call for troops to support operations in Virginia and Tennessee, by early spring 1862 the Florida Parishes and environs had been literally denuded of regular Confederate forces. Governor Thomas Moore protested that no state had done more in terms of providing troops and armaments to support the Confederate war effort, yet no state had been so sorely neglected by the general government. General Mansfield Lovell, commander of the defenses about New Orleans, repeated the objections to the War Department's neglect of Louisiana. Lovell noted that twenty thousand well-trained Louisiana soldiers had been removed to other theaters only weeks before their own state was invaded. Moreover, he warned that to abandon Louisiana entirely "would have a very bad morale effect upon the state," promoting disaffection and encouraging residents to open a cotton trade with the enemy. Rebuffed in his pleas to the War Department, Lovell proposed a solution that Governor Moore heartily endorsed. The plan called for the creation of at least five regiments of partisan rangers to be armed and commissioned by the Confederate government. The purpose of this irregular force would be to "contain the enemy in New Orleans and protect the state from his ravages."[5]

Although different from guerrilla operations, partisan warfare evoked mixed emotions among civilians and military men alike. Many citizens regarded partisans as little more than undisciplined outlaws who often provoked brutal retaliation for their actions yet offered little realistic protection to the civilian population. Military men generally condemned partisans as guerrillas whose uncontrolled activities accomplished little more than keeping qualified soldiers out of the regular army. As early as the summer of 1861 General George McClellan condemned the rebel partisan operations in western Virginia as "a system of hostilities prohibited by the laws of war among belligerent nations." Similarly, Confederate general M. Jeff Thompson noted that most partisan units necessitated the presence of regular troops to make them scout and keep them from stealing. Thompson complained, "Instead of this arm of the service giving us the great advantages that it should, it became a terror to our own people and a disgrace to the true cavalryman or intelligent patriotic ranger." But partisan activities could tie down large numbers of enemy troops. Their hit-and-run tactics necessitated the commitment of significant bodies of troops to garrison duty and escort operations. The memory of the exploits of raiders such as Francis Marion, whether contemptible or heroic, remained fresh to many. And most agreed that in the absence of all else, partisan operations provided a means to strike back at an invader. In June 1861, the Confederate War Department accepted the formation of partisan forces, authorized their inclusion as a branch of the service, and allowed partisan officers to be commissioned. Lingering doubts nonetheless remained, particularly among certain officers who insisted that regular troops were far more effective than partisans. As a result of these doubts, the War Department required that each partisan force receive approval directly from the secretary of war.[6]

Efforts to convince doubters of the effectiveness of partisan rangers continued throughout the war, but Lovell presented a strong case in favor of partisan operations in eastern Louisiana. He pointed out that most of the fewer than three thousand troops that joined him at Camp Moore following the fall of New Orleans consisted of unarmed citizen militia who could not be considered reliable. As a result, without a motivated partisan force in the area, the path would be open for the Federals to proceed up the railroad unmolested and threaten P. G. T. Beauregard's army about Corinth, Mississippi, from the rear. Moreover, Lovell argued that quite probably the Union navy would gain control of most if not all of the Mississippi River, which would necessitate the immediate transfer of all forces from eastern Louisiana to the west side of the river. Both Lovell and Governor Moore recognized the absolute necessity of securing western Louisiana, where the bulk of the state's population and materiel remained concentrated. Finally, Lovell bluntly requested permission to organize "guerrilla parties with authority to act as this is the only available force in the swamps of Louisiana." Lovell's appeal was strengthened by Governor Moore's demand that Louisiana be divided into two departments separated by the river. Moore's insistence that the commands be separated with an emphasis on the defense of the western part of the state, in order to maintain the supplies of beef coming from Texas, reinforced the need for Lovell's partisans east of the river.[7]

Although much skepticism concerning irregular forces remained, the Confederate War Department recognized the logic of Lovell's argument. In early May 1862, General Robert E. Lee, responding for the War Department, gave tacit approval to Lovell's plan. Lee's directive concluded, "You will organize and prepare the troops that you may collect, to act most efficiently against the enemy, should he expose himself in any manner." Three weeks later Lee removed any doubt concerning Richmond's support for Lovell's proposal: "I approve of your purpose to confine the enemy to its [New Orleans] limits as closely as possible and to protect the state from his ravages. The means with which you propose to accomplish this seem to be the best that you can now employ, and I must urge you to put them in operation without delay, soliciting bold and judicious partisans who can raise proper corps."[8]

To provide a structure for the organization of Confederate forces in the region, General Earl Van Dorn, commanding the troops in Mississippi and eastern Louisiana, ordered that a new department be created under the command of General Daniel Ruggles. The orders creating the new Department of Southwestern Mississippi and East Louisiana also contained directions for the formation of partisan units to operate in the area. The instructions stipulated that "no organization less than a regiment, or at least a battalion of five companies," would be accepted as a partisan ranger unit. The partisans were to be trained in the same manner as regulars and held to the strictest discipline in the performance of their operations. According to Van Dorn, "An undisciplined rabble is not dangerous to the enemy, is extremely injurious to the neighborhood where it may be stationed, and is a disgrace to any country." In return for their discipline and satisfactory performance the partisans would be exempted from regular Confederate military service. Although their purpose remained primarily local defense, they could be pressed into service in other theaters. By July 1862, nine companies of partisan rangers had been organized statewide, with at least one, the Ninth Louisiana Partisan Rangers, designated to serve exclusively in the Florida Parishes. During the course of the war at least four partisan units operated in eastern Louisiana, playing a central role in Confederate strategic planning.[9]

Following the capture of Baton Rouge the Federals sought to exploit the demoralized condition of the local residents and the few Confederate troops in the area by moving rapidly to apply irresistible pressure on the Florida Parishes. These operations aimed particularly at the destruction of Camp Moore, the demolition of the New Orleans–Jackson Railroad, and the general subjugation of the region. To further these goals General Benjamin Butler, commanding the department, ordered General Thomas Williams, in charge at Baton Rouge, to mount a series of demonstrations against Camp Moore. Butler's instructions directed Williams to "punish with the last severity every guerrilla attack and burn all the property of every guerrilla found murdering your soldiers."[10]

As a preliminary to his major offensive, Williams launched a series of probing raids into the interior to test Confederate strength and intimidate the population. On June 7, 1862, the Thirtieth Massachusetts Regiment departed on a mission to capture several suspected "guerrillas," a term universally applied to all Confederate forces operating in the area. The raiders failed in their effort to capture any Confederate forces, but they did lay waste several plantations belonging to prominent Confederate sympathizers. The destruction was rapid and complete. At each plantation all buildings and fences excepting the slave quarters were burned, livestock stolen, and ornamental trees cut down. Reporting on the success of his endeavor, the commanding officer reported, "I burnt every building on the estate of these once beautiful plantations, except such as were required to cover the negroes left behind . . . in fact I left nothing but the blackened chimneys as a monument to the folly and villainy of its guerrilla owner."[11]

This destructive mission exemplified the pattern the war would follow in eastern Louisiana for its duration. Similar raids, along with larger scale operations, continued with increasing frequency through late 1862 and into the spring of 1863. By the late summer of 1863 it was apparent that regular Confederate units lacked the strength to repel Union thrusts into the interior of the Florida Parishes. Confederate forces would continue to confront the Federals, but for the remainder of the war the proximity of numerous powerful Union bases would permit speedy reinforcement of any raiding party in trouble. Recognizing their strength and perhaps frustrated by their inability to subjugate the region effectively, the Federals initiated an intensified campaign of terror against the local population. Murder, rape, theft, and unnecessary destruction at the hands of Federal troops became everyday occurrences.

In an 1864 letter to a friend serving in the Army of Northern Virginia, J. M. Doyle described the intensification of Federal actions against the citizens. "The yankees did much more damage this time. Captain Fagan taken off prisoner and much beaten up. Hodges mansion destroyed, all eligible men taken prisoner. McVea's fine dwelling and costly carpets and furniture laid in ashes. Citizens around William's Bridge broken up. Rumor says they are coming again." Robert Tyson likewise expressed outrage at what he termed the "excessive looting" of his fellow Federal soldiers. During a raid coordinated with troops based at Morganza, Tyson watched with aversion as Union soldiers looted every house encountered of all their contents and "disgracefully used" the unfortunate families. He graphically described the devastation inflicted on the population, asserting "the thieving cavalry are a disgrace to the army, the relations and boasts of one of them last evening was disgusting." Tyson noted dryly that their courage as plunderers had failed them as soldiers when they refused an order to confront a small force of Confederate cavalry that attacked their pickets.

Federal colonel Edward Bacon exhibited similar contempt for the Union troops that laid waste the village of Ponchatoula, declaring that the legendary savagery of the Turks could not have been more thorough. Bacon explained that his own soldiers, led by his commanding officer, "seemed transfigured by the evil spirits that possess them, and appeared more like devils of theft and pillage than like mortal men."[12]

During a series of raids around Jackson, Louisiana, in early 1864 at least two women were gang-raped by Federal soldiers who then murdered the chief physician at the Louisiana state insane asylum even as he attempted to produce papers demonstrating that he had taken the Federal oath in order to secure provisions for his patients. Joseph Fluker, sixteen-year-old son of an elderly lady who had lost her husband and six other sons to the war, was clubbed to death in the center of Jackson by Union soldiers who threw the dying young man face down in a gully filled with water. Celine Fremaux described the grieving of regional mothers including one whose son was taken prisoner by a column of Federal soldiers who murdered him shortly thereafter. Union troops who raided the Bowling Green Plantation south of Woodville forced the stunned McGehee family to watch as they smashed everything they did not steal before beating the elderly patriarch and burning the home and all outbuildings. Hatred for the invader consumed the exasperated citizens, who increasingly proved willing to take an active part in operations against the Yankees.[13]

In the spring of 1864 Colonel John S. Scott assumed command of all Confederate forces operating in eastern Louisiana. Scott, at the head of the First Louisiana Cavalry, enjoyed a well-deserved reputation as a cunning and courageous, albeit controversial, commander as a result of his participation in operations in Virginia and Tennessee. More important, Scott, like most of the survivors of his cavalry unit, was a native of the Florida Parishes. The arrival of the First Louisiana Cavalry created great rejoicing among the men of the command and inspired a new confidence among the long-suffering residents.[14]

In order to take pressure off the countryside Scott launched a series of offensive maneuvers that stole the initiative from the Federals.[15] The renewed Confederate operations in eastern Louisiana created consternation among Union commanders in the lower Mississippi region. Outraged Federal officials at Baton Rouge placed a $10,000 bounty on Scott's head.[16] But in a substantive military sense his efforts did little more than provide temporary relief and a bit of hope for the local population. The critical contribution resulting from Scott's command of the department concerns his policy toward citizens under arms.

Little evidence exists to indicate that Scott actively encouraged guerrilla warfare, but that he tolerated such methods of combat is indisputable. Unlike Confederate commanders in other theaters of the war, Scott issued no directives governing, or statements condemning, guerrilla warfare. By adopting a policy of total war, Scott sanctioned a grisly development of enormous consequence for the future of the Florida Parishes.

Proposals to launch a guerrilla war in eastern Louisiana had been entertained as early as the spring of 1862; but guerrilla warfare constituted something far different from partisan operations. Unlike partisan units, whose usefulness resulted from their adherence to the commands of the regular army, guerrillas operated independently. Autonomous bodies of armed men almost always created problems for both friend and foe. A March 1862 proposal recommended, "Let 200 determined men in each county take to the woods with their horses and rifles, swear never to bend their necks to the yoke, but war upon our tyrants and all who give them aid and comfort, night and day, as long as the foot of the Yankee presses upon southern soil." In 1862 this ominous suggestion received little support; by late 1864 the situation proved very different.[17]

Recognizing the odds that faced him, Scott sanctioned the participation of citizens in the war effort by encouraging the formation of citizens' militia. But unlike the militia, which recognized the authority of the regular army, by the fall of 1864 increasing numbers of citizens engaged in attacks upon the Yankees independent of any civil or military control. W. Greene Raoul, a Confederate soldier from Livingston Parish, expressed the exasperated sentiment of these men. "We had as well raise the black flag at once. They [Federals] are fighting almost upon that principle. We, I think ought to take some measure to retaliate. There is no reason to fear that they will do more, for they are doing all they possibly can now."[18]

The *Amite City Daily Wanderer,* one of the few regional newspapers still publishing by the fall of 1864, encouraged guerrilla activity. The *Wanderer* reminded its readers that Spain had survived the burning of its cities and destruction of its armies only to prevail over the French by employing guerrilla tactics. Responding to increasing Federal atrocities, the *Wanderer* urged the people to "strain every nerve to hold in check the northern horde." Beginning in the summer of 1864, guerrillas increasingly preyed upon Union forces operating in the area. Occasionally guerrillas cooperated with regular Confederate units in confronting Union raiders, but in most cases the citizens established prearranged points of ambush and waited in hiding for a Federal patrol. In almost all cases the guerrillas took no prisoners.[19]

These tactics produced fear and outrage among the Federals. The guerrillas proved difficult to catch, and their methods were effective. One group operating in Livingston and lower East Baton Rouge Parishes sought out and killed any Federal stragglers they encountered. The same party frequently ambushed whole patrols, tying up considerable numbers of Union troops in pursuit. Both sides were accused of murdering prisoners and looting homesteads. Confederate guerrillas and partisans wreaked bloody vengeance on Federal soldiers encountered with looted goods. By the fall of 1864 guerrilla activity made considerable portions of the territory unsafe for the Yankees. In response the Federals burned entire towns, executed many Confederate soldiers as suspected guerrillas, and intensified their efforts to arrest every male of combat age. Along the lakeshore and Pearl

River region the war assumed a particularly ugly character. Determined to exterminate one another, guerrilla bands, occasionally operating with Confederate cavalry, and Union forces engaged in wanton acts of murder and destruction. The unfortunate residents became victims of the suspicions and requisitions of both sides. Overcome by the scenes of devastation and mangled bodies by the roadside, Annette Koch lamented, "I have found so much that is bad in the hearts of so many people. They have taken the law in their own hands and do just as they please and I think when things come to that no man is safe."[20]

In early October 1864 the Federals initiated a major offensive designed to drive Scott's force from the territory and exterminate the guerrillas by crushing their base of support. The October raid effectively devastated the region. The Yankees specifically targeted remaining food supplies and other essentials necessary to sustain the population, destroying all crops they encountered and slaughtering or dispersing all livestock. The *New Orleans Daily Picayune* reported that the Federals had destroyed more than forty thousand pounds of bacon, one hundred dozen shoes, and limitless amounts of clothing and other goods, noting that "the general deemed it a military necessity in taking several citizens." Operating under directives outlined in General Orders Number 33, Union forces moved aggressively to disrupt potential sources of sustenance available to the Confederates in order to starve the rebels into submission. The towns of Liberty, Woodville, and Osyka, Mississippi, along with Greensburg, Louisiana, and the Confederate base at Camp Moore, were visited by the raiders. The *Covington Wanderer* reported that the Federals "committed hellish degradations, robbing and plundering indiscriminately." Likewise, the *Amite City Daily Wanderer* declared, "If the yankees continue the destruction and heathenish pilfering that they have practiced heretofore upon the residents in the vicinity of Liberty and the adjacent country, if absolute want and starvation do not ensue, something akin will certainly follow."[21]

Despite the ferocity of the Federal effort, it did not dissuade citizens from attacking Federal soldiers. On the contrary, it seemed to promote continued resistance, which increasingly relied on citizen involvement. In his report concerning his unit's role in the October raid, Major N. F. Craigue, Fourth Wisconsin Cavalry, described his movement through lower St. Helena Parish. His command encountered no regular Confederate units but suffered the heaviest casualties of the raid. Craigue reported that as he departed the region a citizen followed his regiment, killing and wounding several of his men by "firing into them from the bushes." He concluded his report with an ominous note for Federal authorities: "The guerrilla could not be taken." In the Florida Parishes bushwhacking was becoming an art form.[22]

The October raid and corollary operations in the upper Florida Parishes did accomplish a primary Federal objective. As a result of the devastation of the region, Scott, who relied heavily on requisitions from local farmers to feed his troops and horses, withdrew into central Mississippi. But the increasingly aggressive bushwhackers had also accomplished an important goal. The fear they produced helped contain the marauding of small groups of Federals who were more likely to commit atrocities in the absence of a senior officer.[23]

Through the dreary winter of 1864–1865 new Confederate units emerged in eastern Louisiana. The surrender of the Confederate armies under Robert E. Lee and Joseph E. Johnston in April 1865, however, highlighted the reality of failure. Suddenly the Federals adopted a policy of appeasement toward the rebels; yet four years of brutality did not simply disappear. Even after the cessation of hostilities between the regular armies in eastern Louisiana and southwestern Mississippi, guerrilla operations, occasionally on a large scale, persisted. A Federal force traveling through Mississippi and Louisiana to "secure by conciliation and kindness the good will of the people for and toward the representatives of the Federal government" was bushwhacked north of Osyka in late May. The war did not end simply because Washington pronounced it over and staged a great celebration in honor of victory, and in the Florida Parishes the violence had only begun.[24]

In eastern Louisiana the last year of the war served as a microcosm for examining the consequences associated with a conscious decision to resort to guerrilla operations. Unlike in Missouri, where a guerrilla war raged for the duration of the conflict, guerrilla operations in the Florida Parishes emerged only when it became apparent that regular Confederate forces could no longer contain the might of the Union army. A similar debate concerning the value of guerrilla operations occupied the principal Confederate armies shortly before their surrender. Guerrilla tactics in eastern Louisiana demonstrated that bushwhacking could provoke fear of retaliation and contain the marauding of isolated contingents of Federals; but the overwhelming numbers of the Federal army and its willingness to lay waste a region sympathetic to guerrillas illustrated that such tactics would not prevail but instead serve only to increase the horror of the war and prolong the suffering of local residents. Moreover, unlike the operations of regular armies, the activities of guerrillas could not be arrested by official decree, as the bloody postwar events in eastern Louisiana demonstrate.[25]

Ultimately, a successful guerrilla war required an unparalleled degree of commitment from the population sustaining the irregulars. The Federal army demonstrated a commitment to subjugating eastern Louisiana at all costs. With each successful irregular operation on the part of the Confederates, the Federals responded with increasingly brutal depredations on the civilian population. Although the majority of the population and the press of eastern Louisiana continued to support the secession movement, increasing numbers demonstrated the belief that the ultimate price of success might be too high. During the October 1864 raid Scott's cavalry and cooperating partisan units attacked and routed one column of the Federal force along Thompson's Creek in West Feliciana Parish. In response Federal gunboats on the Mississippi River began an intensive shelling of the towns of St. Francisville and Bayou Sara. Just as his forces sought to deliver the coup de grâce to the Yankees, the pleas of local residents, including former Governor Robert Wickliffe, persuaded Scott to break off the engagement. Likewise, in the fall of 1863 Lieutenant C. M. Allen, on a reconnaissance mission along the north shore of Lake Pontchartrain with the Second Arkansas Cavalry, reported that the Federals had so thoroughly decimated the region that the citizens were forced to cooperate with the Yankees in order to survive. Allen noted that many seemed to fear the presence of his cavalry unit would provoke further Federal aggressiveness. In a sorrowful 1863 portrayal of personal conviction balanced by the demands of real life, Mrs. R. J. Causey professed continuing patriotism for the cause to her soldier husband but bemoaned the implications of renewed Confederate operations in the area. Perhaps the most poignant statement of exasperation came earlier from St. Helena resident Abigail Amacker. Reflecting on the loss of so many lives and destruction of so much precious property she confided in her diary, "The suffering the deaths are awful, I pray God we may have peace speedily on any terms. To be subjugated, to be slaves would not be worse than this."[26]

Unlike the Vietcong guerrillas who proved willing to pay a seemingly unlimited price to achieve victory, suffering had its limits in eastern Louisiana. By contrast the Federals demonstrated a propensity to employ any means necessary to achieve total victory, while their vast advantages in men and material and proximity to the scene of the fighting guaranteed a strong popular commitment to eventual success. Although irregulars continued to confront the Yankees in eastern Louisiana for the duration of the war, the increasingly apparent demoralization of the local population coupled with the escalating brutality of the Federals ensured a Union victory. The spirit of most in the Florida Parishes remained committed to the cause, but the prospect of limitless suffering proved a threshold of unobtainable commitment. The southern code of honor required and the residents produced a courageous effort, but ultimately the costs outweighed the benefits of victory.

Notes

1. *War of the Rebellion: Official Records of the Union and Confederate Armies* (Washington: Government Printing Office, 1902) (hereinafter cited as *OR*), ser. 3, 3:148–64; Michael Fellman, *Inside War: The Guerrilla Conflict in Missouri during the American Civil War* (New York: Oxford University Press, 1990), 82–84. Portions of this essay appeared in "Bushwhacking and Barnburning: Civil War Operations and the Florida Parishes' Tradition of Violence," *Louisiana History*, 37 (spring 1995).

2. The Fourth and Sixteenth Louisiana infantry regiments and the First Louisiana Cavalry, among other units recruited largely in the Florida Parishes, suffered heavy casualties at Shiloh and the ensuing skirmishing around Corinth, Mississippi. Eugene Hunter to Stella, June 1, 1862, Mary Taylor to Riah, September 8, 1862, and Mary Taylor Diary, entries for May 6, July 8, 1862, in Hunter-Taylor Family Papers, Louisiana and Lower Mississippi Valley Collections, Hill Memorial Library, Louisiana State University, Baton Rouge (hereinafter referred to as LLMVC). Diary of Abigail M. K. Amacker, April 21, July 9, 1862, in O. P. Amacker Papers, LLMVC; Muster role of the Fourth Louisiana Infantry Regiment in James G. Kilbourne and Family Papers, LLMVC.

3. *OR*, ser. 1, 6:624; Amacker diary, April 26, May 9, 1862; Dear Sister to Edward, May 4, 1862, in John C. Burruss Papers, LLMVC.

4. *OR*, ser. 1, 6:694–95.

5. Ibid., 652–53, 885–90; ibid., 53:805.

6. Ibid., ser. 4, 1:395; *Jackson (Miss.) Mississippian*, February 27, 1863; Virgil Jones, *Gray Ghosts and Rebel Raiders* (New York: Henry Holt, 1956), vi–vii; John D. Winters, *The Civil War in Louisiana* (Baton Rouge: Louisiana State University Press, 1963), 153; M. J. Thompson, *The Civil War Reminiscences of General M. Jeff Thompson* (Dayton: Morningside, 1988), 165; Russell Weigley, *The Partisan War: The South Carolina Campaign of 1780–1782* (Columbia: University of South Carolina Press, 1970).

7. *OR*, ser. 1, 6:885, 889–90; ibid., 53:805.

8. Ibid., 6:652–53.

9. Ibid., 15:768, 1061–62; ibid., 6:889–90; ibid., vol. 41, pt. 2, 141; Winters, *Civil War in Louisiana*, 149, 165.

10. *OR*, ser. 1, 15:24–25.

11. Ibid., 19–21.

12. J. M. Doyle to Eugene Hunter, October 16, 1864, in Hunter-Taylor Family Papers; Robert A. Tyson Diary, September 13–November 24, 1864, ibid.; Edward Bacon, *Among the Cotton Thieves* (Detroit: The Free Press, 1867), 64–67.

13. Celine Fremaux Garcia, *Celine: Remembering Louisiana, 1850–1871* (Athens: University of Georgia Press, 1987), 111–21, 142–55; J. Burruss McGehee to James S. McGehee, February 5, 1904, Eve Brower to James S. McGehee, February 22, 1904, and Carrie McGehee to James S. McGehee, undated, all in James S. McGehee Papers, LLMVC; Nannie C. to Dear Friend Cornelia Stewart, April 1864, and John Connell to Dear Pet, May 1, 1865, both in Albert Batchelor Papers, LLMVC; *OR,* ser. 1, 26:238–40.

14. Steven Ellis to Dear Brother, April 9, 1865, in Ellis Family Papers, LLMVC; Howell Carter, *A Cavalryman's Reminiscences of the Civil War* (New Orleans: American Printing, 1900), 104–7, 117.

15. *Amite City (La.) Daily Wanderer,* December 8, 1864; Serrano Taylor to Eugene Hunter, June 1864, in Hunter-Taylor Family Papers; Tyson diary, February 1, 11, 1864; Tom Ellis to Martina, May 20, 1864, in Ellis Family Papers; Diary of W. W. Garig, April 7, 1864, in W. W. Garig Papers, LLMVC; Diary of Willie Dixon, April 7, 1864, in William Y. Dixon Papers, LLMVC; *OR,* ser. 1, vol. 34, pt. 1, 136–38, 877–79, 906; *OR,* ser. 1, vol. 41, pt. 2, 833, 919, 932; Alex Stuart to Dear Uncle, December 27, 1863, in William R. Bell Papers, LLMVC; Civil War Reminiscences from the Diary of Jane McCausland Chinn, "The Burning of the Barns," 2, LLMVC; Carter, *Cavalryman's Reminiscences,* 107–8.

16. Loving Sister F. P. Wall to Dear Sister, n.d. (1864?), describing reward of $1,000 for the capture dead or alive of Naul and $10,000 for Scott, in Jeptha McKinney Papers, LLMVC; *OR,* ser. 1, vol. 41, pt. 2, 833.

17. *New Orleans Daily Picayune,* March 13, 1862.

18. *OR,* ser. 1, vol. 1, pt. 2, 19; W. Greene Raoul to Pa, May 24, 1863, in W. Greene Raoul Papers, LLMVC; Diary of Mary E. Taylor, April 28, 1863, in Hunter-Taylor Family Papers; *Amite City Daily Wanderer,* December 8, 1864.

19. *OR,* ser. 1, vol. 41, pt. 1, 277–78; John Burruss to Edward, February 18, 1864, in Burruss Papers; Carter, *Cavalryman's Reminiscences,* 113–14.

20. John Burruss to Edward, February 18, 1864, in Burruss Papers; Annette Koch to Christian, September 18, 20, October 3, 9, 1864, February 6, 11, 1865, Elers to Christian, September 20, October 3, 1864, all in Christian Koch Papers, LLMVC; Priscilla Bond Diary, March 6, May 3, 1864, June 16, 1865, in Priscilla Bond Papers, LLMVC; Dominique Pochelu to W. R. Bell, March 23, 1864, and Alex Stuart to Dear Uncle, December 27, 1863, in Bell Papers; *OR,* ser. 1, vol. 41, pt. 1, 294, 880–83.

21. *OR,* ser. 1, vol. 41, pt. 1, 880–83; ibid., pt. 2, 804; *New Orleans Daily Picayune,* October 9, 11, 1864; *Covington (La.) Wanderer,* October 15, 1864; *Amite City Daily Wanderer,* November 29, 1864; James Durnin to Dear Sister, September 13, 1864, in James and John Durnin Papers, LLMVC.

22. *OR,* ser. 1, vol. 41, pt. 1, 881–82; ibid., vol. 39, pt. 1, 831–32.

23. Diary of Eli Capell, March 29, May 28, June 14, July 15, September 6–8, October 25–29, 1864, in Eli Capell Papers, LLMVC; Annette Koch to Christian, September 25, 28, 1864, November 14, 23, 27, 1864, Elers to Christian, October 30, 1864, in Koch Papers; Steve Ellis to

Emily, November 15, 1864, in Ellis Family Papers; Jennings to Dear Wife, May 24, 1863, in Hennen-Jennings Family Papers, LLMVC; St. Helena Parish Succession Records, Succession Bin W-3, numerous entries January–July 1863, and May–June 1864, St. Helena Parish Courthouse, Greensburg, La.; *OR,* ser. 1, vol. 48, pt. 1, 128, 157–58.

24. *Amite City Daily Wanderer,* October 15, 1864; F. P. Wall to Jeptha McKinney, December 17, 1864, in McKinney Papers; Father to Albert Batchelor, September 7, December 26, 1864, in Batchelor Papers; *OR,* ser. 1, vol. 48, pt. 1, 262–64.

25. In the fifty years following the close of the Civil War, Louisiana's Florida Parishes sustained among the highest rural homicide rates ever recorded in American history. See Samuel C. Hyde Jr., *Pistols and Politics: The Dilemma of Democracy in Louisiana's Florida Parishes, 1810–1899* (Baton Rouge: Louisiana State University Press, 1996).

26. *OR,* ser. 1, vol. 41, pt. 2, 880–83; ibid., vol. 26, pt. 1, 313; Mrs. R. J. Causey to Causey, October 14, 1863, in R. J. Causey Correspondence, LLMVC; Amacker diary, April 26, May 9, 1862.

6

THE ONGOING AGRICULTURAL CREDIT CRISIS IN THE FLORIDA PARISHES OF LOUISIANA, 1865–1890

RICHARD H. KILBOURNE JR.

*I*N THE ANTEBELLUM YEARS LOUISIANA'S PORTION OF WEST Florida's panhandle comprised seven parishes to the north of the city of New Orleans on the left bank of the Mississippi River. The district was economically and culturally diverse, with some of the largest slave populations in the South settled in three western parishes and yeomen farmers predominant in the eastern areas. Before the war the parishes were economically part of New Orleans's expansive hinterland, the eastern parishes in particular increasingly drawn into the production of foodstuffs for an expanding urban population. The western parishes along the Mississippi River produced primarily staples for the world market, and in most respects they were fully integrated into the economic and social life of the metropolis.

New Orleans was the point of transshipment for agricultural commodities from the lower Mississippi Valley. It was the financial hub as well for plantation agriculture in the region, and countless planters, country merchants, and even peddlers obtained their stock there and relied on their agents to finance their enterprises by obtaining discounts from city capitalists. Not only planters looked to their agents in the city to mediate their planting risks by obtaining credits and providing profitable investments for idle cash. Small farmers as well were dependent on the city's financial services industry to answer the credit needs of the local merchants who staked their credit needs during the growing and harvesting of crops.

As the 1850s drew to a close, an expanding financial services industry had become one of the primary engines of growth in an environment whose trade area had contracted dramatically in prior decades. Indeed, at the time of the secession crisis the city wielded hegemony over an area that stretched from the Gulf of Mexico to western Tennessee in the north. Mobile and Galveston had increasingly drawn commerce away from the Crescent City on its eastern and western flanks. Still, New Orleans's financial services industry in 1860 could rightly be regarded as the envy of the nation. The banks there had weathered the financial panic of 1857 with comparative ease, being among the only institutions in the country not to suspend specie redemption as contraction spread across the nation.

The occupation of New Orleans by Federal forces in the late spring of 1862 and the city's occupation throughout the remainder of the Civil War effectively decapitated the corpus of economic activity in the region. Existing relationships simply collapsed, and they did not revive in the wake of peace. The region's primary economic activity, staple production, did resume in 1865, but the old ways of financing and spreading the risks of crop failures and low prices came under increasing stress as the decade drew to a close. The old system simply disintegrated, and in its place there arose a highly decentralized production system grounded in share leases and tenancies and local furnishing merchants who assumed all the risk of defaulting farmers.

Pejoratives like "debt peonage" and "from slavery to serfdom" litter the literature of postbellum agriculture. Indeed, the magisterial works of synthetic historians are clumsy when they seek to reconcile the broad themes of postbellum political and social history with the seemingly contradictory findings of economic historians such as Gerald Jaynes. The assimilation of specialized monographs into the general historiography has moved at a glacial pace, but perhaps in another generation the great themes of "exploitation" and "racism" as explanations for the apparent failure of postbellum agriculture to prosper will have run their course.[1]

The literature mostly considers postbellum credit relationships in agriculture as incidental to the revolution in labor relations that was occasioned by the Civil War and the emancipation. This presentation argues for a contrary premise, the primacy of the credit system in shaping labor relationships such as sharecropping and share tenancies. Particular attention is given to the horrendous stresses that confronted the antebellum inheritance and the system that arose to take its place. In 1865 the antebellum inheritance was a residue of worthless claims, but a decade would pass before the implications of this reality could be fully comprehended.

A few assertions about the antebellum agricultural credit system are necessary. Our understanding of technical subjects, such as the system that brings electricity to our homes or the apparatus that allows us to collect and disburse payments without a physical delivery of coin, is much influenced by our own day-to-day experiences. Turning on a light switch or writing a check to a creditor may be the extent of our acquaintance with the vast subjects of public utilities and central banking, and a stream of technical innovations may serve to increase our relative ignorance of what actually is going on.

The incidences of governmental involvement in regulating financial markets over the last one hundred years, for example, has greatly obscured the inner workings of the financial system to everyone except, perhaps, those engaged in managing it. Indeed, it could be said, the Federal Reserve has been so successful that its obligations now not only are the national medium of exchange but are fast becoming the universal one as well. Most financial economists today would argue that gold's monetary importance is an anachronism. But who knows, the yellow dog may yet have its day. Today regulation of financial mediation is so pervasive that the considerations an antebellum planter necessarily kept uppermost in his thoughts, i.e., the solvency of his consignee and banker, are simply absent from the calculus of business relationships. The psychological change has been profound.

The impetus for the revolution in commercial relations in the centuries leading up to the twentieth century are obscure, but financial markets appear to have arisen in part as a response to a need to diffuse the growing risks of vastly more expensive enterprises, such as foreign trade. Commercial banks in the nineteenth century were primary conduits for liquefying the commercial paper market, not for funding the capital needs of solitary business enterprises. The South's commercial banks profited principally from arbitraging commercial paper rates, whether between regions or between nations. Sterling exchange seems to have performed the role of reserve currency for the nation's monetary system up until the Civil War. In 1860 southern staples still provided two-thirds of the nation's foreign exchange; so the region's banks were well situated to arbitrage favorable sterling rates relative to the local currency of account. The sterling exchange business was a direct outgrowth of the southern banking community's wherewithal to support ample local discount lines for the agents of plantation agriculture.[2]

Many of today's great investment houses trace their origins either to the antebellum South's agricultural economy or owe their early prosperity to their ties to the region. Brown Brothers, Lehman Brothers, the Barings, the Rothschilds, all had profoundly important relations with the region. Those firms began not as corporate underwriters but as exchange dealers. Success in this business depended on personal relationships, although the extent of the largest firms' activities reached truly global dimensions. The Browns owned and operated slave plantations in Louisiana and Mississippi, and the Rothschilds owned real estate in antebellum New Orleans. Slave agriculture was the great engine of growth in trade and economic expansion throughout much of the Western world in the antebellum decades.[3]

Southern planters were well positioned to spread their planting risks, not only throughout the region, but to the world's most important money markets as well. Commercial banks were not as numerous in the South as in the North, but they were on average much larger, a good indication of their strategic position in the national and international exchange markets. Emancipation not only bankrupted the planters but muddled every certainty for those who made the market for their commercial paper. Sterling exchange shrank drastically in importance as the price demanded for a very limited supply rose to dizzying heights over the course of the Civil War. In 1864 the premium on the New York money market stood at 400 percent.

The network of business relationships that had spread from the southern heartland to the great money markets of Europe stood hopelessly impaired by the time the war had ended. The principal market makers in the South, i.e., the great factorage houses in New Orleans, Galveston, Charleston, and Richmond, were bankrupt, although the full extent of the insolvency would only become apparent over the succeeding five years. The resumption of staple shipments in the late fall and winter of 1866–1867 did provide a large, much-needed injection of liquidity, but any portents for the future were at best uncertain. Much of the cotton that arrived at places like New Orleans for transshipment was in fact the fruit of an army of speculators who had managed to collect and hoard during the early years of the war. Likewise the price index still stood at nearly three times its prewar average, so much of the liquidity was the result of the lingering effects of wartime inflation.[4]

For the surviving commercial banks in New Orleans, which attempted to resume the prewar way of doing business by discounting for the city's great commercial partnerships, the implications of the revolutionary changes brought by the war and the emancipation were soon clear. On August 1, 1866, for example, the minutes of the board of directors of the Citizens Bank records that the president informed the board that since the war the local discounts had increased from $130,000 to $1,460,000, but "by far the heaviest business ha[d] been dealing in [foreign] exchange. The operations in this line for the year amount[ed] in the aggregate to near $30,000,000.00." But by June of 1868 the bank's representatives found it necessary to importune the firm of Hope and Co. in Amsterdam for a moratorium on redeeming the bank's bonded indebtedness.

> In the summer of 1865 when we applied for an extension of the $4^{1}/_{2}$ Coupons then next maturing, the directory of the Bank fondly expected that the Civil War being just ended, free scope would be left to our planters in Louisiana to repair the disasters inflicted by the loss of four successive crops, the devastation of rural property, the annihilation of value in slaves, and consequent disorganization of labor. That under the newly inaugurated system of labor, unreservedly acquiesced in, an early revival of agriculture would gradually facilitate a liquidation of the debts accumulated during the war, and enable the Bank out of its collections, to meet punctually, not only the then deferred coupons, but also the future interest as it would come due.
> Contrary to this universal expectation, the reorganization of labor has been interfered with by political strifes, and the enforcement of military regulations, rendering field work sadly inefficient, at more cost and less remuneration to the planters. The Levee of the Mississippi, having been wholly neglected during the war, the most fertile districts were left open to partial inundation. Hence the crops fell below one third of an average yield. The last sugar crop was almost a total failure, so that, at the very time when the planters most needed cash resources to repair and restock their devastated plantations & put their lands in working order, their embarrassments were aggravated, & collections in the rural districts rendered temporarily impracticable.

They pleaded a further cause for forbearance: the enormous loss that would be occasioned by any remittances at that time. "In all remittances made to meet the interest on the Bonds during and since the War, three, and at times four dollars collected at home were only equivalent to two dollars paid abroad. The last February dividend was met at an extra cost of 40% premium."[5]

In August of 1870 the *New Orleans Price Current* observed that "the overthrow of the Southern system of labor and the consequent disorganization of our planting interest ha[d] materially changed . . . [the] banking business from the conditions under which it was formally conducted before the war." No longer could lenders look to the collaterals that formerly had supported open-ended credit facilities for planters and their factors. "The proprietary right of the planter in his slaves [had been] . . . the basis on which the entire super structure of all values . . . had rested." Slave labor, "reliable as it was under all emergencies," had made the plantation productive and permitted the banks to extend unlimited credit facilities to the planter and his factor. This, the author concluded, had all been changed by the emancipation. "The proprietary interest of the planter in his slaves ha[d] been destroyed," and the factorage business was attended by hazards heretofore unknown.[6]

By 1870 a reshuffling of credit relationships was under way, so what the *Price Current* observed in that year was by no means at the forefront of developments in the credit markets. In 1865 the great New Orleans factorage houses, which had been the primary market makers for agriculture in the lower Mississippi Valley, were weighted down with worthless bills receivable and discounted commercial paper, which carried the guarantee of every firm partner. Many firms attempted to reorganize by entering liquidation and then forming new partnerships. New partnerships had one important advantage: They could grant priority privileges on shipments to anyone extending credit during the new year without the danger of older claims intervening and obtaining an equality in rank.

This development is especially important because it demonstrates a fundamental change in credit relationships from the antebellum to the postbellum eras. Before the war, credit relationships spanned decades; afterward, a credit relationship was conducted from planting season to planting season. What is first evident in the reconstitution of the New Orleans money market would soon come to characterize such relationships across the entire spectrum of human relations. The city factor, the furnishing merchant in the countryside, the landlord, the cropper, and the tenant all soon entered a credit environment in which the length of any relationship rarely exceeded six or nine months.[7]

The implications of this change are indeed profound, and the labor relationships that became endemic in the postbellum South are best understood as a consequence of the destruction of the South's capital markets and the vast financial network that had permitted antebellum agriculture to spread the risks of staple production to consumers throughout the Western world. In localities across the region planters and their agents attempted to resume production, availing themselves of credit facilities predicated on assumptions inherited from the antebellum era. Clearly there had been fundamental changes in labor relations, but the implications for the credit system were not at all clear in the 1860s.

Typically a planter guaranteed the necessary credit for his labor force to obtain the supplies to carry them through the planting season. Many planters opened stores that extended credit to small white producers and black farm laborers alike. Most of these accounts proved to be uncollectible when the crop was harvested and shipped. Low prices for the staple, poor levels of production, and farm laborers contracting credit facilities with a number of competing sources all but ensured that planters, furnishing merchants, and factors were even more heavily in debt by the time the disastrous decade of the 1860s drew to a close. The weight of the evidence indicates that a similar transformation was under way in the Florida Parishes in the first postbellum decade, although the region's proximity to New Orleans should have sustained some semblance of preexisting relationships.

Conditions only worsened over the course of the succeeding decade as planters and factors attempted with some success to sluff off their debts inherited from the antebellum era, aided by the state in what must be described as wholesale debt repudiation. Measures were taken to prevent farm laborers from contracting multiple facilities with suppliers by mandating recordation of all privileges on standing crops in the parish registry.[8] The first postbellum decade witnessed a rising tide of violence throughout the Florida Parishes in consequence of worsening economic conditions.

Carpetbagger government in Louisiana had experienced a de facto collapse in its creditworthiness sometime before the Battle of Liberty Place and the Bourbon redemption. By 1874 warrants on the state treasury were quoted by the bill brokers at ten cents on the dollar. The redeemers are roundly criticized by historians for cutting public budgets, yet it is well to remember that they followed the only course open to them. Their draconian prescriptions were virtually identical to the ones insisted on today in third world countries by the International Monetary Fund.[9]

By the end of the 1870s the long-distance relationships that had linked wealthy planters in remote and isolated hamlets to the money markets of the world had vanished. Credit for each year's planting was a local affair, contingent on the incidence of wealth in one's own neighborhood. Furnishing merchants in the small towns that dotted the rural landscape could obtain a limited amount of credit by purchasing supplies from wholesalers on sixty- and ninety-day credits. Sometimes, too, a cotton broker in the city would anticipate shipments and make advances on shipments in the months preceding the harvest, but in every case the amount of credit available was paltry and expensive. Usurious interest rates contained a large risk component, and the local furnishing merchant paid his commercial agent 20 percent or more. That the markup for supplies sold on credit to farm laborers sometimes exceeded 50 percent is not surprising. In truth, there are no villains in this story.

This then was the credit environment in which the system of labor relations we call tenancy, share leases, and sharecropping evolved. Decentralizing credit localized planting risks; so rather than being able to spread the risk of poor harvests, low prices, and credit stringencies to consumers throughout the world, land-poor planters limited their exposure to their workers by helping them obtain credit facilities from the local furnishing merchant, who in turn tried to quantify his risks by obtaining guarantees from landlords. A landlord expected to be compensated when he guaranteed the credit facility of one of his tenants, and he was, by the furnishing merchant.[10]

In his book *Pistols and Politics: The Dilemma of Democracy in Louisiana's Florida Parishes, 1810–1899*, Samuel C. Hyde Jr. observes that in the decades after the war politicians and journalists increasingly came to see the cultivation of cotton as a tool for "exploiting the less privileged. Deliverance from the shackles of King Cotton became synonymous with independence in the piney-woods press." Of course Hyde draws important distinctions between the older plantation areas of the Florida Parishes, which were west of the Amite River, and the piney-woods areas to the east.

Still, the sentiment expressed in the local newspapers was not altogether repugnant to what remained of the so-called planter elite, as evidenced by the formation of Grange organizations in places such as Natchez and Clinton, in which leading members of those communities took active roles. Calls for farmers to engage in a kind of subsistence agriculture in the postbellum decades echo much earlier ones: that dependence on staple production placed the farmer at the mercy of the market economy.

No doubt the hardships felt by all after the war were conducive to the misplacement of blame on obvious scapegoats such as the cultivation of cotton and other staple crops at the expense of foodstuffs. Clearly, too, economic historians have shown convincingly that reliance on staple production increased dramatically after the war. The center of cotton production in the South actually moved back from the western frontier to the east. The incidence of white families engaged as sharecroppers also increased dramatically in postwar decades. A combination of powerful forces made this result all but inevitable, the most notable being the loss of liquidity in the financial system and the inability to spread risks beyond a single planting season.[11]

It seems almost paradoxical that land tenures in the Florida Parishes, and throughout much of the Deep South, were becoming concentrated in fewer and fewer hands as the nineteenth century drew to a close, but such indeed was the case. Does this necessarily indicate a widening gulf between rich and poor, between landlords and the landless? Land prices actually declined in the two decades after the war, a consequence of a national deflation that necessarily preceded the resumption of a specie standard. But the national deflation was not the only cause for falling land prices. Predictable income streams from land, the primary factor for determining price, were an impossibility in the wake of the emancipation. Anyone who bought land was doing so as a speculation; so it is not surprising that the "robber baron" Jay Gould invested heavily in Louisiana timberlands. The same impetus motivated local citizens to invest in land that had little or no immediate income potential.

The East Feliciana planter and lawyer James G. Kilbourne, for example, owned between two and three thousand acres of prime lands at his death in 1893, and in the years after the war he bought and sold land on a large scale. He certainly did not consider himself a wealthy man, however, at least when compared with the level of wealth he had achieved in the antebellum decades. In the 1850s he usually grossed ten thousand dollars a year from his plantation, and his law practice brought him a few thousand more. He ran the plantation with an overseer, and he personally had little to do with its day-to-day management. In one letter to his son, a student at the University of Louisiana in New Orleans during the 1870s, Kilbourne reflected that "the times . . . [were] hard and . . . [he] suppose[d] would remain so. [He saw] no reasonable grounds of hoping ever to be in flourishing circumstances again."[12]

C. Vann Woodward's paradigm that the destruction of the planter class made room for a new professional elite simply does not apply in the case of the Feliciana Parishes and probably has limited application elsewhere in the Florida Parishes. Very often the great planters were themselves lawyers and doctors by education who had derived the bulk of the income from their plantations. Many practiced their professions in earnest after the war, their sole means of earning a livelihood. I do not think this is what Woodward had in mind, but his writing to some extent reflects a time when statism was seen as a positive good and the social sciences were attempting to answer the question why the South's economy was so retrogressive even in the 1930s and 1940s.[13]

Gavin Wright has written that the southern labor market operated outside the national economy well into the twentieth century, that it remained localized and regressive when compared to nationalizing tendencies evident elsewhere. Paradoxically slavery had given the South the nation's first truly regionwide labor market in the antebellum decades in consequence of a highly liquid market for slaves. Michael Tadman has given us some tantalizing insights into that market, and it is clear that the slave market's huge financing requirements provided a lucrative business for financial intermediaries. These same financial intermediaries also made the market for southern staples by spreading the risks of each year's planting to consumers in the North and in Europe. The existence of international networks more or less guaranteed that slave agriculture would remain profitable even if crop prices were low and production disappointing.[14]

In the postbellum decades, despite the fact that a far greater percentage of each season's earnings was given over to debt service and market fluctuations, staple production remained the profitable pursuit for southern agriculture, irrespective of the size of the planting unit involved. A money economy was part of the antebellum inheritance, and it was not going to go away simply because most of the wealth had vanished from the region. It is strangely contradictory that historians have argued that one of the failings of postbellum agriculture was a lack of self-sufficiency in foodstuffs, a consequence of overspecialization in staple production, and the lack of investment in infrastructure by state and local government. Without heavy concentration in staple production there would have been no tax base to support even a paltry level of public services such as segregated schools, the beginnings of road systems, and, in the case of Louisiana, the critically important levees along the Mississippi.

It is possible to estimate the annual default rates among tenants and sharecroppers in parishes like East Feliciana and St. Helena, at least in the decade of the 1870s, by comparing the crop mortgages and privileges recorded in the mortgage registry in the spring of each year with the judgments recorded in the late fall and subsequent winter. In the case of East Feliciana Parish there is the Meyer Brothers Store Records, located in the Louisiana and Lower Mississippi Valley Collections at Louisiana State University in Baton Rouge. The Meyer Brothers Store Records represent perhaps the only complete collection of furnishing merchants records that has survived anywhere in the South for this critical period in southern agriculture. Its existence is all the more remarkable because no complete set of records for a single New Orleans factor exists today; indeed, even business records from the early decades of the twentieth century are scarce.[15]

An examination of the Meyer Brothers ledgers indicates that in the years 1875 and 1876 their payables tripled from previous years and that each year they were carrying forward larger and larger balances. On May 1, 1876, the deficit totaled $54,702.53, of which only $16,073.48 represented new payables. On average they provided about $12,000.00 a year in credits for almost two hundred customers. That their carryovers from previous years should have ballooned in the wake of the 1874 panic is perhaps not surprising, but certainly by modern accounting standards, the firm would have been judged insolvent. The rate of defaults among their customers was staggering, perhaps as high as 50 percent on a year-to-year basis. By 1879 they had reduced their deficit with their factor, but they still owed more than $26,000.00, a sum well in advance of the annual credits they afforded their customers.

The Meyer Brothers creditors chose to forbear because they had little choice if they hoped to recover their investment. Fortunately for the Meyers, their factor had the means to support their credit needs and recognized that foreclosing on them would not ensure a recovery of what he was owed. But their experience was the exception. Plenty of other furnishing merchants failed. They were simply more fortunate than most, but their relationship with their factor seems to have put a great deal of stress on everyone involved.

The literature on furnishing merchants in the rural South suggests that the amount of credit afforded by the Meyers was about average. In East Feliciana Parish the short-term credit facilities afforded growers was never more than about 10 percent of what it had been in the antebellum decades. Long-term financing simply vanished from the scene. Indeed, the average credit facilities afforded by a typical furnishing merchant for a clientele of hundreds in the postbellum decades was about what had been available to a medium-size planter in the 1850s.

As the 1870s drew to a close the Meyers were providing smaller and smaller credits to many more growers. These growers were primarily freedmen who settled their accounts with bales of cotton, and on average they produced from one to six bales each. The Meyers might ship as many as three hundred bales to their factor over the course of the season, but they were forced to reduce the cotton to cash as soon as it arrived in the market at New Orleans. Every grower, then, was at the mercy of powerful market forces well beyond his control. At every level the system for financing production was a costly one; so it is not surprising that furnishing merchants had to charge dearly for what credit they could provide. It is difficult to imagine a more fundamental change than that which occurred in the system for financing staple production from antebellum to postbellum eras.[16]

While the Meyer Brothers collection is an invaluable source for quantifying available credit facilities in one locale in the postbellum decades, it is possible to reconstruct a great many credit accounts from the judicial archives, especially for the Florida Parishes. Until 1878 most financing agreements between furnishers and their clienteles were recorded, especially where the borrower was in a share-lease agreement with a landlord. The numbers of transactions are manageable, and these can then be compared and contrasted with collection suits, which would have been filed immediately after the harvest. Debts more than a season old were de facto uncollectible; so an inference can be made about default rates in the critical decade of the 1870s.

The decade of the 1880s is more problematic. After 1878 it was possible to mortgage a standing crop apart from the land, and more furnishers preferred this arrangement to recording evidence of a crop privilege. As the local economy gained stability the number of recordings declined, which is not surprising given the expense of making a recordation. Also, furnishers increasingly relied on guarantors to insure any advance of credit; so we may infer that conditions improved enough to attract risk takers. Still, there are telling indicators of how retarded the postbellum credit system remained for the rest of the nineteenth century.

In 1860 the combined capitalization of New Orleans's commercial banks aggregated to about $25 million. As late as 1890 that capitalization still barely exceeded $7 million. A portion of this decline, moreover, is attributable to postwar developments, i.e., the return of capital to stockholders by managements that could find no profitable riskless outlet for investing idle capital. Also, it should be noted that much of the banking activity in the city by 1890 involved financing of governmental and municipal debt, as well as lending to various manufacturing enterprises. Never again would the city's financiers see their primary role as mediating the risks of staple agriculture.[17]

The old critics of carpetbagger misrule, so often pooh-poohed by today's sagacious pundits, deserve to be reappraised in light of what we are gradually coming to understand about the consequences of the economic revolution wrought by war and emancipation. Profligacy is not too strong a description of the tax-and-spend practices of a government that seems to have had little or no awareness of the hardships borne by the vast majority of its citizens. It is little wonder that the greatest challenge facing state government over the last decades of the nineteenth century was rationalizing the bonded indebtedness. A careful reading of the state constitutions of 1879 and 1898 certainly sharpens the image of an organization in the throes of debt distress.[18]

Debt distress was the predominant theme in agriculture in the two decades after 1865. It should be clear that nothing of the antebellum system for spreading staple production risks survived the war and emancipation. Economic historians have certainly noticed a major decline in productivity, which Roger Ransom and Richard Sutch argued was a consequence of the freedmen withdrawing a portion of their labor from production, as well as refusing to allow their wives and daughters to toil in the fields. That may have been true in the immediate aftermath of the war, but as the nineteenth century drew to a close evidence of long work days and women as well as men in the fields is available in abundance.

Even had staple production been as productive as in the antebellum decades, the likelihood of a system emerging for spreading planting risks over several seasons was remote. The antebellum system was highly centralized and well capitalized. The planter was in a position to command credit resources from consumers everywhere. No amount of cotton in the postwar decades would have restored this balance to the marketplace.

The high incidence of violence in the eastern Florida Parishes, which Samuel Hyde attributes in large part to the social and economic chaos that accompanied endemic violence during the war, no doubt aggravated social and racial tensions in those areas. But the drift into sharecropping by white farmers as well as blacks also was a source of anxiety and frustration. In this respect small white farmers saw a precipitous decline in their economic status and independence from that of antebellum years. Hyde notices the relatively lower incidences of racial and political violence in the western parishes, where the old elites remained somewhat in the ascendancy. But it is important to note that even the relatively wealthy were not doing especially well anywhere in the Florida Parishes from 1870 to 1890. For most residents of the area a connection with the metropolis to the south was as fanciful as the imaginings of the three sisters in Chekhov's play by that name about some future life in Moscow, a city not all that distant from them.

Notes

1. Gerald David Jaynes, *Branches without Roots: Genesis of the Black Working Class in the American South, 1862–1882* (New York: Oxford University Press, 1986); Eric Foner, *Reconstruction: America's Unfinished Revolution, 1863–1877* (New York: Harper & Row, 1988).

2. The specie standard is indeed an arcane subject in today's monetary theory. The best contemporary treatment is Lawrence H. Officer's *Between the Dollar-Sterling Gold Points: Exchange Rates, Parity, and Market Behavior* (Cambridge: Cambridge University Press, 1996). The standard work on antebellum planters and their factors remains Harold D. Woodman's *King Cotton and His Retainers: Financing and Marketing the Cotton Crop of the South, 1800–1925* (1968; reprint Columbia: University of South Carolina Press, 1990). See also Richard H. Kilbourne Jr., *Debt, Investment, Slaves: Credit Relations in East Feliciana Parish, Louisiana, 1825–1885* (Tuscaloosa: University of Alabama Press, 1995), and "The Business of Arbitraging Exchange Rates and Its Influence on Louisiana's Early Law of Bills and Notes," in *Louisiana: Microcosm of a Mixed Jurisdiction,* ed. Vernon Valentine Palmer (Durham: Carolina Academic Press, 1999).

3. Stanley Chapman, *Merchant Enterprise in Britain, from the Industrial Revolution to World War I* (Cambridge: Cambridge University Press, 1992), and *The Rise of Merchant Banking* (1984; reprint London: Gregg Revivals, 1992); George D. Green, *Finance and Economic Development in the Old South: Louisiana Banking, 1804–1861* (Stanford: Stanford University Press, 1972); Larry Schweikart, *Banking in the American South from the Age of Jackson to Reconstruction* (Baton Rouge: Louisiana State University Press, 1987); Ralph W. Hidy, *The House of Baring in American Trade and Finance: English Merchant Bankers at Work, 1763–1861* (1949; reprint New York: Russell & Russell, 1970); *Pickersgill & Co. v. Brown,* 7 Louisiana Annual Reports 297 (May 1852).

4. *New Orleans Price Current,* 1865.

5. Board of Directors to Messrs. Hope and Co., June 6, 1868, in Citizens Bank Collection, Minute Book, p. 674, Louisiana and Lower Mississippi Valley Collections, Hill Memorial Library, Louisiana State University, Baton Rouge (hereinafter cited as LLMVC).

6. "Money Market," *New Orleans Price Current,* August 31, 1870.

7. See generally Kilbourne, *Debt, Investment, Slaves.*

8. Ibid.

9. Namely, cutting public expenditures and taxes. The twin burdens of public and private debt in postbellum Louisiana were staggering. The memorial for the first Redeemer mayor of New Orleans, Edward Pillsbury, noted that he had cut the city's budget by 50 percent after taking office, perhaps his greatest achievement. But see Roger W. Shugg, *Origins of Class Struggle in Louisiana* (1939; reprint Baton Rouge: Louisiana State University Press, 1972), and William Ivy Hair, *Bourbonism and Agrarian Protest: Louisiana Politics, 1877–1900* (Baton Rouge: Louisiana State University Press, 1969). Isidore Newman to James G. Taliaferro, July 29, 1972, in James G. Taliaferro and Family Papers, box 5, LLMVC.

10. Kilbourne, *Debt, Investment, Slaves;* Michael Wayne, *The Reshaping of Plantation Society: The Natchez District, 1860–1880* (Baton Rouge: Louisiana State University Press, 1983).

11. Samuel C. Hyde Jr., *Pistols and Politics: The Dilemma of Democracy in Louisiana's Florida Parishes, 1810–1899* (Baton Rouge: Louisiana State University Press, 1996), 153. Gavin Wright, *Old South, New South: Revolutions in the Southern Economy since the Civil War* (New York: Basic Books, 1986), 84–91.

12. Judge James G. Kilbourne to Charles Kilbourne, February 8, 1878, in James G. Kilbourne and Family Papers, LLMVC.

13. C. Vann Woodward, *Origins of the New South, 1877–1913* (1951; reprint Baton Rouge: Louisiana State University Press, 1994), 85–97.

14. Wright, *Old South, New South;* Michael Tadman, *Speculators and Slaves: Masters, Traders, and Slaves in the Old South* (Madison: University of Wisconsin Press, 1989).

15. Meyer Brothers Store Records, LLMVC.

16. Ibid.

17. *Gardner's New Orleans Directory 1860* (New Orleans, 1859); *Soards' New Orleans Directory for 1885* (New Orleans, 1886).

18. Roger L. Ransom and Richard Sutch, *One Kind of Freedom: The Economic Consequences of Emancipation* (Cambridge: Cambridge University Press, 1977); *West's Louisiana Statutes Annotated, Treaties and Organic Laws, Early Constitutions* (St. Paul: West, 1997), Constitution of 1879, 3:127, Constitution of 1898, 3:182.

7

THE LEGENDARY LONGLEAF PINE FORESTS OF THE FLORIDA PARISHES

Historic Character and Change at the Hand of Man

LATIMORE SMITH

A DRAMATIC INTERSECTION OF HUMAN HISTORY AND NATURAL history has played out in the piney woods of the eastern Florida Parishes from the early 1800s to the present day. During this period, a once magnificent natural treasure of the region, the longleaf pine (*Pinus palustris* L.) forest, has been reduced by human endeavor from the dominant forest type of the area to what is today an endangered ecosystem.[1] Most current residents of the area have little understanding of the magnitude of the changes that have been wrought to their local native forests, most of which have occurred in the last one hundred years. Today on the whole, thick pine-hardwood forests, agriforestry plantations of pines other than longleaf, agricultural fields, and developed landscapes stand in the place of the virgin longleaf "piney woods." There remain, however, a few areas that support very significant longleaf pine habitats and an incredible diversity of native species.

More than 2 million acres of longleaf pine forests and savannas were historically present in the hills and flatwoods of the eastern Florida Parishes when white settlers first arrived in the area.[2] Longleaf-dominated forests stretched almost unbroken from the Pearl River in the east to just past the Amite River in the west (in the hills), thence down through the eastern flank of Livingston Parish. They occupied the great majority of the land area in St. Helena, Tangipahoa, Washington, and St. Tammany Parishes, and approximately the eastern third of East Feliciana Parish, the far northeastern corner of East Baton Rouge Parish, and about the northeastern third of Livingston Parish.

These forested systems arose many millennia ago on the nutrient-poor, sandy, silty soils of the outer coastal plain and occupied a vast region of the southern United States from Virginia to east Texas at the time of European settlement.[3] The original forests were almost pure stands of longleaf pine, stretching for mile upon mile, broken only by hardwood-lined creek and river bottoms and by wet depressions.

The longleaf forests of the rolling hills that characterize the northern and middle latitudes of the eastern Florida Parishes were densely stocked with trees, but they were invariably parklike, with long, scenic vistas of up to one-half mile or more across the forest floor, carpeted by grass and wildflowers.[4] The wet longleaf pine savannas of the flatwoods that typify the southern latitudes of the area were open expanses of grassland and wildflowers with very scattered longleaf pine trees. Seasonal wetness of surface soils in the flatwoods created very special conditions for plant growth.

Longleaf trees of the virgin forests commonly lived well over two hundred years (some approached five hundred years) and grew to a maximum size of around forty inches in diameter as measured 4½ feet above the ground.[5] The loamy soils of the eastern Florida Parishes were well-suited to the development of majestic stands of longleaf pine, forests that, in general, were more densely stocked than longleaf forests in more easterly states.[6]

As counterintuitive as it seems, fire is the primary natural force that created and maintained these incredible forests.[7] Frequent lightning-generated fires associated with thunderstorms during the growing season swept regularly through the grassy understory, burning away shrubs, hardwoods, and other pines that would otherwise have overtaken the area. While a few relatively fire-adapted hardwoods, such as southern red oak *(Quercus falcata)*, post oak *(Q. stellata)*, blackjack oak *(Q. marilandica)*, and mockernut hickory *(Carya alba)*, were sprinkled in among the longleaf pine, most woody species indigenous to the area were generally confined to steep slopes, stream bottoms, and other places more or less protected from fire.

Fires originating from lightning are estimated to have burned through the forests and savannas once every two to four years on average.[8] While Native Americans of the area practiced burning long before white men arrived, and indeed shared their knowledge of the beneficial effects of fire on longleaf forests with the early settlers,[9] the fire-maintained longleaf system had been in place for tens of thousands of years before the arrival of the aboriginals. Indian burning is believed by most students of the longleaf ecosystem to have had little overall effect on the structure and composition of the type, although their conflagrations could have spread longleaf pine over time into some areas (e.g., "finger ridges" in uplands) that otherwise would not have supported the type.[10]

Fires in the longleaf forest were almost exclusively confined to the ground, burning through grasses and pine needles, and very rarely burning into the tops of trees. Thus, catastrophic blazes that killed large trees were quite rare. Longleaf pine is arguably the most fire-adapted tree in North America, possessing numerous characteristics that render it resistant to fire.[11] The adaptations of longleaf pine to withstand fire include thick, fire-resistant bark that insulates the tender growing tissues underneath, long needles that protect terminal growth buds from excessive heat, and a special growth strategy in its early years that allows it to tolerate fire as a young sapling.

All species, both plant and animal, indigenous to longleaf forests and savannas evolved over millennia with frequent light ground fires, and most depend on the habitat conditions produced by fire for perpetuation. Among other effects, fire stimulates flowering and seed production by many plants that otherwise do so only sporadically (if at all), deters invasion by fire-intolerant woody vegetation, such as sweet gum *(Liquidambar styraciflua)* and water oak *(Quercus nigra)*, and exposes the mineral soil needed for seedlings of grasses, wildflowers, and longleaf pine to become established.[12]

The grasslands encouraged by frequent burning favor numerous wildlife and plant species that prefer open pinelands. Wildlife such as northern bobwhite *(Colinus virginianus)*, red-cockaded woodpecker *(Dendrocopos borealis)*, eastern bluebird *(Sialia sialis)*, Bachman's sparrow *(Aimophila aestivalis)*, Henslow's sparrow *(Passerherbulus henslowii)*, Bachman's fox squirrel *(Sciurrus niger bachmanii)*, gopher tortoise *(Gopherus polyphemus)*, and many others were historically found in relative abundance in open longleaf pine forests and savannas of the Southeast.[13] Judging from the best remaining longleaf forests and savannas in the Florida Parishes today, hundreds of native sun-loving plant species, many found only in regularly burned longleaf pine habitats, undoubtedly thrived in the virgin, open pinelands of the area.

EARLY SETTLERS OF THE PINEY WOODS

Beginning slowly in the late 1700s and early 1800s, white settlers began to populate the magnificent longleaf piney woods of the eastern Florida Parishes.[14] Immediately west of the longleaf range, beginning not far west of the Amite River in East Feliciana Parish, lay rich uplands that were well-suited to agriculture. In contrast, the lands of the longleaf country were not particularly conducive to crop-raising.[15] This difference in soil productivity for farming greatly influenced the human occupation and use of the longleaf piney woods for many decades.

The earliest settlers of the piney woods were almost invariably lone pioneer families who carved out small homesteads, usually near streams where small clearings could be made to grow a few crops in the relatively richer soils of the bottoms. While agriculture was attempted on a somewhat larger scale in the piney uplands early in the 1800s, it soon became apparent that the soils of the longleaf hills were too poor to raise bountiful crops, and many would-be farmers who had settled the area moved on in search of more fertile lands.[16] While farming in the bottoms was quite risky because of the threat of flooding, it was the best option available to the early pioneer settlers. Because the longleaf piney woods were not conducive to the general development of agriculture, the virgin forests and savannas of the area were essentially untouched for much of the antebellum 1800s, except for the minor incursions of the few hardy homesteaders and some small towns and trading centers.

The mainstays of these early settlers were the livestock brought to range free in the open, grassy woods, and the abundant game that thrived in the virgin forests.[17] The abundance of grass and game were the two principal fundamentals that shaped the basic lifestyle and economy of the piney woods folk for much of the 1800s. The words of William H. Sparks provide a colorful description of the piney woods people who lived in nearby Mississippi and who almost certainly derived from the same stock and lived in the same manner as their contemporaries in the piney woods of the Florida Parishes:

> Most of them were from the poorer districts of Georgia and the Carolinas. True to the instincts of the people from whom they descended, they sought as nearly as possible just such a country as that from which they came, and were really refugees from a growing civilization consequent upon a denser population and its necessities. They were not agriculturalists in a proper sense of the term; true, they cultivated in some degree the soil, but it was not the prime pursuit of these people, nor was the location sought for this purpose. They desired an open, poor, pine country, which forbade a numerous population.

Here they reared immense herds of cattle, which sustained exclusively upon the coarse grass and reeds which grew abundantly among the tall, long-leafed pine, and along the small creeks and branches numerous in this section. Through these almost interminable pine forests the deer were abundant, and the canebrakes full of bears. They combined the pursuits of hunting and stock-minding, and derived support and revenue almost exclusively from these....

Along the margins of the streams they found small strips of land of better quality than the pine forests afforded. Here they grew sufficient corn for bread and a few of the coarser vegetables, and in blissful ignorance enjoyed life after the manner they loved. The country gave character to the people: both were wild and poor.[18]

Cattle, sheep, and hogs were common possessions of the early settlers and were allowed to range freely throughout the virgin forests and savannas. Large groups of these animals were common in the piney woods throughout much of the 1800s.[19] Many ecologists believe these non-native animals had a significant impact on the native vegetation of the open pine-woods grasslands and the stream bottoms. The large numbers of cattle almost certainly greatly diminished the abundance of preferred forage grasses such as big bluestem *(Andropogon gerardii)* in the hills and also referred to at the time as "reed") in the bottoms, an effect that lingers to this day in remnant longleaf pine stands.[20] Sheep actively forage on a variety of different vegetation, including the leaves and buds of young longleaf pine, and hogs root up sapling longleaf pine to eat the sweet inner bark of the root. The loss of the bison *(Bison bison)*, historically present in the area,[21] interrupted the dynamic ecological interplay of native grazer and native vegetation that had evolved over thousands of years in the piney woods. While cattle and sheep in some fashion duplicated the effects of bison on native vegetation, their grazing habits are fundamentally different than those of the historic native grazers.

The early stockmen of the Florida Parishes regularly burned off the piney woods in the early spring to freshen the growth of native grasses and improve grazing conditions for their livestock.[22] Such burning supplemented natural lightning fires.

Usually within a few years of a settler's arrival his herd would have grown large enough to provide sufficient manure to enrich a few upland acres for crop production, and the pioneer and his family would be able to move out of the flood-prone stream bottoms and onto the hills. Although this shift subjected some of the piney woods soil of Florida Parishes to the plow, the vast majority of the virgin longleaf forests were unaffected by agriculture through most of the 1800s. The great majority of agriculture during this period remained confined to the stream bottoms.[23]

While this pastoral lifestyle prevailed for much of the nineteenth century in the piney woods, by the late antebellum period strong forces were growing that would soon change the life of splendid isolation in the virgin pine wilderness.[24] Population was steadily increasing throughout the piney woods, particularly near the railways. The large herds of livestock possessed by most piney woods families had by this time begun to dramatically reduce the summer range through overgrazing, and cane, the primary winter food for the free-ranging herds that had originally thrived along the creeks and river bottoms of the area, was disappearing. Game that was once so abundant and easy to take was becoming scattered and gun-shy. Most important, the vast, virgin longleaf pineries of the South were attracting ever-increasing attention from a rapidly growing and industrializing society. In the Florida Parishes, as elsewhere throughout the South, it was the arrival of the railroad in the piney woods that eventually spelled the end of the virgin forests and of the grass-and-game economy of the plain folk of the pinelands.

DEVELOPMENT OF THE LOCAL LUMBER INDUSTRY

Even prior to the coming of the railroad in the mid- to late 1800s, "turpentining" and timbering had been fairly major enterprises in the Florida Parishes. "Turpentining," the gathering of raw gum from longleaf pine trees for the production of pitch, tar, turpentine, and other products, was one of the oldest economic endeavors practiced throughout the virgin piney woods of the South.[25] Since most of these products were used extensively in wooden sailing vessels for waterproofing seams and for cordage, they were referred to commonly as "naval stores." When a pine's bark is cut, gum exudes from the wound. Turpentiners scarred trees in a particular way using implements specially designed for the purpose and gathered the crude gum to be processed into naval stores and turpentine. Although some turpentining had been practiced for several decades almost everywhere in the piney woods that had access to market, the peak of the industry's activity generally moved in a wave from east to west across the South in the late 1800s. The industry began to increase locally after about 1870 with the construction of the railroads, the general depletion of the virgin timber in the eastern states, and the arrival of eastern turpentiners seeking fresh forests in which to practice their trade. It became standard practice for the large land-owning timber companies to tap their timber holdings for naval stores for a few years before harvesting the trees. The peak of the local naval stores industry in the Florida Parishes was around 1900 or shortly thereafter,[26] though it persisted until the last of the virgin timber was removed.

The great majority of early timber operations were confined to areas near streams. The earliest lumber mills were water-powered, located on suitable streams to power the mill. Even as late as 1880, thirty water-powered sawmills were present in St. Helena Parish.[27] Overall, very little lumber was manufactured from the piney woods in this fashion. The coming of the steam engine in the early 1800s saw a significant increase in the capacity of mills to produce lumber. The early steam sawmills in the Florida Parishes were all situated on waterways concentrated near the northern shore of Lake Pontchartrain in southern St. Tammany and Tangipahoa Parishes. Streams were of critical importance for the transport of logs to the mills by rafting and for transport of milled lumber and other products to market by sailing and steam vessels. Before the coming of the railroad, commercial timbering and lumber production would have been next to impossible without readily available water transportation. Rafting of logs to mills was a major, often adventuresome feature of the prerail lumber industry. Trees were cut by axe or saw and then dragged to the stream by oxen or mule teams, where the logs were formed into rafts. Using this laborious method, the maximum distance from which it was practical and economical to haul logs to streams was no more than three or four miles.[28] This meant that the great majority of the virgin longleaf forest that covered the hills and flatwoods was still beyond the reach of the timberman. A number of forces were coming together, however, that would shortly render this apparent seclusion illusory.

Expanding development of lumber markets after the Civil War, steadily improving mechanizations employed by the mills, migration of northern timber interests and capital into the great remaining pineries of the South upon the commercial depletion of the eastern white pine *(Pinus strobus)* forests of the Great Lakes region, and the arrival of the railroad in the region all acted in concert to spur on dramatic growth in the local timber industry of the late 1800s.[29] Almost everyone in the backcountry of the longleaf pinelands came to depend on the timber and lumber industry to a greater or lesser degree for their livelihood. Many people of the piney woods, perhaps with mixed emotions, abandoned their simple pastoral lifestyle in the virgin forests to join the burgeoning lumbering enterprise that would soon profoundly alter their forested home and a forest ecosystem that had existed for untold millennia.

RAILS IN THE PINEY WOODS

The full development of the lumber industry in the interior of the Florida Parishes was almost completely reliant upon development of the rail system. Hundreds of thousands of acres of virgin longleaf pine, one of the greatest timber trees the world has ever seen,[30] stood waiting and provided the impetus for the construction of railroads in a land where agriculture was generally hardly better than subsistence farming.

The first railroad constructed in longleaf piney woods of the Florida Parishes, the New Orleans, Jackson, and Great Northern (later the Illinois Central), began operating in the early 1850s.[31] This railway, serving as a ready conduit for lumber products, stimulated rapid development of commercial lumbering along the piney woods portion of its route that passed around the west side of Lake Pontchartrain, and thence more or less due northward to the Mississippi line in the north-central portion of the Florida Parishes. Amos Kent's mill, erected in 1853 at what later became Kentwood, was one of many that sprang up along the railroad. Although commercial lumber production was interrupted by the Civil War, timber interests recovered rapidly in postbellum years, and by the early 1880s there was a sawmill at virtually every train stop along the railroad. In 1886, thirty-one small mills sat adjacent to the Illinois Central Railroad along its traverse in Louisiana.[32] By this time, a wide swath of the virgin timber had been cut from both sides of the railroad along its entire length through the Florida Parishes.

With the removal of the timber near the main tracks, lumbermen constructed tram roads, smaller side-track lines often called "dummy lines," to access the remainder of the forest. By the late 1800s, numerous millmen on the Illinois Central were operating tram roads, and by 1905, timber for all the large backcountry mills was brought in over dummy lines. In order to access the timber, an average of six spurs per square mile extended into the woods from the tramline.³³ Once the timber was removed from an area, the spur lines were taken up and relaid in uncut timber.

In addition to the New Orleans, Jackson, and Great Northern, a number of other significant railroads operated in the Florida Parishes in the great lumbering era. These included the New Orleans and Great Northern, which ran between Slidell, Bogalusa, and Jackson, Mississippi (initiated in 1909 and owned by the Goodyear family of the Great Southern Lumber Company); the East Louisiana, which mainly operated in St. Tammany Parish (initiated in 1887, owned originally by Poitevent and Favre lumber interests but later acquired by the Goodyear family); the Kentwood, Greensburg, and Southwestern, which ran between Kentwood, Greensburg, and Freiler (initiated in 1910, owned by the stockholders of Amos Kent enterprises); the New Orleans, Natalbany, and Natchez, which operated between Natalbany and Pine Grove (initiated in 1902, owned by the Denkman lumber interests, e.g., Natalbany Lumber Company); and the Kentwood and Eastern, which ran in areas east and southeast of Kentwood (initiated in 1896, owned by the Brooks-Scanlon Lumber Company).³⁴ By 1910, the railroad system had penetrated essentially the entire backcountry piney woods of the Florida Parishes.

THE LARGE MILLS AND THE END OF THE VIRGIN FOREST

The boom of railroad construction in the late nineteenth and early twentieth centuries coincided with technical innovations that rapidly improved the ability of millmen to produce lumber and with the development of large, efficient mills. While numerous small sawmills continued to operate during this time, large mills with ever-increasing capacity dominated the industry. Among the largest in the Florida Parishes were the Great Southern Lumber Company in Bogalusa, the Natalbany (Denkman) Lumber Company in Natalbany, the Brooks-Scanlon Lumber Company in Kentwood, the Salmen Lumber Company in Slidell, and the Poitevent-Favre Lumber Company in Mandeville and Mississippi. The larger mills could cut huge amounts of lumber in a single day.³⁵

The Great Southern Lumber Company mill in Bogalusa, built in 1908, was one of the largest, if not the largest, lumber mill in the world at that time and was "the showplace of the south."³⁶ By 1915, this facility was milling 1 million board feet of lumber in a twenty-four-hour period, a volume of production that far exceeded the capacity of the largest mills of the late

1800s. To produce such incredible volumes required tremendous numbers of logs to be brought to the mill every day, some from as far away as one hundred miles. It is likely that at least two thousand trees per day would have been required to sustain this level of production. While the other large mills of the area did not individually achieve quite this fantastic level of productivity, considered in union, and further considering the combined activities of the numerous small sawmills still operating, it becomes easy to comprehend the sheer speed and scope of dissolution of the virgin longleaf forests of the Florida Parishes, once thought to be "inexhaustible."

In addition to the railroads and the revolutions in mill technology, one more mechanical innovation deserves special mention for its contribution to the massive escalation of the pace of logging in the region: the "steam skidder." For decades prior to the early 1900s, all logs brought to streams for rafting or to railside for loading on railcars were dragged by teams of oxen, mules, or horses—an inherently slow process.[37] With this new technology, introduced to the region just after 1900 and readily adopted by most (but not all) loggers, logging outfits could hasten their work many times over. Steam skidders, mounted on special railcars, were hauled along with the logging trains and set up along the spur tracks to retrieve cut logs. Steel cables, wound on large drums, would reach out one thousand feet or more when stretched their full length. These cables were attached to groups of logs to be dragged back to the train through the steam-driven action of the revolving drums. As many as fifteen logs could be retrieved on one pull-in.[38] It was commonplace for one of these machines to fetch and load more than five hundred trees in a day. Such heavy-handed logging was extremely damaging to the land and young timber of unmerchantable size, and it left behind vast, barren landscapes essentially denuded of all trees, both large and small.

Longleaf pine logging and lumber production in the Florida Parishes peaked shortly after 1910. While there were some calls for conservation in the early 1900s by some who foresaw the end of the virgin pine resource, the allure of the virgin timber was too great and logging continued unabated[39] and at a furious pace. The timber was rapidly being cleared, however, and the end of the virgin longleaf forest was near. By the early 1930s, virtually all the virgin forest had been taken down and the last of the big mills ceased operations, thus marking the ignominious end of the "cut out and get out" era in the longleaf pine country. It is probable that well over one million acres of virgin longleaf pine forest in the interior of the Florida

Parishes were logged out from 1890 to 1930. A magnificent forest that had stood for thousands of years was now little more than a memory. In its place, a stark, forlorn landscape remained, and the vast, virgin forests, the true home of the piney woods folk, was forever lost.

MAJOR LAND USE PATTERNS AFTER THE VIRGIN TIMBER BOOM

Most lumbermen of the day had little incentive to attempt reforestation after the virgin timber was removed. Most people believed such a venture was at best a long, drawn-out process, likely to be expensive and subject to failure. Some, however, such as the Great Southern Lumber Company, became actively involved in reforestation in the early 1920s and planted what was later called the largest man-made forest in the world.[40] The great majority of the acreage planted in these early reforestation efforts, however, was replenished, not with longleaf pine, but with slash pine *(Pinus elliottii)* or loblolly pine *(Pinus taeda)*, species that were found to be much easier to establish than longleaf. Because the particular requirements for successful establishment of longleaf pine were obscure in the early years of the reforestation effort, a bias developed against planting longleaf pine.

Many lumbermen, reluctant to reforest their cut-over lands and perceiving them to be of little value, initiated grand promotional campaigns prior to 1920 to dispose of land to would-be farmers from other sections of the country, and even from foreign countries.[41] Misleading and overblown descriptions of the agricultural capacity of the land lured many prospective colonists to purchase land for farming. Typically within a year or two of arrival, these newcomers discovered that the glowing claims of bountiful harvests would not be realized from this poor pineland soil, and they quickly abandoned their small fields in disillusionment.

Not all agricultural attempts in the pine flats and hills failed, however. A significant truck farming industry, mainly involved in strawberry cultivation, had by the late 1800s developed in the cut-over pinelands along the Illinois Central railroad in Tangipahoa Parish.[42] This industry was bolstered by the arrival of Sicilian immigrants in the area. Although it has declined from its heyday in the early 1900s, the truck industry remains a significant pursuit in the region.

The dairy industry grew steadily in the hills of the north-central Florida Parishes after the Extension Department of Louisiana State University demonstrated a reliable system for establishing pasture grasses in the cut-over pine hills,[43] and with the encouragement of local citizenry in the vicinity of Kentwood seeking to bolster the local economy with the loss of the virgin pine forest. The dairy industry became the largest agricultural pursuit in the former piney woods of the Florida Parishes. It is probable that the overall acreage occupied at one time or another by the dairy and livestock industry in the northern Florida Parishes is in excess of 400,000 acres, the vast majority having been placed into permanent pasture of bahia grass *(Paspalum notatum)* and bermuda grass *(Cynodon dactylon)*, and annual winter pasture of rye grass *(Lolium perenne)*.[44]

Some areas of cut-over pineland were planted to tung-oil tree *(Aleurites fordii)* orchards in the 1930s, particularly in Washington and St. Tammany Parishes.[45] Tung-oil tree, a native of China, produces an oil in its seeds that has been highly valued for use in quick-drying paints and varnishes and as a wood finish oil. While this industry was short-lived in the area, it is still common to see tung-oil trees in many places in the former piney woods of the eastern Florida Parishes.

Commercial plantation forestry started slowly but grew quickly in the piney woods of the Florida Parishes over the course of the twentieth century. The establishment of plantation forests of pines other than longleaf had its beginnings in the Florida Parishes in the early 1920s with the fourteen-thousand-acre planting project of the Great Southern Lumber Company. This planting used slash pine rather than longleaf. Because early efforts to establish longleaf pine met with little success, planters chose to use loblolly and slash pine, which were easier to obtain and to grow.[46] This preference for loblolly and slash over longleaf pine continued as the commercial pine plantation industry began to slowly expand in the 1930s and early 1940s, and more and more acres of cut-over longleaf pine woods were planted to these other pines. By the late 1940s and early 1950s, commercial plantation forestry was becoming big business in the Florida Parishes. Large acreages were being planted almost exclusively to loblolly pine in the hills and slash pine in the flatwoods. These agroforests were destined to become "short rotation" stands, which typically are allowed to grow for only thirty to thirty-five years or less between harvests. Few, if any, of these planting projects used longleaf pine throughout this period and beyond. More than 200,000 acres of the original longleaf pine country of the Florida Parishes have been planted to pine agroforests over the last several decades. While these forests sustain some of the original complement of native plants and animal species originally present in the longleaf piney woods, many species, particularly those adapted to open pinelands or that require old pines, cannot persist in these thickly stocked monocultures of young pines.[47]

Most of the land that originally supported longleaf pine was not converted to agriculture, planted to tung-oil, or replanted with other pines after the cut-out, and most of the acreage produced a heavy growth of young longleaf pine saplings within a few years, particularly where woods burning was prevalent. Vigorous forest-fire-suppression campaigns began in the early 1900s, however. Led by well-intentioned but misinformed agencies that believed fire to be one of the worst enemies of the forest, the effort began to dramatically reduce the number of people practicing woods burning. This reduction in burning, combined with the activities of the "piney woods rooter" (feral hogs), allowed other pines and hardwoods to begin to overtake many of the "second growth" longleaf pine stands.[48] Over the next few decades, most of these forested areas that had started out as young longleaf stands evolved, with continued fire suppression and regular timber harvests, into dense forests of loblolly or slash pine mixed with various hardwoods, or even essentially pure hardwood forests in the uplands. Longleaf is seldom seen in most of these stands. Such anthropogenic forests, far removed from their original condition of open longleaf forests and savannas, are today everywhere to be seen in the Florida Parishes. Few people recognize the fact that such forests, and the pine plantation agroforests discussed above, are completely the result of human actions, and that these altered modern stands bear little resemblance to the original forests and savannas of the area, the majority of which were present as recently as one hundred years ago.

Burgeoning residential and commercial development is a last major land-use pattern that must be considered when assessing change to the former longleaf piney woods of the Florida Parishes. Most of this development has occurred in the flatwoods of the southern portions of St. Tammany and Tangipahoa Parishes. There has been explosive growth of residential subdivisions and concomitant commercial enterprises to service this proliferating population of the "North Shore." Although most of the growth has been in the southern zone of the Florida Parishes, a considerable degree of growth has been seen in areas farther to the north, particularly in locales that have ready access to major highways or interstates. This expanding land occupancy has directly and significantly reduced the area of residual longleaf pine habitat in the Florida Parishes.

LONGLEAF ENDANGERED

From a natural history perspective, by far the most significant result of the massive exploitation and development of the piney woods landscape in the Florida Parishes is the reduction of the area's once-dominant longleaf pine ecosystems to the point where they are today imperiled. While it is still common to see individuals or small groups of longleaf pine in the eastern Florida Parishes today (typically in such places as dairy fields, yards, on fence rows, and scattered in dense mixed forests), ecologically functioning longleaf pine forests and savannas that approach at least in some moderate degree the structure, and in large degree the composition, of the original habitats, are exceedingly scarce. It is estimated that not more than twenty thousand acres remain in the Florida Parishes that can be considered relatively high-quality, residual longleaf pine habitat.[49] These residual areas are places that were not converted to agriculture or agriforests, and that somehow burned sufficiently over the years to encourage young longleaf to grow and to prevent overgrowth by other trees and shrubs. Such burning also maintained a diverse native ground-cover community of grasses and wildflowers. That areas supporting very diverse native herbaceous plant communities remain is testament to the reality that early land-use activities of livestock grazing, logging, and turpentining in the 1800s and early 1900s were not terribly disruptive to the native ground-cover communities of longleaf forests and savannas, although some damage was undoubtedly done. Further, it appears that logging with steam skidders either was not excessively damaging to the native herbaceous plants on the ground or was not used everywhere in the interior pinelands.

Our residual longleaf pine forests and savannas of the Florida Parishes provide extremely important habitat for a plethora of plant and animal species and serve as reminders, museum pieces actually, of the type of landscape the original piney woods folk occupied. Hundreds of native plant species, the great majority herbaceous, are found in regularly burned longleaf forests and savannas of the area, many of which are found nowhere else in the Florida Parishes. It is not uncommon to encounter more than one hundred plant species on one acre of high-quality remnant longleaf habitat. Upland longleaf pine forests found in the hills of the Florida

Parishes are dominated by many kinds of grasses, but mainly little bluestem *(Schizachyrium scoparium)*. Numerous kinds of plants in the sunflower family (asteraceae) and pea family (fabaceae) also thrive there, as well as an incredible variety of other plants. The pine savannas of the flatwoods in the southern part of the Florida Parishes, and the floristically closely related hillside seepage bogs in the hills, support an amazing contingent of plants, including many unusual species. These include carnivorous plants (pitcher-plants, *Sarracenia* spp.; yellow butterwort, *Pinguicula lutea*; and others), plants in the lily family such as the death-camus *(Zigadenus leimanthoides)*, and more types of native orchids than any other habitat in Louisiana. In addition, the pine savannas of southeast Louisiana support more species of rare plants than any other habitat in the state.[50]

Numerous animal species may be found in these forests and savannas, many of which are rare today. Northern bobwhite (quail), a species of much interest to many and a bird once ubiquitous in the longleaf piney woods, has become quite scarce in recent decades. Many who once enjoyed "bird hunting" have reluctantly given up the sport. Red-cockaded woodpecker, a bird highly dependent on old, living pine trees, was once almost certainly abundant in our virgin longleaf forests but today is extremely rare in the piney woods of the Florida Parishes because of the lack of old pine trees and open, piney woods. Bachman's sparrow and Henslow's sparrow are two rare birds that are restricted to high-quality open piney woods. Many other examples could be given of this pattern of modern rarity. While most animals that reside in or use remnant longleaf forests and savannas are not rare, many are found most commonly in these environs.[51]

RECENT CONSERVATION EFFORTS AND HOPE FOR THE FUTURE

For most of the twentieth century, the need for conservation of longleaf pine habitats and the many species they support was not recognized in the Florida Parishes, despite the massive losses this ecosystem has suffered. In recent years, a number of important steps have been taken for longleaf conservation in the area. Important remnant longleaf pine habitats in the hills and flatwoods of the area, totaling more than four thousand acres, have been acquired by the Louisiana Department of Wildlife and Fisheries and the Office of State Lands over the last twenty years. The U.S. Fish and Wildlife Service has purchased land in St. Tammany Parish and established wildlife refuges, parts of which contain important longleaf areas, including some that support the endangered red-cockaded woodpecker. A number of private and public owners of important longleaf habitats have engaged in conservation management of their lands, working in cooperation with groups such as the Nature Conservancy, the Louisiana Natural Heritage Program, and the State Office of Forestry. The Nature Conservancy has done more than any other private group for the direct conservation of longleaf pine in the area, acquiring more than three thousand acres in the pine flatwoods for conservation of longleaf pine savannas and associated habitats. Through the conservation efforts of many, a program of common purpose is in place to restore and maintain longleaf pine habitats in many places across the Florida Parishes. While we will never see forests akin to the vast virgin longleaf stands that once dominated our landscape, we can hope that through the combined efforts of many, we can sustain the multitude of species that call these forests and savannas home, and maintain small vestiges of the great piney woods of our ancestors.

Notes

1. Latimore Smith, "Louisiana Longleaf: An Endangered Legacy," *Louisiana Conservationist* (May/June 1991): 24–27.

2. Charles Mohr, *The Timber Pines of the Southern United States*, U.S. Department of Agriculture, Division of Forestry, Bulletin no. 13 (Washington, D.C., 1897), 43.

3. W. G. Wahlenberg, *Longleaf Pine: Its Use, Ecology, Regeneration, Protection, Growth, and Management*, Charles Lathrop Pack Foundation in cooperation with the Forest Service, U.S. Department of Agriculture (Washington, D.C., 1946), 45.

4. Samuel H. Lockett, *Louisiana As It Is* (1874), ed. Lauren C. Post (Baton Rouge: Louisiana State University Press, 1969).

5. Mohr, *Timber Pines*, 59; William J. Platt, Gregory W. Evans, and Stephen L. Rathbun, "The Population Dynamics of a Long-lived Conifer (Pinus palustris)," *American Naturalist* 131 (1988): 491–525.

6. Mohr, *Timber Pines*, 43.

7. Kenneth H. Garren, "Effects of Fire on Vegetation of the Southeastern United States," *Botanical Review* 9 (1943): 617–54.

8. Wahlenberg, *Longleaf Pine*, 57.

9. Garren, "Effects of Fire on Vegetation," 617.

10. David L. Martin and Latimore M. Smith, *A Survey and Description of the Natural Plant Communities of the Kisatchie National Forest: Evangeline and Catahoula Districts* (Baton Rouge: Louisiana Department of Wildlife and Fisheries, 1993), 3.

11. Wahlenberg, *Longleaf Pine*, 57.

12. J. Larry Landers, Nathan A. Byrd, and Roy Komarek, "A Holistic Approach to Managing Longleaf Pine Communities," *Proceedings of the Symposium on the Management of Long-*

leaf Pine, April 4–6, 1989, Long Beach, Mississippi, U.S. Forest Service General Technical Report SO-75 (New Orleans, 1990), 135–66; Smith, "Louisiana Longleaf," 24–27.

13. R. Todd Engstrom, "Characteristic Mammals and Birds of Longleaf Pine Forests," *Proceedings of the 18th Tall Timbers Fire Ecology Conference—The Longleaf Pine Ecosystem: Ecology, Restoration, and Management* (Tallahassee, Fla.: Tall Timbers Research Station, 1993), 127–38; Craig Guyer and Mark A. Bailey, "Amphibians and Reptiles of Longleaf Pine Communities," ibid., 139–58.

14. Samuel C. Hyde Jr., *Pistols and Politics: The Dilemma of Democracy in Louisiana's Florida Parishes, 1810–1899* (Baton Rouge: Louisiana State University Press, 1996), 3.

15. Eugene W. Hilgard, *Report on the Cotton Production of the State of Louisiana, with a Discussion of the General Agricultural Features of the State*, U.S. Department of the Interior, Census Office (Washington, D.C., 1884), 21–27.

16. Nollie Wade Hickman, "History of Forest Industries in the Longleaf Pine Belt of East Louisiana and Mississippi, 1840–1915" (Ph.D. diss., University of Texas, 1950), 8.

17. Ibid., 12.

18. William H. Sparks, *The Memories of Fifty Years*, ed. J. W. Burke, 3rd. ed. (Macon, Ga., 1872), 331–32.

19. Hickman, "History of Forest Industries in the Longleaf Pine Belt," 13–18.

20. Dr. William Platt, interview by author, July 1999, Louisiana State University, Baton Rouge.

21. Mohr, *Timber Pines*, 62; George H. Lowery Jr., *The Mammals of Louisiana and Its Adjacent Waters* (Baton Rouge: Louisiana State University Press, 1974), 501.

22. Hilgard, *Report on the Cotton Production of the State of Louisiana*, 65.

23. Hickman, "History of Forest Industries in the Longleaf Pine Belt," 15; Hilgard, *Report on the Cotton Production of the State of Louisiana*, 34.

24. Hickman, "History of Forest Industries in the Longleaf Pine Belt," 19.

25. Mohr, *Timber Pines*, 29; Hickman, "History of Forest Industries in the Longleaf Pine Belt," 189.

26. Hickman, "History of Forest Industries in the Longleaf Pine Belt," 199–206, 208.

27. Ibid., 24; Milton B. Newton Jr., "Water-Powered Sawmills and Related Structures in the Piney Woods," in *Mississippi's Piney Woods: A Human Perspective*, ed. Noel Polk (Jackson, Miss.: University Press of Mississippi, 1986), 156, 164.

28. Hickman, "History of Forest Industries in the Longleaf Pine Belt," 40, 60.

29. Ibid., 241–88.

30. Wahlenberg, *Longleaf Pine*, 8.

31. Hickman, "History of Forest Industries in the Longleaf Pine Belt," 82; Hyde, *Pistols and Politics*, 78.

32. Hickman, "History of Forest Industries in the Longleaf Pine Belt," 92.

33. Ibid., 93, 256.

34. Ibid., 346–56.

35. Ibid., 249.

36. Ibid., 284, 287.

37. Ibid., 258.

38. Ibid., 260.

39. H. B. Steer, *Lumber Production in the United States*, U.S. Department of Agriculture, Miscellaneous Publication no. 669 (Washington, D.C., 1948), 12–147; Hickman, "History of Forest Industries in the Longleaf Pine Belt," 441.

40. Hickman, "History of Forest Industries in the Longleaf Pine Belt," 439, 452; Jeff Hughes, Crown Zellerbach employee, interview by author, August 1999, Bogalusa, La.

41. Hickman, "History of Forest Industries in the Longleaf Pine Belt," 443.

42. C. Howard Nichols, ed., *Tangipahoa Crossings: Excursions into Tangipahoa History* (Baton Rouge: Moran, 1979), 33, 45, 59.

43. Donald McDaniel, *Soil Survey of Tangipahoa Parish, Louisiana*, U.S. Department of Agriculture, Soil Conservation Service (Washington, D.C., 1990), 2.

44. Nichols, *Tangipahoa Crossings*, 50.

45. Claire A. Brown, *Trees and Shrubs of Louisiana*, Louisiana Forestry Commission Bulletin no. 1 (Baton Rouge, 1945), 155.

46. Hughes interview.

47. Don Feduccia, Louisiana State Office of Forestry employee, interview by author, August 1999, Baton Rouge.

48. Thomas C. Croker, *Longleaf Pine: A History of Man and a Forest*, U.S. Forest Service, Southern Region, Forestry Report R8-FR7 (1987), 7.

49. Smith, "Louisiana Longleaf," 24–27.

50. Information provided by the Louisiana Natural Heritage Program, Louisiana Department of Wildlife and Fisheries, Baton Rouge.

51. William Vermillion, nongame biologist, Louisiana Natural Heritage Program, Louisiana Department of Wildlife and Fisheries, interview by author, March 1999, Baton Rouge.

III | CHALLENGES LESS SPOKEN

8

AFRICAN AMERICAN LUMBER WORKERS IN THE FLORIDA PARISHES LUMBER INDUSTRY, 1900–1925

BILL WYCHE

*O*N SEPTEMBER 1, 1919, CITIZENS OF BOGALUSA AND NEIGHBORING hamlets of Washington Parish, Louisiana, witnessed a remarkable event for a southern lumber community. Bogalusa, the parish's largest city, celebrated its first Labor Day parade, with marches by more than 2,500 workers, including 800 African Americans. This parade ranks as an extraordinary development in southern history, for both black and white workers, about to commence a long, turbulent strike, demonstrated a unity uncommon for labor in the South. The local newspaper, the *Enterprise and American,* noted the excitement:

> The working man was in the saddle Monday in Bogalusa's first Labor Day celebration. The blue overall was prominent and the families of the men who run the wheels of industry shared in a day that was one continuous round of pleasure. Stores were closed, all mills and factories were shut down and not one job was operated that could be avoided. The day was ideal, and there was not a hitch to mark the perfect success of the celebration.
> At 10 A.M., with a little spare time in order to make the parade natural, the boys headed from Labor Temple in Northeast Bogalusa for the Avenues. Every union in Bogalusa was represented, and headed by Jep Smith, grand marshal, city officials, and the Y. M. C. A. band, the parade moved forward. Just how long it was is uncertain, but the men marching in twos extended practically two miles. There were 2,500 men in the lines, according to L. E. Williams, President of the Local Federation, 800 of whom were colored union men.[1]

The parade revealed several important truths about labor in the Florida Parishes: Lumber ranked as the major industrial employer, African Americans formed a major component of that industry's work force, and the solidarity of the marchers challenged the widely accepted premise of an insurmountable barrier between white and black workers in the South.

Washington and the other Florida Parishes of Louisiana boasted numerous assets and natural resources, including a mild winter climate, rich soil, an abundant water supply, and immense quantities and varieties of wild game. But the key to understanding the explosive pattern of social and economical development was the area's most vital resource: massive stands of longleaf, yellow pine.[2] Consequently, between the years of 1900 and 1925, lumber companies flourished in the region, helping to make Louisiana a national leader in lumber production. By 1910, Louisiana ranked first among the states in lumber production and counted more than 43,000 workers in the industry; by 1921 the state included a remarkable cut-over area totaling 12,725,000 acres. In 1917 Louisiana produced 4.21 billion board feet of lumber, which represented 11.7 percent of the total production for the United States.[3] The Florida Parishes accounted for a significant portion of this production, boasting impressive production facilities such as the Great Southern Lumber Company in Bogalusa (the "largest lumber mill in the world"), the Natalbany mill near Hammond, and the Amos Kent Lumber Company in northern Tangipahoa Parish, along with numerous smaller concerns.[4]

Lumber manufacturing served as a dramatic catalyst affecting not only the region's economy but also population mobility and social attitudes, particularly of African Americans who represented more than 50 percent of the industry's labor force.[5] Although black lumber workers throughout the South often competed with rural whites for the lowest paying, unskilled jobs, employers in the Florida Parishes at times utilized extraordinary strategies to hire or to retain African Americans.[6] In 1913 George Bloomington of Isabell, Louisiana, petitioned the Department of Justice in Washington, D.C.:

> Dear Sir,
> Can't you do something to help us colored people here. When a man goes and hires to the Great Southern Lumber Co. here [he] is just like a slave or worse. He is held under the big guns and whipped and can't leave unless he can run away. . . . I have jest got away but they are still holding a lot of men yet. Please look into this. I don't know where else to write to.
> Yours truly
> George Bloomington, Colored[7]

The response, if any, to this plea is unknown, but perhaps forceful retention of African American lumber workers proved counterproductive and legally risky, for five years later, during World War I, advocates for the Great Southern Lumber Company attempted to use persuasion in order to keep black workers. On January 11, 1917, the *Bogalusa Enterprise and American* reported that "a Negro who had a good reputation" had contracted pneumonia while living and working in Chicago because of the bad weather. The newspaper cautioned that "Southern Negroes cannot endure the weather which is existing in the North and East and the Negro who goes to those sections during the next four months is flirting with the undertaker."[8]

Both Bloomington's appeal and the newspaper warning reflected the demand for African American lumber workers in the Florida Parishes, and this demand affected population mobility. The region, like Louisiana, could count a significant African American population dating back to the pre–Civil War era, but the lumber industry in the early twentieth century caused some parishes to retain and even to attract black citizens while the state overall registered a percentage decrease.[9] In 1900, Louisiana's races stood almost evenly divided, with a black population of 47.1 percent and a white population of 52.8 percent; by 1920, the population had changed to 38.9 percent black and 61 percent white.[10] The addition of foreign-born whites who entered the state in the early years of the twentieth century accounted for a minuscule portion of the percentage increase for that group.[11] In the Florida Parishes, East Baton Rouge Parish experienced a significant decrease in the percentage of African Americans, dropping from over 66 percent to 51.9 percent, but the explosion in the white population, no doubt due to industrial expansion and state government employment, accounts for this change. By comparison, the African American percentage in two parishes with large lumber manufacturing facilities, Tangipahoa and Washington, remained constant.[12]

Washington Parish presents an excellent model to document lumber's importance in retaining and attracting African American workers. The Great Southern Lumber Company commenced operations in this parish in 1906, and between 1900 and 1910 the African American population almost doubled, increasing from 2,776 to 5,458. Because of equally impressive growth in the white population, percentages remained constant, although the African American population registered a slight increase, from 28.8 to 30.6 percent, between 1910 and 1920.[13] Again, these changes occurred during the period that Louisiana experienced a decrease in the percentage of African Americans in the population. Moreover, a survey of 1910 census numbers for Washington Parish's Fourth Ward, which includes Bogalusa, indicates that only a minority of black workers claimed Louisiana as their place of birth, with the majority migrating from southern states such as Mississippi, Alabama, Texas, Arkansas, Florida, and Georgia, and a few from distant areas such as California, Vermont, and England.[14]

The African American percentage of the population in both Washington and Tangipahoa Parishes remained constant in these years because of the lumber industry, which required thousands of black workers. Louisiana early established a governmental agency to investigate labor conditions, and this office issued a number of valuable and informative reports. The *Ninth Biennial Report* of the commissioner of the Department of Labor and Industrial Statistics for the years 1916–1918 provides a wealth of information about industrial development in the state, wages and hours of workers, labor conditions, and the racial composition of the employees in various industries.[15] A survey of twenty-two lumber mills in the Florida Parishes, based on the *Ninth Biennial Report,* indicates that African Americans represented at least 50 percent of the work force in several establishments and 90 to 100 percent at other facilities. These twenty-two mills employed more than 6,700 workers, including more than 4,000 African Americans. Only one mill had no black employees, while African Americans accounted for at least 50 percent at the other twenty-one operations. Several large mills, including Lacombe Lumber at Lacombe, Amos Kent in Kentwood, and Dendenger in Madisonville, counted 80 percent or more African American employees.[16]

Employers selected these workers because of availability, low wages, and the valuable labor that African Americans could provide in this industry. Contrary to the popular assumption of a surplus in the southern labor force, accurate in terms of other industries such as textiles, Louisiana officials and employers often expressed concern about a shortage of workers, particularly for agriculture and unskilled jobs in lumber.[17] The *Ninth Biennial Report,* analyzing the issue during World War I, expressed concern about the exodus of common labor, particularly African Americans, and concluded that poor treatment caused much of the migration.[18] In May 1923 the *New Orleans Times-Picayune* also considered the black exodus from the South but, in an overly optimistic and inadequate explanation of the problem, attributed this development to an improvement in skills that would allow the race better jobs in the North.[19] Amos Kent, descendant of his namesake who established both the town of Kentwood and the lumber company, noted the competition with farmers for this labor.[20]

Regional lumbermen advanced conflicting opinions about the proficiency of black workers, and both advocates and detractors often reflected a racist rationalization. An official of a southern Mississippi company complained that black workers were "becoming more no-account and trifling every day." Others accused blacks of being unreliable, willing to work only long enough to buy necessities, and warned that high wages only contributed to the problem.[21] A 1907 letter to the *Southern Lumberman* castigated the black worker by claiming that he would rather live in the city than work in the fields and that, with his freedom, had "grown careless, improvident, indigent, and altogether unreliable."[22]

Others expressed a different, albeit racist view, of the African American worker. Many who favored black workers borrowed from the old arguments used by defenders of slavery, particularly the view of African Americans as stronger. One employer offered, "The average Negro, unspoiled by education and life in the city, was, if dealt with properly, the best type of mill labor, as patient as an ox and as reliable as a steam engine." Another lumberman observed: "I would rather have one black man in a sawmill than two white men, for he will perform just as much labor as two Anglo-Saxons and will do it willingly and even joyously. All he wants is three square meals a day and his wage paid to him every Saturday night."[23]

In the Florida Parishes, black workers might compete with other than Anglo-Saxon whites. During the 1908 anti-Italian frenzy in Natalbany, Louisiana, one observer offered this backhanded approval of African American workers:

> I don't understand them [Italians], although I have tried my best. They don't understand us because they don't seem to want to. As a laborer give me a Negro every time. I know his ways and he knows mine. I can handle him and get results out of him. But I can never tell what an Italian is going to do next. In dealing with him I always make a mental reservation.[24]

Regardless of these less-than-enlightened views, employment statistics demonstrate the preference and demand for African American lumber workers in the Florida Parishes.

Labor historians generally acknowledge that black workers in the southern lumber industry were restricted to low-wage, unskilled jobs and consequently received, on the average, less pay than did their white counterparts.[25] However, pay was not the sole factor in evaluating worker compensation, for many companies provided benefits such as housing and even medical care for white and black workers.[26] The Pearl River Valley Lumber Company, for example, in addition to providing housing, built a dance hall and a church for black employees.[27] Such subsidies for blacks paled in comparison to benefits offered to whites, but African Americans undoubtedly considered conditions superior to alternatives offered in southern agriculture.[28]

Although usually restricted to unskilled work, black workers possessing extraordinary talent, intellect, or energy occasionally broke through the race barrier and gained the better-paying skilled positions. In reminiscing about conditions at the Natalbany Lumber Company in Tangipahoa Parish, white executive John O. Stamps acknowledged several outstanding, skilled black workers. Henry Levi served as a block setter, George Long as "an able edgerman," and Ollie Walker as a grader for pattern stock, especially flooring. Perhaps one of the more exceptional employees at Natalbany was Columbus Crosby, who worked as a "green chain grader." Crosby could not read, and when the Southern Pine Association made changes in the rules for grading lumber, his employer would read the changes to Crosby, who would then memorize the new regulations. Trimming lumber in the sawmill often resulted in waste, but Stamps remembered Si Simmons as a black craftsman who left practically no waste.[29] A study of census reports for Ward 6 of Tangipahoa Parish, location of the Natalbany Lumber Company, indicates a few black workers holding skilled positions with whites controlling most of those jobs. Two black workers worked as sawyers, the top skilled job in the lumber industry. Other skilled or semiskilled black workers included eight edgermen, three graders, three block setters, one checker, one saw filer, six trimmers, one pipe setter, one fireman, and one re-sawyer.[30]

Louis William Golden of Killian, Louisiana, represents an African American who served the industry in a rather unconventional way. Golden, 104 years old when interviewed in 1974, was born in Texas and lived for a time in Wisconsin before moving to Louisiana. As a young man, he first worked in a sawmill and later as a boat pilot for the Salmen Lumber Company of Slidell, Louisiana. His job at Salmen was to pilot the boats pulling logs across the waterways of south Louisiana and into the company's Slidell facilities. According to Golden, the logs tied together would sometimes extend to one-half mile, a situation requiring considerable ability on the part of the pilot.[31] The exploits of Golden and other skilled African American workers do not refute the thesis that blacks were generally restricted to unskilled, low-wage jobs. These examples do indicate, however, that even in this era of extensive racism and inadequate legal remedies for discrimination in the workplace, some black workers broke through the racial barrier and achieved status and skills.

Employment in the lumber industry influenced not only economic and population changes but social attitudes as well, and the 1919 strike against the Great Southern mill in Bogalusa challenged the traditional premise of a persistent, economic rivalry between white and docile, compliant black workers. Labor organizations in this era, particularly the American Federation of Labor, presented a poor record of admitting black workers, with many unions deliberately and systematically excluding them. Consequently, black workers often considered the employer a better friend, and in turn, companies might use these workers as strikebreakers.[32] Rejected by white-dominated unions, the black worker often had little choice but to support the employer, who, after all, did provide jobs and housing. When white workers went on strike at the Natalbany Lumber Company in June 1910, strikers warned African American employees to "keep away" from the mill, while the employer demanded that they either work or vacate company housing.[33] Caught in the cross fire between strikers and employers, the black worker often sided with management, causing labor to denounce him as an undependable ally in strikes.

Nevertheless, black workers, if recruited and included, might support a strike, and one of the more significant efforts to enlist these workers in labor protest occurred in 1919 at the Great Southern Lumber Company. Proclaimed as "the largest sawmill in the world," the operations in Bogalusa employed almost three thousand workers and in 1915 set a world record by cutting more than 1 million feet of lumber in one twenty-four-hour period.[34] The general manager of the company and mayor of Bogalusa, William H. Sullivan, ran an efficient, paternalistic, controlled operation, but in September 1919 workers, unhappy over wages, rent increases for housing, and company domination of their lives, commenced a three-month-long, tumultuous strike.[35] Two American Federation of Labor unions, the International Union of Timber Workers and the Brotherhood of Carpenters and Joiners of America, rapidly enrolled the great majority of workers. African Americans represented at least 50 percent of the work force, and union leaders recognized the necessity of recruiting these employees for the effort.[36] The unions selected Sol Dacus, a black official of the Timber Workers local, to organize African American workers, and his success weakened the company's ability to defeat the strike by exploiting racial differences.[37]

Racial tensions, often a factor in southern labor, worsened in August 1919 with the lynching of a black man accused of assaulting a white Bogalusa housewife. The local newspaper and company booster, the *Enterprise and American,* condemned this assault as "one of the most hideous crimes ever attempted in the history of Washington Parish." Reminding readers of recent race riots in Washington, D.C., and Chicago, the *Enterprise and American* considered the South the safest area for the Negro but also admonished that "it is only those members of the race who desire social equality and other things which he has never had and never will have, who stir up trouble." The paper also accused the militant International Workers of the World (IWW) of attempting to stir up racial prejudice and incite violence.[38] The articles and editorials presented an argument often advanced by antilabor forces in the South: Unions caused violence and wanted to upset the near-sacrosanct practice of racial segregation in the region.

The articles and editorials convinced neither white nor black workers. The Great Southern, however, would not agree to collective bargaining, and in late September, an accident that damaged the engine drive for the main plant provided the company with an excuse to shut down operations and lock out union workers.[39] Bogalusa now experienced a violent, turbulent strike with both racial and economic issues dividing the community.

Racial division would not defeat this strike. White and black workers remained united and steadfast throughout October and early November. Sol Dacus, who may well rank as the most famous African American in the Florida Parishes during this era, soon became the center of a raging controversy. On Friday, November 21, city officials, obviously with company encouragement, issued a warrant for the arrest of Dacus, charging that he was "a dangerous and suspicious character."[40] The next day, two white union members, Porter Bouchillon and S. L. O'Rourke, armed with shotguns, protected Dacus as the three marched defiantly down the main street and toward the office of L. E. Williams, the strike leader. For the first time in American history, white union members had risked their lives by offering protection to an endangered black labor leader.[41] Later that day, a "special police force" arrived at the office and, in a controversial shootout, killed Williams and several other union leaders. This brought terror to union members and ultimately defeated the strike, but both black and white workers had remained unwavering allies in this effort.[42]

The Bogalusa strike confirmed that southern black workers, if included, would support collective bargaining and organized labor. Although a failed effort, the strike reflected a maturing of social attitudes among both black and white workers while demonstrating the necessity for unity and biracial cooperation in battling for better working conditions. *Crisis,* the publication of the National Association for the Advancement of Colored People, reprinted an editorial from the *New York Age* that suggested that the Bogalusa strike represented a breakthrough in labor relations: "It gives promise that the day will come when the white workingmen of the South will see and understand that their interests and the interests of the black workingman of the South are identical."[43] That day would arrive much later, but black and white workers in Bogalusa offered an early preview of that promise.

African Americans in the Florida Parishes served as an essential source of labor for the lumber industry, which in turn sustained black workers. This industry not only served as a vital source of revenue for the region but also influenced social change by offering workers an opportunity to abandon a rural, agricultural economy and gain entry into an industrial society. The work, although demanding and low-paying, represented the only opportunity for these workers to participate in the "new economy" of this era. And despite suffering from limited educational opportunities and usually restricted to low-paying, dead-end jobs, some African Americans did break through racial barriers by acquiring status and skills. Additionally, the Florida Parishes gained significantly as young men seeking employment would not have to migrate to the industrial centers of the North, and wealth created by this industry could be utilized to build the economy of the region. Perhaps most significant, experiences in an industrial setting influenced racial attitudes, a social milestone demonstrated by the Bogalusa strike and the uncommon display of solidarity among southern black and white workers rejecting the traditional creed of economic rivalry and separateness. Without question, African Americans served as a crucial pillar for the industry and this industry significantly affected the livelihood, location, and social attitudes of these workers as well as the overall progress and prosperity of the Florida Parishes.

NOTES

1. *Bogalusa (La.) Enterprise and American*, September 4, 1919.

2. Louisiana Department of Conservation, *The Why and the How of Forestry in Louisiana*, Bulletin no. 7 (1921), map insert; Nollie Wade Hickman, "The Yellow Pine Industries in St. Tammany, Tangipahoa, and Washington Parishes, 1840–1915," *Louisiana Studies* 5 (summer 1966): 75–88.

3. Louisiana Department of Conservation, *The Why and the How of Forestry in Louisiana*, map insert; Hickman, "Yellow Pine Industries," 75–88; U.S. Bureau of Labor Statistics, *Wages and Hours of Labor in Lumber Manufacturing, Mill Work, and Furniture Manufacturing, 1890–1912*, Bulletin no. 129 (Washington, D.C., 1913), 14; Jack Cook Wimberly, "Labor and Collective Bargaining in the Louisiana Lumber Industry" (M.A. thesis, Louisiana State University, 1960), 2; Rachael Edna Norgress, "The History of the Cypress Lumber Industry in Louisiana," *Louisiana History* 30 (July 1947): 1045.

4. Louisiana, Department of Commissioner of Labor and Industrial Statistics of the State of Louisiana, *Ninth Biennial Report, 1916–1918* (Baton Rouge: Department of Commissioner of Labor and Industrial Statistics of the State of Louisiana, n.d.), 124–34; *Kentwood (La.) Commercial*, March 9, 1906; "Two of Louisiana's Finest Lumber Mills Located Here," *Ponchatoula (La.) Enterprise*, March 11, 1921.

5. La. Department of Commissioner of Labor, *Ninth Biennial Report*, 124–34.

6. Nollie Wade Hickman, "History of Forest Industries in the Longleaf Pine Belt of East Louisiana and Mississippi, 1840–1915" (Ph.D. diss., University of Texas, 1950), 397–98; Lorenzo J. Greene and Carter G. Woodson, *The Negro Wage Earner* (1930; reprint New York: AMS Press, 1970), 124–28; Sterling Spero and Abram L. Harris, *The Black Worker: The Negro and the Labor Movement* (New York: Columbia University Press, 1931), 331; John Reed Tarver, "The Clan of Toil: Piney Woods Labor Relations in the Trans-Mississippi South, 1880–1920" (Ph.D. diss., Louisiana State University, 1991), 110; F. Ray Marshall, *Labor in the South* (Cambridge: Harvard University Press, 1967), 9–11.

7. George Bloomington to U.S. District Attorney, November 4, 1913, in Federal Bureau of Investigation Files, file number 7282, National Archives, Washington, D.C.

8. *Bogalusa Enterprise and American*, January 11, 1917.

9. J. D. B. De Bow, *Statistical View of the United States*, vol. 5, *Demographic Monographs* (1854; reprint New York: Gordon and Breach, 1970), 248.

10. Bureau of the Census, *Thirteenth Census of the United States, 1910, Abstract of the Census, Supplement for Louisiana* (Washington, D.C., 1913), 588–641; Bureau of the Census, *Historical Statistics of the United States: Colonial Times to 1970*, pt. 1 (Washington, D.C., 1975), 28.

11. Bureau of the Census, *Fourteenth Census of the United States, State Compendium, Louisiana* (Washington, D.C., 1924), 34.

12. Department of Agriculture and Immigration, *Louisiana, 1927–1928* (Baton Rouge: Department of Agriculture and Immigration, n.d.), 115–17, 153; *Fourteenth Census, State Compendium, Louisiana*, 25–30, see p. 17, table 1.

13. *Thirteenth Census, Supplement for Louisiana*, 598, and *Fourteenth Census, State Compendium, Louisiana*, 30.

14. Bureau of the Census, *Thirteenth Census of the United States, 1910, Washington Parish, Louisiana, Fourth Ward*. For the purpose of specificity, these statistics are based on citizens designated as "black" and do not include those classified as "mulatto."

15. Louisiana, Department of Commissioner of Labor and Industrial Statistics, *Ninth Biennial Report*.

16. Ibid., 124–34. See p. 8, table 2.

17. For a brief analysis of labor in the southern economy, see C. Vann Woodward, *Origins of the New South, 1877–1913* (Baton Rouge: Louisiana State University Press, 1971), 291–320; see also Edward L. Ayers, *The Promise of the New South: Life after Reconstruction* (New York: Oxford University Press, 1992), 104–31.

18. Louisiana, Department of Commissioner of Labor and Industrial Statistics, *Ninth Biennial Report*, 15–18.

19. *New Orleans Times-Picayune*, May 12, 1923.

20. Amos Kent, interview by Joy J. Jackson, August 1974, tape 8005, Oral History Collection, Southeastern Louisiana University Archives and Special Collections, Hammond (hereinafter cited as SLU).

21. Hickman, "History of Forest Industries," 398–400.

22. Ibid., 402.

23. Ibid., 403.

24. *New Orleans Times-Democrat*, July 24, 1908.

25. Hickman, "History of Forest Industries," 397–98; Greene and Woodson, *The Negro Wage Earner*, 124–28; Spero and Harris, *The Black Worker*, 331; Tarver, "The Clan of Toil," 110; Marshall, *Labor in the South*, 9–11; U.S. Bureau of Labor Statistics, *Wages and Hours of Labor*, Bulletin no. 129, 16–21.

26. Auditor's report for year ending December 31, 1922, Apollonia Lumber Company, Pearl River Valley Lumber Company, and the Marietta Lumber Company, Hans Schneider Collection, box 1, folder 9, SLU; "Two of Louisiana's Finest Lumber Mills," *Ponchatoula Enterprise*, March 11, 1921; *Bogalusa Enterprise and American*, June 5, 1919.

27. Auditor's report, Schneider Collection, SLU.

28. Ervin Mancil, "An Historical Geography of Industrial Cypress Lumbering in Louisiana" (Ph.D. diss., Louisiana State University, 1972), 209–18; Tarver, "The Clan of Toil," 622.

29. Recollections of J. O. Stamps, April 23, 1969, New Orleans, in Schneider Collection, box 2, folder 1, SLU.

30. Bureau of the Census, *Thirteenth Census of the United States, 1910, Ward 6, Tangipahoa Parish, Louisiana*.

31. Louis William Golden, interview by Joy J. Jackson, tape recording, February 15, 1974, at his home in Killian, La., tape 0003, Oral History Collection, SLU.

32. F. Ray Marshall, "The Negro in Southern Unions," in *The Negro and the American Labor Movement*, ed. Julius Jacobson (Garden City, N.Y.: Doubleday, 1968), 128–54; Melvyn Dubofsky, *We Shall Be All: A History of the Industrial Workers of the World* (Chicago: Quadrangle Books, 1969), 213–19.

33. *New Orleans Times-Picayune*, June 9, 1910.

34. *Bogalusa Enterprise and American,* December 9, 1915.

35. Billy H. Wyche, "Paternalism, Patriotism, and Protest in 'The Already Best City in the Land': Bogalusa, Louisiana, 1906–1919," *Louisiana History* 40 (winter 1999): 63–84.

36. Ibid.

37. Labor's version of strike in *United Paper,* January 30, 1958; Marshall, *Labor in the South,* 99.

38. *Bogalusa Enterprise and American,* September 4, August 14, August 7, 1919.

39. Ibid., September 25, 1919; Vernon H. Jensen, *Lumber and Labor* (New York: Farrar and Rinehart, 1945), 92.

40. Testimony of T. Abner Magee, *Williams v. Great Southern Lumber Company, et al.,* No. 16,377, U.S. District Court, Eastern District of Louisiana, New Orleans, April 20–May 5, 1925, typewritten transcript, p. 430.

41. Philip S. Foner, *First Facts of American Labor* (New York: Holmes & Meier, 1984), 110.

42. Wyche, "Paternalism, Patriotism, and Protest," 80–82.

43. "On Bogalusa," *Crisis* 19 (February 1920): 208.

9

WASHINGTON PARISH AND ITS BLACK COMMUNITY
Horace Mann Bond's Study of 1934–1935

ADAM FAIRCLOUGH

> When I asked a Louisiana librarian for a history of Washington Parish, he shook his head with scarcely concealed contempt for my ignorance. "Nothing has ever happened in Washington Parish. Natchitoches? St. Martinville? The Teche Country? Opelousas? There's plenty of history I can give you about those places. But *nothing* ever happened in Washington Parish!"
> —HORACE MANN BOND, "Forty Acres and a Mule," 1935

Washington Parish is one of the least-known parts of a neglected region of Louisiana. It lacks Creole flavor or Cajun spice. Even though it was settled well before the Civil War, it cannot boast the picturesque antebellum mansions that have long attracted tourists to the Felicianas. Bordered on two sides by Mississippi, it seems one of the least Louisianian of the state's sixty-four parishes. Today, moreover, Washington Parish is an economic backwater. Its principal industry, papermaking, employs only a fraction of its former work force, and the loss of jobs has not been offset by inward migration. Whereas the growth of Baton Rouge and the settlement of the northern lakeshore by former New Orleanians have expanded the population of East Baton Rouge, Livingston, St. Tammany, and Tangipahoa Parishes, Washington Parish has not participated in the suburban boom. Indeed, it is one of the few parishes to have experienced population decline over the past forty years. It receives few migrants and not many visitors.[1]

Yet Washington Parish is hardly a place without a history. Indeed, on at least three occasions local events there came to the attention of the nation. The first event was the Bogalusa strike of 1919, when the Great Southern Lumber Company used brute force to crush the paper mill workers' union, a clash that left the union's president and two other union men dead. The second was the lynching in 1935 of Jerome Wilson, a young black man. The third occasion when Washington Parish impinged upon the national consciousness was in 1965, when the civil rights movement in Bogalusa led to a violent standoff between the Deacons for Defense, an armed black organization, and the Ku Klux Klan. The situation became so explosive that the federal government intervened to curb the activities of the Klan.[2]

Given the character of these incidents, one might be forgiven for concluding that Washington Parish has been a lawless and violent place where blacks and whites have lived in a state of permanent tension. But civil rights–era stereotypes of a racially polarized South can be misleading. In 1934, when a young black historian and his wife settled into a cabin a few miles from Franklinton, the parish seat, it was the *absence* of racial tension that impressed them. Horace Mann Bond discovered that personal relations between whites and blacks varied tremendously from place to place, and that to generalize about Washington Parish, small as it was, was as dangerous as generalizing about the vast South. In the Star Creek area, for example, easy familiarity between black and white seemed to be the rule.

> To me it came as a shock to hear a Negro call a white man . . . by his first name, to observe white families visiting Negro families and "taking coffee" with them, to see a white man sit down to dinner at "hog killing time," while across the table sat a Negro man who was, genuinely, his friend; and who, quite as genuinely, was also eating with no consciousness of the violation of a taboo almost as fundamental as those involved in sex mores.

Here, where black farmers were numerous and formed distinct communities, race relations differed markedly from those in the "whiter" sections of the parish, and were different again from race relations in Bogalusa, a company town that drew migrants from Mississippi as well as immigrants from Europe.[3]

During their three-month stay in Washington Parish, Bond and his wife observed the daily interactions between blacks and whites, delved into the family histories of their black neighbor, and took copious notes. Bond became so fascinated by the material they accumulated that he tried turning it into a book. In "Forty Acres and a Mule," begun in 1935, he attempted to trace the history of a rural black community from slavery to the present. The narrative pivoted upon a single family, the Wilsons—the family of lynching victim Jerome Wilson. But Bond never finished the book: Taking up the post of dean at Dillard University, administration crowded out research and writing. Nevertheless, Bond's extensive research notes, as well as his unfinished book manuscript, constitute an invaluable source of information on Washington Parish.

How and why did Horace Mann Bond come to write this material? Bond and his wife, Julia Washington Bond, went to Washington Parish at the behest of the Julius Rosenwald Fund. This Chicago-based philanthropic foundation had helped to finance the construction of five thousand black schools across the South. With its building program complete, in 1934 it initiated a study called the Rural School Exploration Project. The Rosenwald Fund wanted to find out what was going on *inside* the schools it had sponsored, concerned that it been so focused on the erection of decent buildings that it had scarcely considered the extent to which impressive-looking structures might hide ill-equipped classrooms, poorly trained teachers, and undernourished pupils.

With a view to evaluating black rural schools and improving them, the Rosenwald Fund selected about a dozen southern communities, including Washington Parish, for close study. The "Explorers" were expected both to participate in community life and to act as observers. Reflecting the growing sophistication of the social sciences, and in line with its interest in the wider context of race relations, the Rosenwald Fund told the Explorers to investigate family life, economic conditions, political structures, class relationships, religious culture, voluntary activities, interracial contacts, and folklore. The Explorers were expected to take detailed notes and to write them up in the form of a diary. Confusion of purpose, however, dogged this effort. Although the Rural School Exploration Project amassed a wealth of data, the information it gathered yielded few practical results.[4]

Bond's approach to his assignment to Star Creek, in Washington Parish, may have reflected that confusion of purpose. In any case, it is clear that he soon developed a research agenda of his own. Although he had a deep interest in black education—his first book, *The Education of the Negro in the American Social Order* (1934), made him a nationally recognized authority on the subject—Bond found his remit both vague and limiting. He wanted to produce research that was solid and publishable. At first, encouraged by Robert E. Park, the eminent University of Chicago sociologist who was a mentor to him, Bond entertained the idea of turning his Star Creek diary into a book of social anthropology along the lines of *Deep South*, a study of Natchez, Mississippi, then being undertaken by black sociologist Allison Davis. Yet Bond, while at home in the social sciences, was at heart a historian, and he gradually became aware of the narrative possibilities presented by a dramatic incident that had taken place on his very doorstep.

Upon arriving in Star Creek, Bond learned of a shooting affray that occurred on a farm owned by John Wilson, a respected black landowner, on July 21. The incident, sparked by an apparently trivial dispute over the dipping of a mule against Texas fever tick, left two people dead: sheriff's deputy Delos Wood and John Wilson's thirty-five-year-old son, Moise. Three other Wilson children, two sons and a daughter, suffered wounds. The entire family had then been jailed. Soon afterward, in a trial at the courthouse in Franklinton, one of the Wilson sons, Jerome, was convicted of murder and sentenced to death. Because of the confused circumstances of the shootout—it was not clear who started the shooting, nor was it certain who fired the shot that killed Deputy Sheriff Wood—the New Orleans branch of the National Association for the Advancement of Colored People (NAACP) retained a white attorney, G. Wray Gill, to appeal the verdict. Gill argued that whites in Washington Parish had been so inflamed over the slaying of the deputy sheriff that the trial had been held with undue haste in order to avert mob violence; this gave the defense inadequate time to prepare its case and rendered a fair trial impossible. The case was still on appeal, and Jerome Wilson languished in the Franklinton jail alongside his brother Luther, when Bond and his wife arrived in Washington Parish.[5]

Bond soon encountered members of the extended Wilson family. He became intrigued by the story of the shooting affray and fascinated by the black farmers in the Franklinton area. Here, in contrast to common stereotypes of dirt-poor sharecroppers and loose, mother-centered families, black farmers comprised stable communities of landowners and patriarchal families. As a devotee of social history, Bond could not help but be impressed by the resilience and strength of these families, most of which descended from a small number of slaves and were in some way related to each other. How these families succeeded in acquiring land piqued his curiosity. He was also struck by the fact that so many black and white families shared the same surnames—Graves, Bickham, Burris, Crane, and Magee—and surmised that extensive miscegenation, not merely sentiment, explained this coincidence. While attending to his Rosenwald Fund duties, therefore, Bond researched the history of Washington Parish and, more important, interviewed his neighbors in order to reconstruct the family histories that, to a large extent, constituted the history of the black community itself. Before long, Bond and his wife had compiled detailed genealogies for half a dozen black families, as well as rougher sketches for a dozen more.

It was only in January 1935, however, while spending the Christmas season elsewhere, that Bond hit upon something that might enable him to convert this raw data into a book. That something was the murder of Jerome Wilson in the Franklinton jail on the night of January 11. Entering the jail unopposed, half a dozen men bludgeoned Jerome Wilson with a hammer, dragged his body outside, placed it on a truck, and then dumped it in a ditch outside town. Three days earlier, the Louisiana Supreme Court had upheld Jerome Wilson's appeal and ordered a new trial, which was scheduled to begin the day Wilson was murdered.

Had it happened two decades earlier, the murder of Jerome Wilson would have aroused little interest or indignation beyond the local black community. By the 1930s, however, lynching was becoming discredited and had declined in frequency. The antilynching propaganda of the NAACP had forced white southerners onto the defensive. Moreover, the Communist Party's spirited defense of the Scottsboro boys—nine black youths who were convicted of rape and sentenced to death on the basis of false testimony—demonstrated that even when blacks escaped the mob they could expect scant justice in southern courtrooms. The state supreme court's reversal of Jerome Wilson's conviction, and the furtive nature of Wilson's murder, illustrated the contradiction between a growing recognition that accused blacks should receive formal "due process" and a lingering attachment to lynch law.

Lynching had declined, in part, because an increasing number of law enforcement officials decided to face down lynch mobs. Indeed, the Association of Southern Women for the Prevention of Lynching, founded in 1930, campaigned to secure written "pledges" from southern sheriffs that they would protect blacks in their custody. In Washington Parish, however, Sheriff J. L. Brock made light of Jerome Wilson's killing—even though the victim had been inside his jail. "There wasn't any lynching," he told reporters. "There wasn't any mob either. They were just about six or eight men who were going about their business." Senator Huey Long, speaking to the NAACP's Roy Wilkins, was also unrepentant. "This nigger got hold of a smart lawyer somewhere and proved a technicality. He was guilty as hell."[6]

The killing of Jerome Wilson so unnerved Horace Mann Bond that he and his wife decided against returning to Star Creek, cutting short what should have been an eight-month project. Nevertheless Bond, now ensconced at Dillard University, a safe eighty-five miles away in New Orleans, was reluctant to abandon his Washington Parish research. "I . . . hope to be able to link this happening with the material I had already obtained," he told a colleague. "We had just gotten to the point where daily observation and recording of life in the community was lending insight into events and details which at first had been meaningless or without any social significance."[7]

Bond's personal involvement with the Wilson family spurred him to shape his Washington Parish material into a coherent historical narrative. In March 1935 Bond spent the better part of two weeks interviewing John Wilson—who, having lost two sons, had now been forced to sell his land. The encounter left him brimming with excitement. "I got . . . his unvarnished story of his life, the families in his community, and of the lynching," he informed Robert Park. "He is an exceptionally intelligent man, and talks with great power—if I could only transcribe exactly what he says, it would be a rare piece of literature." His interviews with Wilson enabled Bond to fill out the genealogies he began at Star Creek, and he realized that he had captured something rich and possibly unique. "The life histories of each member of these families is enough to make even [sociologist E. Franklin] Frazier turn green with envy." Putting aside his Ph.D. dissertation (a study of Negro education in Alabama), Bond set about writing a book. Using the history of John Wilson's family as a narrative core, Bond proposed to trace "the development of the idea of 'Forty Acres and a Mule,' the gradual acquisition of land by the Negroes, the effect of urbanization on members of the family who moved to the cities, and the tragic denouement furnished by the lynching in January."[8]

If he entertained fleeting visions of writing a best-seller, Bond started the book from unselfish motives. If the Wilson family was forced to move north, he feared, the pressures and unfamiliarity of big-city life would destroy it. He tried to enlist the help of the NAACP, the Rosenwald Fund, and various individuals in finding the Wilsons a farm elsewhere in the South. Royalties from "Forty Acres and a Mule," he hoped, would help facilitate that plan. Bond's good intentions came to nothing, however, for at some point he abandoned the book and lost touch with the Wilsons.[9]

For sixty years the unfinished manuscript remained unknown and unread. Finally rescued from obscurity, "Forty Acres and a Mule" was published in 1997, along with some of Bond's other writings on Washington

Parish, under the title *The Star Creek Papers*. "Forty Acres and a Mule" arguably represents the most valuable source of evidence for the period between the Civil War and the Second World War. Together with Bond's research notes, now readily available on microfilm, it constitutes an important contribution to the study of the black family. Indeed, it provides something that in 1935 may have been unique and which is still rare: detailed evidence of miscegenation between white and black families.[10]

John Wilson, born in 1880 to former slaves of Hezekiah Magee, was blessed with a sharp mind and a keen memory. In his interviews with Bond, he recounted family folklore about slavery and about the Yankee cavalry raid of 1864. His information assumes greater importance as historical evidence, however, when he called upon his own memories. For example, Wilson provided a firsthand account of a major outbreak, the Balltown riot of 1901. Now almost forgotten, the Balltown riot created a sensation at the time. The violence erupted shortly after hundreds of whites witnessed the burning alive of Bill Morris, an African American, in the hamlet of Balltown. Morris was accused of assaulting and attempting to murder Mrs. John Ball, whose husband operated a grocery store. "The Balls got their water from a spring," Wilson recalled, "real nice place fixed in cistern form. They say the boy caught the old lady at the spring and knocked her in the head to get some money. He thought he had killed her but she lived long enough to tell who did it."

The ensuing riot seems to have been caused by white fear of black retaliation. When blacks held a camp meeting near Balltown at Live Oak Church, alarmed whites, worried that this yearly religious gathering might be used to plot revenge for Bill Morris's lynching, decided to attend. "White folks and colored folks were there from all sections of the country," Wilson told Bond. "The people came there in wagons, buggies, walking, and on horses." The presence of whites at such meetings was not all that unusual, but on this occasion mutual fear and hair-trigger tempers produced a deadly confrontation. "Some drunken white and colored boys got in a 'spute along the road," Wilson recalled. "The white and the colored boys started to fighting." The resulting gunfight claimed over a dozen lives. A black preacher named Conerly was killed coming out of a church—wielding a shotgun, according to white reports—and three black women perished when whites set fire to a house. News of the battle traveled like electricity: A sheriff arrived from Mississippi with a posse of whites; the sheriff of Washington Parish telegraphed Governor William Heard to send troops.

Blacks suffered the bulk of the casualties, and scores sought refuge with white families or fled the area altogether. Yet a black folk memory arose that portrayed the riot in rather different terms. Wilson told Bond that "more white people were killed than colored, but they did not make it known." According to Wilson, "Old Man Crea Lott killed about six [whites]" and claimed that he would have killed more had his wife not hidden his ammunition. "When he couldn't find no more ammunition, he just walked [out] of the house and said, 'Well, boys, here I am.' They just riddled him to pieces." Wilson's memories raise some interesting questions. Did whites really suppress the extent of their casualties, or was Wilson's claim a post-riot myth of the kind that flourished after the Watts riot of 1965, when many blacks, in spite of figures to the contrary, insisted that more whites than blacks had lost their lives?[11]

The Louisiana constitution of 1898 had disfranchised most black voters, and the Balltown riot can be seen as a bloody coda to the political conflicts of the Reconstruction era. But political memories were long. Wilson recalled how a group of black Republicans, including his father-in-law, Wade Hampton Magee, had controlled the post office at Franklinton long after Reconstruction, a remnant of black political influence deeply resented by local whites. Although Louisiana boasted a mere eight hundred black voters in 1935, some whites still harbored suspicion of John Wilson because he and his family had been prominent Republicans.[12]

Wilson's detailed description of farming, and his explanation of the precarious economics of raising cotton, supplies a season-by-season account of a black farmer's typical year, including his commercial dealings with white sellers, buyers, and creditors. Wilson provides insight, too, into the process whereby black farmers acquired—and sometimes lost—land. According to Wilson, the Great Northern Lumber Company and the syndicates that preceded it sometimes cheated black homesteaders out of land. "They would come to you and you sign a contract with them to [sell] 40 acres of timber.... [But] when they cut the timber they cut the timber off of two 40 acres." Illiteracy, explained Wilson, meant that many of these gullible farmers did not understand the contracts they were signing.

Still, the relative ease of homesteading public lands, and the willingness of many former slaveholders to sell land, enabled a high proportion of Washington Parish's black farmers to become owners. Bond estimated that

325 of the 769 black farm families, 45 percent, owned their own homes, "a percentage unusually high in rural southern counties and almost unique when the high percentage of Negroes in the population is concerned."[13]

This statistic supplied one of the principal themes of "Forty Acres and a Mule." Bond was convinced that miscegenation helped to explain the exceptionally high rate of black landowning in Washington Parish. Former slaveholders sold and sometimes gave land to their mulatto children and often assisted them in other ways. Of course, there were plenty of half-white children in the South who received no such favors—Booker T. Washington, the most famous mulatto of his time, never discovered who his white father was and never received any help from him. Many slaveholders shunned their mulatto progeny. Yet paternal benevolence was sufficiently common to provide mulattos with a distinct advantage over other blacks, and after Emancipation they became the backbone of the emerging black upper class of teachers, ministers, professionals, federal employees, and landowners. Better educated than the black majority, mulattos were more likely to form long-lasting marriages and build stable families. Sociologist E. Franklin Frazier dubbed the most successful members of this group "Black Puritans"—families that practiced a Victorian moral code of sobriety, thrift, and self-improvement, values that reinforced their cohesion and intergenerational stability. Bond himself, whose grandfather was white, and whose mulatto father had bequeathed him a passion for learning, came from a quintessentially "Black Puritan" family.[14]

Miscegenation, of course, was the South's worst-kept secret. A blatant contradiction of the slavemasters' professions of paternalism and racial purity, it had been a staple of abolitionist propaganda. Yet in the 1930s white southerners were engaging in collective amnesia—or, as we might put it today, denial—about the extent of miscegenation. Shame, embarrassment, and racism all contributed to that denial, as did fear of being categorized as "colored" when so many light-complexioned blacks "passed" into the white population every year. Blacks, too, although aware of their white ancestry, were often reluctant to talk about it. Bond sometimes found his research into family history stymied when people clammed up, telling him, "I am *not* going to tell anyone about all of those white folks mixed up in my background." From his interviews with John Wilson, however, Bond was able to trace, in some detail, the history of miscegenation in the Franklinton area of Washington Parish, a history that began with slavery but continued for several decades after slavery's demise.[15]

According to the genealogies drawn up by Bond, many of the leading white citizens of Washington Parish had fathered mulatto children. Slaveholder John Magee, an early settler, fathered Wade Hampton Magee, John Wilson's father-in-law, by a slave named Keziah. Two of John Magee's sons, Jacob and Fleet, between them fathered nine mulatto children by seven women. Fleet Magee's mulatto children were all born after the Civil War. Former slaveholder and clerk of court William Burris fathered two mulatto sons, both born during Reconstruction, by the mulatto daughter of slaveholder Nathaniel Graves. William Burris's brother, James, who operated a merchant's store in Franklinton and who served as mayor, parish judge, and superintendent of education, sired a mulatto child by Lucy Ellis, a slave who also bore a son by a prominent white doctor. Bond identified numerous other mulattos and their parents, but there is no need to extend the list here for the point to be made. To be sure, Bond's genealogies contained errors. Yet insofar as they can be verified by looking at census records from 1870 to 1920, his identification of mulatto children and their white fathers was remarkably accurate.[16]

What can we learn from this? It is impossible to discover if miscegenation in Washington Parish was unusually common. The records that might enable us to compare rates of miscegenation from one county to another simply do not exist. Rather than being exceptional, however, as Bond believed, Washington Parish may have been a microcosm of the South.

Louisiana was well-known for having a large number of very light-skinned mulattos, a fact often attributed to the fact that French and Spanish Catholics had viewed miscegenation in a permissive light. Before the Civil War, the free colored Creoles (especially those who lived along the Cane River in Natchitoches Parish and the much larger group that resided in New Orleans) had acquired education, accumulated property—including slaves—and formed distinct societies. Indeed, Bond and his mentor, sociologist Robert Park, were keenly interested in the tightly knit mulatto communities that had persisted into the twentieth century, forming "racial islands" scattered along the Gulf Coast.

Yet miscegenation may well have been just as common in areas of the South that had been settled by Anglo-Saxon Protestants. No doubt it was more flagrant in some areas than others. In Alabama, for example, certain counties were recognized for having a large percentage of mulattos, as well as the kind of open acknowledgment of black-white kinship that Bond witnessed in Washington Parish. Black teacher Jacob L. Reddix recalled moving from the Mississippi Gulf Coast to Wilcox County, Alabama, in 1907: "I was amazed to see so many light-skinned colored people in the rural community. . . . I will never forget seeing a planter ride his horse to the school, dismount, and enter the principal's office to pay the year's expenses of a very light-skinned girl, who was said to be his daughter." Bond attributed racial miscegenation to frontier conditions and believed that in areas like Washington Parish it had been "an accepted pattern of life."[17]

It is hard to estimate the social significance of the tangled bloodlines that Bond documented in Washington Parish. Like Frazier, he argued that blood relationships between black and white families were sometimes tacitly acknowledged and that they helped to humanize an unjust racial system, or at least to mitigate its inhumanity. The fact that black families adopted the family names of their former owners lent support to his argument, as did the persistence of occasional examples of concubinage into the twentieth century. By the 1930s, open concubinage had died out. Yet, Bond noted, "there were still living in the community old [white] patriarchs who directed the destinies of both white and black children and grandchildren whom they had brought into being."[18]

Perhaps Bond exaggerated the extent of affective kinship between blacks and whites. How far were the facts of miscegenation shared knowledge between the races? John Wilson knew full well which women had given birth to mulattos by which white fathers. There is a lack of evidence, however, as to whether such information was common knowledge in the white community. Shared ancestry is devoid of social significance, a pure abstraction, if it remains unknown. For example, Jerome Wilson, lynched in 1935, was a distant cousin of Delos Wood, the deputy sheriff whom he allegedly shot dead: They shared two great-great-grandparents, slaveholding Magees. It seems fanciful to suppose, however, that either man knew of the relationship, let alone felt a sense of kinship with the other.

Had "Forty Acres and a Mule" been published in the 1930s, its frank description of miscegenation would have made it highly controversial. It might even have made Bond *persona non grata* in Louisiana. As William Ivy Hair has written, the flagrancy of interracial sex in the Pelican State "made questions about ancestry even more explosive than in other southern states." Dr. Carl Weiss, it should be remembered, was so incensed by the suggestion that his father-in-law had Negro blood that he killed the man who was peddling the rumor, one Huey Pierce Long.[19]

Yet folk memory insists that some whites continued to openly acknowledge their black kin. Moreover, in the mere fact of documenting black-white kinship ties—insofar as such things could be documented—Bond performed a valuable service. By "naming names," as it were, he gave miscegenation a human face. In the post–civil rights era, when racial intermarriage is increasingly common, even in the South, there are signs that whites, as well as blacks, are ready to recognize that the two races are biologically as well as historically intertwined, and that the whole notion of fixed races is untenable.[20]

Bond was well aware that the South is not, and never has been, a monolith, and in writing about Washington Parish he took great care to emphasize the distinctiveness of this corner of Louisiana. Yet the central theme of "Forty Acres and a Mule," the history of the Wilson family, can be seen as a metaphor for the entire South. Former slaves Isom Wilson and Mandy Daniels had a long and successful marriage, acquired land, and raised eleven children into adulthood. The daughters married landowners, and the sons, too, became independent farmers. "The entire family," Bond believed, "is a good example of what a Negro owner family can become—unsophisticated, of course, but honest, industrious, ambitious people."[21]

In tracing the history of the Wilsons, Bond was pioneering a new form of scholarly inquiry. Until relatively recently, the black family was a subject of near universal neglect. As Bond complained in 1953, "In all of the state and county libraries and court house record rooms that I have worked in—from Massachusetts to Alabama—I have never in all my born days seen a Negro looking up his family history, while I have seen thousands of white people doing that." Now the situation is quite different, as a visit to the microfilm reading room at the National Archives in Washington, D.C., on any Saturday will attest. The civil rights movement and *Roots,* the book and television series, stimulated new interest in black family history, and the Internet revolution, combined with rising levels of prosperity and education, have made genealogical research something of a popular pastime, one that transcends former boundaries of race.[22]

Yet in 1953 Bond's lament that only whites researched their family histories was largely true. For many African Americans, still suffering disproportionately from poverty and illiteracy, research into genealogy was an unaffordable luxury and a practical impossibility. In the Jim Crow South, moreover, state archives and county record offices did not welcome blacks, and county courthouses were intimidating places. Access, however, was only part of the problem: In many cases records simply did not exist, or did not exist in a useful form. The U.S. Census, for example, listed slaves by age and sex and also tried to identify mulattos; but there are no names, and family groups are hard to discern. Legal documents, found in abundance in courthouses across the South, help to remedy these omissions, and Gwendolyn Midlo Hall, who has rescued such documents from moldering neglect, has compiled a database of Louisiana slavery that opens rich possibilities for genealogical research. Yet the ravages of flame and flood can frustrate even the most diligent researcher. Fire destroyed most of the 1890 U.S. Census. The Washington Parish courthouse burned down in 1897, destroying virtually all legal records pertaining to slavery. As Bond once admitted, "Genealogy, at best, is a difficult subject for Negroes . . . [and] the difficulties of tracing families are in some cases beyond solution."[23]

For historians and other scholars, the black family scarcely existed as a topic of serious investigation. Few whites wrote about the black experience; most of those who did regarded the family life of African Americans as an object lesson in degradation and immorality. Philip A. Bruce's *Plantation Negro as a Freeman,* published in 1889, expressed the commonly held view that life among blacks was a riot of unrestrained sexuality: "Lasciviousness has done more than all the other vices of the plantation negro united, to degrade the character of their social life since they were invested with citizenship." Fifteen years later, Virginia-born novelist Thomas Nelson Page agreed that "the great body of the [Negro] race has scarcely any knowledge of the foundation principles of pure family life." Images of unbridled sexuality colored and even dominated white images of African Americans well into the twentieth century. Writing in 1935, Mississippi planter and author David Cohn believed that "life is a long moral holiday" for the Negro, whose sexual desire "is to be satisfied when and wherever it arises."[24]

Even the more scholarly writings of sociologists dwelt upon the allegedly libidinous immorality of black families. Willis D. Weatherford, a YMCA official who authored a widely used college textbook on race relations, wrote that "a terrible moral corruption . . . eats at the vitals of the negro race," citing an anonymous black physician who told him that at least 98 percent of Negro men were "socially impure." Arthur W. Calhoun, who wrote the first scholarly history of the American family, believed that "unbridled sexuality" was one of the "prevalent characteristics" of the Negro.[25]

Paradoxically, black scholars also lamented sexual laxity in black families. Stressing the barbarity and crippling legacy of slavery, they argued that bondage had stripped blacks of their African culture, subjected slave women to sexual exploitation, robbed black men of their patriarchal status, spawned a host of bastard mulattos, and rendered normal family life impossible. "Sexual immorality is probably the greatest plague spot among Negro Americans," wrote W. E. B. Du Bois in 1908, "and the greatest cause is slavery." Thirty years later, in a book that became the single most influential study of the subject, sociologist E. Franklin Frazier restated these themes, presenting the history of black families as one of repeated disruptions and dislocations, leading to a dominant family type that was looser, less stable, and more matriarchal than the typical white family. Despite the grimness of his interpretation, Frazier's work represented state-of-the-art sociology in the 1930s, and his ideas held sway well into the 1960s. Frazier exerted a strong influence on Horace Mann Bond, as is particularly evident in the emphasis that "Forty Acres and a Mule" places upon miscegenation, family instability, and the destructive effects of northward migration.[26]

A contending influence, however, informed Bond's treatment of the Wilson family, that of Booker T. Washington. Although sometimes accused of perpetuating demeaning stereotypes of black people, Washington actually depicted the black family in a more positive light than Du Bois, his militant critic. "In studying the negro as a race," Washington argued, "especially as you find him in his normal, regular life in the rural districts of the South, you will find that the negro, for the most part, is not a degraded human being. He may be an ignorant human being so far as books are concerned; but there is a great difference between degradation and pure simple ignorance." Washington cited the caring nature of the extended Negro family, pointing out that the sick, the aged, and the orphaned always found homes. "The negro, in some way, has inherited and has had trained into him the idea that he must take care of his own dependents, and he does it to a greater degree than is true, perhaps, of any other race in the same relative stage of civilization."[27]

Bond's description of the Wilsons as sturdy, upright, and hardworking people owed much to Washington's idealization of the black peasant as a yeoman farmer. "It is principally because I have such a deep respect for the latter class—the Negro folk—that I can think so highly of Booker T. Washington," Bond admitted. "He spoke their language, and they agreed that he was a great man." Bond's friendship with Robert Park, who had worked closely with Washington as a researcher and ghostwriter, reinforced his belief in the simple decency of rural black southerners. That decency Bond found in abundance in the black families he encountered at Star Creek. They were "honest, self-respecting, [and] hard-working, . . . my idea of what human beings ought to be." Washington, and Bond, anticipated modern scholarship. Many historians now contend that black families emerged from slavery with far more strength and cohesion than Frazier and others had believed. And a recent study by Stewart Tolnay, focusing on rural blacks between 1910 and 1940, argues that Frazier's characterization of southern black families as matriarchal, with high degrees of instability and high rates of illegitimacy, was considerably overstated. Families such as the Wilsons were by no means rare.[28]

One of the keys to both family stability and economic success was the ownership of land. Implicit in Bond's treatment of the Wilson family was his belief that the failure of the federal government to redistribute land after the Civil War—to give every black family "forty acres and a mule"—had been an egregious error. Throughout the Black Belt, black farmers faced great difficulty in acquiring land; without it, most black farmers became trapped in tenancy and sharecropping, conditions that made it hard for them to put down roots and rendered them vulnerable to be blown off the land altogether by the winds of economic change. Even in Washington Parish it took exceptional persistence and industry to survive as an independent operator.

Landownership by itself would not have protected black farmers from the chill blast of change: The economics of agriculture became increasingly unfavorable to the small farmer, especially those dependent upon cotton production. By the 1940s the era of agribusiness, encouraged by federal policies, was well under way in the South; between 1945 and 1965 eleven million southerners, white and black, left the farm. It does not follow, however, that distributing land to the freedmen after the Civil War would have been futile. Had black families enjoyed the benefits of landownership over several generations, they might have climbed higher, faster; they might also have been better equipped to withstand the successive shocks of economic depression, migration, and urbanization.[29]

In May 1935, four months after Jerome Wilson's death by lynching, Bond delivered the commencement address at Washington Parish Training School, the black secondary school in Franklinton. His theme was "The Road to Freedom." He told the assembled children and guests about "Old Henry," a slave who, after emancipation, became a "slave to work" in order to provide for his family and see them settled on the land. "Such men as old Henry led our race out of legal slavery, and fought for the freedom that beckons way down the road yonder where we cannot see." Old Henry, of course, was Isom Wilson, the former slave of Hezekiah Magee who by 1880 owned eighty acres of land. Never mentioning the lynching of Jerome Wilson and the departure of the Wilson family from Washington Parish—a family tragedy that would have made nonsense of this parable of racial uplift—Bond addressed his concluding remarks to the white guests—ministers, school board members, the head of the American Legion. "Why do we need to quarrel, and fight, and suspect each other—when all of us, black and white, want Freedom? Isn't there enough to go round in this world of ours so that every one can have his share?"[30]

In the course of editing *The Star Creek Papers* I was able to establish the history of the Wilson family after Bond lost contact with them in 1935. In brief, John Wilson sold his two farms and left Washington Parish. Although he stayed in the South, settling in Baton Rouge, his wife and six surviving children migrated to Chicago. They led modest but successful lives in the North. In typical American fashion, the descendants of Isom Wilson and Mandy Daniels have scattered; they can be found in California, New York, Illinois, Washington, and Texas. Some, however, still farm land in Washington Parish.

NOTES

1. Population figures obtained through State Census Data Center, www.state.la.us/census.

2. Stephen H. Norwood, "Bogalusa Burning: The War against Biracial Unionism in the Deep South, 1919," *Journal of Southern History* 63 (August 1997): 591–628; Adam Fairclough, *Race and Democracy: The Civil Rights Struggle in Louisiana, 1915–1972* (Athens: University of Georgia Press, 1995), 26–29, 344–80.

3. Horace Mann Bond and Julia W. Bond, *The Star Creek Papers: Washington Parish and the Lynching of Jerome Wilson*, ed. Adam Fairclough (Athens: University of Georgia Press, 1997), 12.

4. "Memorandum for the Rosenwald Explorers to be Used as an Incomplete Guide for the Research Part of Their Activities" [1934], in *Horace Mann Bond Papers*, ed. John H. Bracey Jr. (Ann Arbor: University Publications of America, 1998), microfilm, 98 reels; "News Letter to Rural Explorers," November 1934, Julia W. Bond Papers, private collection; John C. Dixon to John J. Coss, March 6, 1935; Coss to Dixon, March 11, 1935, in box 1, series 12–6–62, Division of Negro Education, Georgia Department of Archives and History, Atlanta; Bond to Ambrose S. Caliver, January 9, 1935, in *Bond Papers*, reel 5, ser. 1.

5. *Franklinton Era-Leader*, July 26, 1934; *New Orleans Times-Picayune*, July 31, August 3,

August 7, 1934; D. W. Taylor and James E. Gayle to NAACP, August 11, 1934, in box I-C-357, NAACP Papers, Library of Congress; "Mr. John Wilson's Account of What Happened" [March 1935], Horace Mann Bond, "The First Lynching of 1935," draft of article, 1935, both in *Bond Papers*.

6. *New Orleans Times-Picayune*, January 11, 1935; *State v. Wilson*, 181 La. 62, 158 So. 621 (1935); Roy Wilkins, "Huey Long Says—An Interview with Louisiana's Kingfish," *Crisis* (February 1935): 41, 52.

7. Horace Mann Bond to Robert Redfield, January 17, 1935, in *Bond Papers*, reel 1, ser. 5.

8. Bond to Robert E. Park, April 2, 1935, ibid.

9. Bond to Robert M. Labaree, March 20, 1935, Bond to Robert E. Park, April 2, 1935, Bond to Frederick Lewis Allen, March 13, 1935, all ibid.

10. Bond and Bond, *Star Creek Papers*.

11. Horace Mann Bond, Notes of interviews with John Wilson, and "Cause of Balltown Riot," Julia W. Bond Papers; E. Russ Williams Jr., *History of Washington Parish, Louisiana, 1978–1992* (Monroe, La.: Williams Genealogical and Historical Publications, 1994), 1:291–93; [New York?] *Record-Herald*, November [?] 1901, Tuskegee Institute clippings file, microfilm, Perkins Library, Duke University.

12. Bond, Notes of interviews with John Wilson, Julia W. Bond Papers.

13. Ibid.; Horace and Julia Bond, "A Description of Washington Parish," 1934, p. 3, Julia W. Bond Papers.

14. E. Franklin Frazier, *The Negro Family in the United States* (Chicago: University of Chicago Press, 1939), 190–205.

15. Bond, *A Study of Factors Involved in the Identification and Encouragement of Unusual Academic Talent among Underprivileged Populations* (Washington, D.C.: HEW, 1967), 13–14.

16. Bond and Bond, *Star Creek Papers*, 96–115; Bond, Notes of interviews with John Wilson, notes on the Wilson and Magee families, Julia W. Bond Papers.

17. Joel Williamson, *New People: Miscegenation and Mulattoes in the United States* (New York: Free Press, 1980), 14–27; Horace Mann Bond, "Two Racial Islands in Alabama," *American Journal of Sociology* 36 (January 1931): 552–67; Horace Mann Bond to Robert E. Park, June 2, 1936, in Julia W. Bond Papers; Bond and Bond, *Star Creek Papers*, 11; Jacob L. Reddix, *A Voice Crying in the Wilderness: The Memoirs of Jacob L. Reddix* (Jackson, Miss.: University Press of Mississippi, 1974), 61.

18. Bond and Bond, *Star Creek Papers*, 11, 15–16.

19. William Ivy Hair, *The Kingfish and His Realm: The Life and Times of Huey P. Long* (Baton Rouge: Louisiana State University Press, 1991), 303–4, 320–22. To this day, blacks in Louisiana recount a quip (possibly apocryphal) by Long: "You could feed all the pure whites in Louisiana with a nickel's worth of red beans and a dime's worth of rice."

20. After hearing this paper, a white member of the audience recounted his memory of a white merchant who kept a framed photograph of his mulatto son on the wall of his store.

21. Bond and Bond, *Star Creek Papers*, 14; Bond to W. P. Dabney, March 20, 1935, in Julia W. Bond Papers.

22. Horace Mann Bond, "The Sons and Daughters of Academic Freedom," speech at Alabama College, Montevalla, Ala., June 10, 1953, microfilm copy in Horace Mann Bond Papers, Library of Congress. Typing "African American Genealogy" into an Internet search engine yielded 17,148 Web sites.

23. Gwendolyn Midlo Hall, ed., *Databases for the Study of Afro-Louisiana History and Genealogy, 1699–1860: Computerized Information from Original Manuscript Sources,* CD-Rom ed. (Baton Rouge: Louisiana State University Press, 2000); Bond, *A Study of Factors Involved in the Identification and Encouragement of Unusual Academic Talent among Underprivileged Populations,* 13–14.

24. Philip A. Bruce, *The Plantation Negro as a Freeman* (1889; reprint Williamston, Mass.: Corner House, 1970), 17; Thomas Nelson Page, *The Negro: The Southerner's Problem* (1904; reprint New York, Johnson Reprint, 1970), 81; David L. Cohn, *Where I Was Born and Raised* (Boston: Houghton Mifflin, 1935), 79.

25. Willis D. Weatherford, *Negro Life in the South: Present Conditions and Needs* (New York: Association Press, 1910), 23–24; Arthur W. Calhoun, *A Social History of the American Family,* 3 vols. (1919; reprint New York: Barnes and Noble, 1960), 3:43.

26. W. E. B. Du Bois, ed., *The Negro American Family* (Atlanta: Atlanta University Press, 1908), 21–22, 41; Frazier, *The Negro Family in the United States.*

27. Booker T. Washington, "An Address before the White House Conference on the Care of Dependent Children," January 25, 1909, in *The Booker T. Washington Papers,* ed. Louis R. Harlan et al., 14 vols. (Urbana: University of Illinois Press, 1972–89), 10:18–20; Booker T. Washington to William P. Blake, December 12, 1911, ibid., 11:413.

28. Roger M. Williams, *The Bonds: An American Family* (New York: Atheneum, 1972), 93–94; Bond to John J. Coss, February 15, 1937, in *Bond Papers,* reel 5, ser. 1; Bond, "The Road to Freedom," May 5, 1935, p. 1, *Bond Papers,* reel 10, ser. 4; Herbert G. Gutman, *The Black Family in Slavery and Freedom* (New York: Pantheon, 1976); Orville Vernon Burton, *In My Father's House Are Many Mansions: Family and Community in Edgefield, South Carolina* (Chapel Hill: University of North Carolina Press, 1985); Ann Patton Malone, *Sweet Chariot: Slave Family and Household Structure in Nineteenth-Century Louisiana* (Chapel Hill: University of North Carolina Press, 1992); Stewart E. Tolnay, *The Bottom Rung: African-American Family Life on Southern Farms* (Urbana: University of Illinois Press, 1999), 100–19, 152–67.

29. Horace Mann Bond, "Forty Acres and a Mule," *Opportunity* 13 (May 1935): 140–41, 151; Pete Daniel, *Lost Revolutions: The South in the 1950s* (Chapel Hill: University of North Carolina Press, 2000), 39.

30. Bond, "The Road to Freedom," 2–4.

10

ENVIRONMENT, ECONOMY, AND QUALITY OF LIFE IN LOUISIANA'S FLORIDA PARISHES

PAUL H. TEMPLET

INTRODUCTION

THE FLORIDA PARISHES OF LOUISIANA ARE A GROUP OF EIGHT parishes that extend generally westward in two tiers from the Mississippi state line north of Lake Pontchartrain to the Mississippi River. Although the extent of their economic development varies, they have a common history and similar cultural traits. The parishes are at a crossroads: While the region is developing rapidly or seeking to develop economically, many people there wonder if the Florida Parishes must sacrifice a clean environment to maintain and secure jobs. Economic developers and government officials often take the traditional, short-term view that environmental quality and resource conservation are adversarial and contradictory to job creation and economic development—a belief that has achieved the power of myth. In developing economies, where increasing pollution and an improving economy can coexist, this myth may be sustained.[1] In developed countries, however, a substantial and growing body of empirical evidence demonstrates that, in fact, economic development and job creation are positively correlated with a clean environment and good environmental management. This chapter investigates the myth by presenting the evidence and exploring the complementary relationship between the environment and the economy using the United States as a model. To the best of my knowledge there are no empirical studies demonstrating a negative impact on the public sector because of environmental policies, although all agree that there are costs involved. The purpose of this type of analysis is to demonstrate not only that environmental quality and economic prosperity are compatible but that areas with poor environments are much less likely to be able to sustain economic growth. The reasons for the positive relationship between environment and economy are many and varied: A clean environment leads to a more productive work force and a location more attractive to other people and businesses; fewer public subsidies for pollution-related causes mean more dollars for additional public services such as education; health expenditures are lower when pollution is lessened. These factors help to create a better economy and a better place to live.

This essay also presents a new way to think about quality of life for the Florida Parishes. The concept of "quality of life" is subjective, but it can be measured objectively to some extent. Quality of life is characterized as our total wealth, as long as we are willing to think big about wealth. In this view total wealth is the sum of natural capital, social capital, and man-made capital, where natural capital is what the environment contributes to us, social capital is the quality of our communities, schools, government, and other institutions, and man-made capital is factories, production, and income. This new view of economic development takes the approach that good development includes improving natural and social, as well as man-made, capital.[2] None of the three capitals is sacrificed for the others because total wealth is the sum of the capitals; therefore, a loss of any of the three diminishes the whole and our quality of life. In addition, public decisions are to be made in such a way that at least two of the capitals are improved and the third is not diminished—a new type of economic goal (in economics, the term is *optimality*). Unless our communities, income, and environment provide us with a good quality of life, which includes more than man-made capital, economic development fails to improve public welfare.

BACKGROUND

Many economists agree that externalizing environmental costs to the public sector is a bad idea, since it distorts prices and the market, resulting in market failure.[3] One common theme in ecological economics is that laissez-faire free-market activities, using common resources, lead to market failure and environmental abuse primarily because of externalities, or spillover costs.[4] Environmental commons are resources that are not privately owned and whose use is largely uncontrolled, e.g., air, water, some public lands, or even the public itself. Externalities occur when unwanted, and sometimes unintended, costs (normally caused by production) of one party are visited upon another party who is outside of the decision process that created the costs: Hence the term *externalities*.[5] Such costs are also outside the price system, and market signals are therefore incomplete and inadequate,[6] which leads to "market failure." Some economists believe that government intervention—generally in the form of regulation, incentives, or disincentives—should be implemented to correct the failure.[7]

A principal reason for the complementary relationship is that economic systems function within a larger environment that provides "free" services (e.g., clean water and air and other resources) to the economy and accepts wastes when the resources are discarded as pollution. These services are essential to a smoothly functioning economy; without them the economy cannot operate. An *environmental* base thus negatively affected or diminished, therefore, reduces the long-term economic welfare because it can contribute less service to the economy. For example, industrial discharges that exceed the assimilation capacity of the environment can accumulate in fish and wildlife and inhibit commercial and sport fishing, often resulting in the loss of more jobs than are created by the economic activity responsible for the discharge. Acid rain and other air pollution slows crop and tree growth and economically retards agriculture and forestry. Cities and regions that maintain clean air and an appealing aesthetic environment have a better chance of attracting tourists and their dollars. The environment can be viewed as an infrastructure that contributes to the economy in the same fashion as the more traditional infrastructure of roads and other public services. The public welfare suffers if electrical and water systems are abused, and environmental abuse will also result in lowered public welfare.

The Tangipahoa River is a case in point. During the early 1990s, while I was secretary of the Louisiana Department of Environmental Quality, exceedingly high coliform counts were found in the river after rainstorms, evidence of sewage contamination. State law required that the condition be posted, and DEQ officials did so by putting up signs along the river, over the objections of many. The posting caused several "float" rental businesses to close because people no longer came from the adjacent parishes and New Orleans to drift lazily down the river on a hot summer afternoon. A negative economic impact from the pollution had occurred. The cause of the contamination was traced to inadequately treated sewage from some communities and camps and from many dairies located in the river's watershed. In fact, the volume of cattle waste discharged into the watershed area was very large. Cattle waste does trigger the action level for coliform, just as human waste does, since a number of diseases can be passed from cattle to humans. The DEQ proposed a program in which cattle waste would be collected into pits and then sprayed over fields so the organics could be oxidized, the bacteria killed by sunlight and air, and the nutrients removed by the grasses. The department also provided technical assistance for the dairies, and the federal government provided grants and loans to dig ponds and buy equipment. Natural capital was improved because the river became cleaner; it is open for use once again. The dairy operations improved because the cattle waste became a resource to improve fertility, and the fields and hedges provide cover for other species. Recreation is improved—one does not have to float down contaminated rivers—thus improving social capital. Financial capital, while suffering a short-term loss, was enhanced over the long term, and the area's quality of life improved.

GENESIS OF THIS WORK

In 1987 a reform-minded, Harvard-trained candidate, Buddy Roemer, was elected governor of Louisiana on a "revolution" platform. (When asked about his Harvard background, Roemer usually replied, "Don't hold that against me.") In a *Wall Street Journal* ad, he called for applications from people interested in cabinet positions, an unusual approach in a state where political patronage usually fills appointed jobs. As a university scientist interested in the environment (I had spearheaded Earth Day at Louisiana State University in 1970 and headed up the development of the state's coastal-management program in the mid- to late 1970s), I applied, along with some two hundred other people, for secretary of the DEQ. I had never met the new governor, but liked what I heard him say about pollution. A committee interviewed me; then the governor interviewed me and two other applicants. He offered me the job, and I accepted, expecting to last about six months. My motivation? It was time for me to put up or shut up. I had been complaining for years about the environmental destruction taking place in Louisiana and finally had an opportunity to do something about it.

Once the new administration was in office, we began pushing for new laws and putting new regulations in place, increasing the effectiveness of the DEQ (in 1987 the DEQ had only twenty personal computers for 350 employees) and carrying out rigorous enforcement. Nearly every time we tightened up on pollution we heard from the industrial sector's representatives and economists that we would run jobs and investments out of the state. That claim did not make much sense to me, since Louisiana had neither jobs nor much investment nor a clean environment at the time. In 1987 our unemployment rate was 12 percent, the highest in the United States, and we were first in toxic discharges. The Environmental Protection Agency's first Toxic Release Inventory (TRI) came out in 1989, and Louisiana was top polluter in the nation—a dubious honor. It seemed to me that the relationship between a good environment and a good economy must be positive, but I had no data or analysis to back up my hypothesis that a clean environment is good for people *and* the economy. The only studies at that time were traditional economic analyses that used no data and held that pollution control slowed economic growth. By the end of Roemer's first term, and with much controversy, we had lowered toxic discharges by 50 percent and had put a number of new rules and laws in place, including our own Air Toxics Law, enacted a year before the 1990 Federal Clean Air Act. In addition, enforcement went up by a factor of five, and we began to condition industrial property tax exemptions on environmental criteria.[8] Investments and jobs went up as pollution declined because industrial spending for pollution control increased by a factor of six. Many other socioeconomic indicators also began to improve.[9] I sensed that some unrecognized system-level effects were occurring and began research on these issues when I returned to LSU in 1992.

To my surprise I had lasted a full four-year term, the first secretary of the Louisiana DEQ ever to complete a term. Roemer lost his bid for a second term, a defeat aided by much soft-money spending by industry. Some of our reforms, including the Environmental Scorecard (which rated the discharges from industry, declaring them environmentally friendly or not), were eliminated by the next two governors, but others remain in place. Reformers do not last long in Louisiana, but the fruits of Roemer's reforms are now an integral part of discussions about Louisiana's future.

THE EVIDENCE

To demonstrate the relationship between the economy and the environment, a measure of environmental impact needs to be related to commonly measured indicators of public welfare. It is difficult to determine the final effects of many processes and consequent exposure to technological risks. We can, however, measure the relative risks involved with certain activities, such as pollution discharge levels. The emissions-to-jobs ratio (E/J)[10] is derived by dividing the toxic emissions for a sector of the economy by the number of jobs in the same sector. The E/J is a measure of relative risk; that is, those manufacturing industry types[11] with a high E/J are inherently riskier than those with a low E/J (see table 1).[12] Table 2 shows the manufacturing E/J ratio for each state in 1990. The wide variation in E/J across states can be attributed to a number of possible causes, including excessive emissions levels, energy use and efficiency, state and corporate policies, and industry substructure (e.g., level of automation). A leading cause of a high E/J, however, is underspending on pollution control by the emitting sectors.[13] For example, those states whose chemical industries[14] underspend on pollution abatement relative to the national average for a particular level of emissions generally have a high E/J ratio as pollution costs are externalized to the environmental commons. If the pollution discharges exceed the environment's assimilation, capacity ambient pollution levels will rise and the public will incur increased risk.

The question for public planners and managers is this: Is there a commensurate benefit to a municipality or state for the cost of assuming the risk? The question can be stated another way: Given the variation in relative environmental risk across industry types, is this risk related positively or negatively to economic welfare? What we observe is, in fact, that *poorer* economic conditions exist where environmentally risky activities are more intense. If allowing more pollution resulted in better economic conditions,

TABLE 1. TOTAL TRI RELEASES/SECTOR JOBS FOR THE MANUFACTURING INDUSTRY

Sector	Releases (lbs/job)	Sector	Releases (lbs/job)
Apparel	2	Miscellaneous	65
Food	28	Fabr. Metals	91
Machinery	28	Leather	104
Printing	34	Transportation	110
Measure/Photo	35	Furniture	120
Textiles	55	Plastics	222
Lumber	56	Paper	460
Electrical	57	Primary Metal	799
Tobacco	61	Petroleum	1,048
Stone/clay	63	Chemicals	1,859

TABLE 2. 1990 EMISSIONS-TO-JOBS (LBS/JOB) RATIOS FOR THE FIFTY STATES

State	Releases	State	Releases	State	Releases
Vermont	23	Illinois	118	Oklahoma	198
Mass.	39	Nevada	128	Florida	214
Hawaii	41	N. Dak.	129	Arkansas	264
Colorado	41	Michigan	131	Indiana	274
N.J.	41	Minn.	132	Alabama	306
California	46	Georgia	138	Arizona	398
R.I.	52	Maine	144	Tenn.	412
New York	53	N.C.	149	Miss.	444
Conn.	62	Kentucky	152	Texas	444
Maryland	76	Ohio	155	W. Va.	465
Wisconsin	82	Missouri	163	Kansas	471
Pa.	88	Nebraska	175	N. Mex.	818
N.H.	90	Iowa	177	Wyoming	1,135
S. Dak.	99	S.C.	183	Utah	1,236
Delaware	100	Virginia	188	Alaska	1,513
Oregon	105	U.S.	188	Montana	2,134
Wash.	113	Idaho	190	Louisiana	2,496

there might be an argument for allowing poor environmental policies and practices. What the data show, however, is that higher unemployment and poorer, not better, economic conditions exist in those states where pollution levels and the E/J are higher. The strategy of allowing more pollution results in fewer jobs and, of course, more pollution—a lose-lose situation. For example, across the United States, statistical analysis (a cross-sectional analysis, analyzing data from all fifty states at a particular time) shows that as a state's pollution levels (or E/J) rise, income per capita drops; poverty, unemployment, and energy use increase; and the environmental indicators reveal a poorer environment (see table 3). A more detailed multivariate analysis shows that poor environmental conditions, weak environmental policies, and high emission-to-jobs ratios are all negatively related to indicators of economic welfare across states. Thus, the data from the fifty states demonstrate that the environment and the economy are complementary, not adversarial.[15]

Economic development indicators worsen with increased pollution. A telling statistic for economic development is the one between the E/J and

TABLE 3. E/J REGRESSION RESULTS

State Variable	Pearson's r	"t" statistic
*Environmental**		
Green Condition Score	0.28[a]	2.02
Green Policy Score	0.42[b]	3.23
Green Index Score	0.42[b]	3.25
Energy		
Energy (mill. Btu)/capita	0.81[c]	9.61
Energy (Btu)/$ GSP	0.67[c]	6.31
Socioeconomic		
Personal Income ($/yr.)	−0.28[a]	−2.00
Income Disparity (20% top/bottom)	0.32[a]	2.33
Poverty (% below)	0.31[a]	2.26
Unemployment (%)	0.52[c]	5.05
Economic Development		
Economic Health Score (A = 4), CED	−0.32[a]	−2.33
Retail Sales Growth %(1982-88)	−0.61[c]	−5.27
Business Failures/10K Concerns	0.42[b]	3.27

[a]significant at p<0.05, [b]p<0.01, [c]p<0.001
* "Green" scores are taken from Hall & Kerr, 1992

the rankings and grades assigned to states by the Corporation for Enterprise Development,[16] which define a state's economic health. States are graded and ranked on economic performance, business vitality, and development capacity, using more than seventy economic indicators. My statistical analysis finds that there are significant *inverse* relationships between a state's E/J and its economic grade. In other words, as E/J increases, the economic performance grade decreases and the ranking moves toward fiftieth, the lowest rank. Thus, those states that allow pollution to be excessively externalized to the environment find themselves less attractive to prospective businesses, not more, as they might have hoped. The polluted environment acts as a de facto barrier to entry and results in a less diversified economy. The E/J is also positively related to the rate of business failures in a state. As E/J rises the failure rate also rises, indicating that the economic health for *existing* businesses declines as pollution increases. A note of caution is in order: Statistical analyses such as these do not establish the direction of causation; they do indicate the compatibility of a good economy and a clean environment and suggest how we can have both.

Lest the reader think I am promoting the E/J as the indicator to end all indicators, let me say that E/J is probably tracking a larger measure of economic/environmental interactions: externalization. One way for an individual or firm to increase profits is to externalize costs, that is, to pass them on to something or someone else. An externalized cost generally results in a subsidy, sometimes hidden, which accrues to whoever is doing the externalizing. Pollution is an example of a cost that is passed on to the environment and ultimately to the people of an area while the avoided pollution abatement costs (the subsidy) are retained by the polluting industry. Other examples of externalized costs are regressive taxes and low energy costs, which provide an implicit subsidy for one economic sector while other sectors and the public bear the cost. I have calculated the amount of the subsidies caused by pollution, regressive taxes, and energy pricing for the fifty states as a means of measuring externalities and compared them to other indicators of a state's general welfare.[17] As externalities, and hence subsidies, increase, socioeconomic, energy, environmental, and economic development measures all worsen. Table 4 shows the average of a number of measures for two groups of states, those with high subsidies (and high externalities) and those with low subsidies (and low externalities). In general, the high externality states are poorer; use more energy less efficiently; have more pollution, fewer jobs, less economic development, and poorer political health; and are no more economically competitive than low externality states.

The indicator of poor political health requires some additional explanation. If subsidies are being created by increasing externalities, how do special interests create them? One possibility is that through campaign contributions and other means, private firms can influence the voting patterns of elected representatives to promote subsidies for themselves and externalization of their costs to the public. As subsidies rise across states, campaign contributions to federal elections, and presumably state election campaigns, increase while the voting records of congressmen decline, at least from an environmental perspective.[18]

One other troubling result from a political health perspective is that voting participation by citizens in federal elections[19] declines significantly in states with high subsidies. In the 1988 federal elections, for example, voter participation in high subsidy states was on average 15 percent lower

TABLE 4. STATES GROUPED BY SUBSIDY SIZE

Group Subsidy Type	Group Means		% Differences
	Low	High	
State Variable			
Total Subsidy ($)/Capita	−252	274	209[c]
Environmental			
T Waste (lbs)/capita	2,772	4,686	69[a]
Haz. Waste Generated(lbs)/cap.	763	2,817	269[a]
Total Toxic Releases (lbs)/capita	17	32	88[a]
Toxic Emissions/Total Jobs	40.21	80.17	99[a]
Green Conditions	4,248	4,674	0
Green Policies	1,747	2,639	51[c]
Energy			
Energy (Mill. Btu)/capita	312	394	26[a]
T Energy/TJob (Bill. Btu/J)	0.71	0.97	37[a]
GSP($)/Mill. Btu	59.82	43.83	−27[c]
Socioeconomic			
Personal Income ($/yr.)	13,880	11,788	−15[c]
Income Disparity (20% top/bottom)	8.01	9.22	15[b]
Poverty (% below)	11.20	14.91	33[c]
Unemployment (%)	4.84	6.15	27[a]
Economic Development			
Economic Health Score (A = 4)	2.64	1.79	−32[b]
Retail Sales Growth %(1982–88)	42.60	31.93	−25[b]
Business Failures/10K Concerns	73	110	51[b]
Economic Competitiveness			
Value Added (manufacturing)/Job	67,970	69,624	2*
GSP ($)/capita	17,183	16,000	−7*
GSP ($)/Job	38,355	39,037	2*
GSP Growth %(1982–89)	33	27	−18*
Political Health			
Party Contributions($)/US Rep.	2,819	4,566	62[b]
Congressional Voting Record	62	43	−31[c]
Voter % in '88 Fed. Rep. Election	52	44	−15[b]

*no significant difference, [a]significant at $p<0.05$, [b]$p<0.01$, [c]$p<0.001$
Significance of the differences in the means is determined by a two-tailed t test.

than in other states. Perhaps citizens in high subsidy states perceive that special interests command an elected representative's attention and that voting will not change anything. In short, voters feel "disenfranchised." This analysis does not establish cause-and-effect relationships between campaign contributions, congressional voting, and citizen participation in elections, but this area appears to be ripe for future political science research.

An argument could be made that there are other factors causing the poor economic performance seen in Louisiana. One could point to the state's education achievements, which are below the U.S. average, as the reason businesses stay away and our economy is poor; but while education undoubtedly plays a role, it too suffers from overgenerous subsidies that result in pollution and poor education. The two factors are linked. The state grants about $350 million each year in property-tax subsidies to industry under the Ten Year Industrial Property Exemption program administered by the Louisiana Department of Economic Development (DED). These subsidies are moneys that would have been paid to parishes for property taxes and used for local government purposes, of which education is a large part. Instead the money stays with the manufacturing industry, which is creating most of the state's pollution. The result is poor schools and more pollution. Louisiana is the only state that does not even grant local governments a voice in the decision. The stated purpose of the subsidy is to create more jobs, but it is failing in that regard. Since 1980 the state has *lost* twenty thousand manufacturing jobs and paid out about $7 billion in subsidies. The money would have been better spent on schools.

OTHER STUDIES ABOUT ECONOMY-ENVIRONMENT RELATIONSHIPS

The relationship of the environment and the economy has attracted considerable interest of late. Stephen Meyer[20] of the Massachusetts Institute of Technology has found that, over time, those states with good environmental programs have better employment, productivity, and economic growth than do states with poor environmental programs. He noted that "states with stronger environmental policies consistently out-performed the weaker environmental states on all the economic measures." A Bank of America study[21] found similar results. States ranked environmentally "strong" had higher economic growth rates and lower rental vacancies than states ranked environmentally "weak." The Bank of America study listed three reasons a clean environment is good for business:

1. The quality of life is improved. Providing an improved environment is similar to providing any consumer good or service: It fulfills the needs of the citizens and improves the quality of life.
2. Resources are better managed. Environmental regulations allow for the side effects of using resources. For example, if a factory pollutes a river and water quality is not enforced, the water in the river may be unsuitable for use by other factories and cities downstream. Regulating pollution enhances overall economic efficiency and productivity.
3. Long-term growth is maintained. Environmental protection will sustain long-term economic growth. Short-term exploitation of resources can result in unsustainable growth because current market prices do not take future resource limitations into account. Only specific environmental protection can ensure that resources will be available for sustainable economic growth.

A 1994 study entitled *Gold and Green*[22] investigated the relationship of economy to environment by ranking states according to both their economic and their environmental health using twenty indicators of each. The economic indicators emphasized job opportunities, working conditions, protection for disabled or unemployed workers, and job creation. The environmental indicators focused on toxic emissions, recycling efforts, and state spending to protect natural resources. The state rankings on the two lists were remarkably similar. Louisiana was last on both lists, and southern states and those reliant on mineral extraction generally ranked low on both. The New England and Upper Midwest states rank best on both sets of indicators. A correlation of the *Gold and Green* scores shows them to be positively related, another indicator that a good economy is compatible with a good environment. Given that the economy is a subset of the larger environment and relies on it for services, it is becoming clear that a clean environment is a necessary condition for a good economy, at least when the long term is considered.

SUSTAINABILITY

A sustainable economy recognizes the need for the long-term viability of a culture and is being promoted by the United Nations and most countries.

To be sustainable,[23] a society must integrate environment with economics in its planning and policies. Sustainable economic development is usually defined as a means of satisfying the needs of today without sacrificing the needs of future generations. Another way to look at it is that we should live off the income from our capital rather than the capital itself. Living off the income from our stock of capital is sustainable living; endlessly drawing down the stock of capital will bankrupt us. In much the same way as our stocks of money, equipment, and other assets are *man-made capital* from which we create wealth, the environment is *natural capital* essential to wealth creation. If depleted, the environment will not contribute its income—resources and waste disposal—to our economic system or its life support to us.

Although the concepts of sustainable development are still being worked out, H. E. Daly[24] has proposed some operational principles. Table 5 contains a partial list of Daly's sustainability conditions and some recommended variables to measure them at the state level.[25] Some of the variables, such as poverty level as a measure of the sustainability goal of poverty reduction, need no further explanation. Wealth inequality across states can be adequately measured by the disparity index, which is a ratio of the average income of the top 20 percent of wage earners divided by the average income of the bottom 20 percent of wage earners.[26] Energy efficiency can be measured by such means as energy use per capita and per job and Gross State Product (GSP)/unit energy. For materials, the most convenient surrogate efficiency measure is waste/capita because a composite measure of material resource consumption is not readily available. As efficient use of material resources increases we would expect waste/capita to decline. Waste/capita can be expressed as hazardous waste generated/capita and total waste/capita. Total waste is the sum of solid, hazardous, and toxic wastes. Industrial energy use per state is used to measure energy throughput (amount used in a year), and toxic releases by state is used as a surrogate measure of material resource use, since aggregate resource use is difficult to measure. Waste should decline as resource use throughput declines within a state if efficiency of materials conversion is constant or increasing. The unemployment rate will be used to measure the full employment sustainability condition.

Daly[27] proposes three conditions for sustainability as a way to protect the environment from overuse: economic scale, waste emissions within capacity, and harvest rates equal to regeneration. If achieved, these conditions will lead to improvements in environmental quality, which I propose to measure by the Green Index's environmental conditions and environmental policy scores.[28] The Green scores are a broad index of environmental conditions and policies across states and incorporate 256 environmental indicators. One group of 179 indicators represents "conditions," while another group of 77 represents "policies." The two scores together make up the Green Index score. In my experience, the Green Index measures adequately reflect the general environmental quality of a state.

The question we are asking here is whether sustainability is enhanced or retarded by externalities such as high pollution levels. To find out we must statistically compare total subsidies/capita (our externalities measure discussed above) with the state variables across the fifty states. Table 5 indicates that each of the sustainability conditions are better satisfied by *low* subsidies/capita, i.e., low externalities. Low externalities means lower pollution levels, less reliance on regressive taxes, and equitable energy prices. Decreases in poverty, income disparity, inefficiency of resource use, resource throughput, and unemployment, which are all necessary for sustainability, occur with *decreases* in subsidies/capita. Environmental quality, as measured by the Green Index, improves with decreasing subsidies. The general result is that externalization, and its subsidies, is negatively related to sustainability. According to this analysis lower externalities and subsidies generally mean more sustainability.

One disturbing result of large externalities is increased income disparity, which deserves further comment. Income disparity is the gap in average income between the top 20 percent of incomes and the bottom 20 percent. The disparity increases significantly as externalities and subsidies increase. In fact, the gap between rich and poor has been increasing in the United States for some time. During the 1980s the gap widened in forty-three states; in twenty-seven of those states the average income of the bottom 20 percent *declined* while the top 20 percent increased.[29] The widening gap indicates that externalities are increasing over time in the United States, an unfortunate situation for a developed country. Large income disparities are usually characteristic of a developing country. Income disparity also shows a significant relationship with a composite crime score using sixteen crime statistics.[30] As the disparity index increases so do the crime statistics, perhaps indicating that large income disparities promote societal dysfunction. The income disparity between the *middle* 20 percent (the center of the "middle class") and the rich also widened during the 1980s in forty-six

TABLE 5. SUSTAINABILITY INDICES AND SUBSIDIES

Sustainability Condition	State Variable	Relationship to Subsidy/Cap.		Sustainability Condition Satisfied by
		Pearson's r	t	
Poverty Reduction[a]	% below poverty level	0.58	4.92	low subsidy or externality
	personal income ($/yr)	−0.56	−4.71	low subsidy or externality
Limiting Wealth Inequality[a]	income disparity index (20% top/low)	0.49	3.90	low subsidy or externality
Increased Efficiency of Resource Use[a]	energy/capita (mill. Btu's/person)	0.37	2.73	low subsidy or externality
	energy/job (bill. Btu's/job)	0.46	3.58	low subsidy or externality
	GSP/energy ($/mill. Btu's)	−0.59	−5.03	low subsidy or externality
	hazardous waste/capita (lbs/person)	0.33	2.42	low subsidy or externality
Reduced Resource Throughput[a]	total waste/capita (lbs/person)	0.30	2.19	low subsidy or externality
	industrial energy use (10^{12} Btu's)	0.24	1.70	low subsidy or externality
	total toxic releases (lbs), 1990	0.50	3.96	low subsidy or externality
	toxics/capita, 1989	0.51	4.17	low subsidy or externality
Economic Scale Matched to Ecology[a] Waste Emissions within Assimilation Capacity[a] Harvest Rates Equal Regeneration Rates[a] Environmental Quality[b] (Hall & Kerr 1992)	Green Conditions	0.46	3.64	low subsidy or externality
	Green Policies	0.64	5.82	low subsidy or externality
Full Employment (Templet & Farber 1994)	Unemployment Rate (%)	0.53	4.30	low subsidy or externality

[a]Source is Daly 1990.
[b]Assumed to result from previous 3 conditions.
The relationships are all significant at the 95% confidence level, except for industrial energy use significance at the 90% level.

states, which probably led to the "shrinking middle class" phenomenon. The disparity between the middle and top income segments is also significantly related to the crime score.

Louisiana's income disparity is the highest in the United States: At 14.5, it is 67 percent above the U.S. average of 8.6. Mississippi is the next nearest state at 11.1. Between 1979 and 1989 Louisianians with the bottom 20 percent of incomes *lost* $2,789, or 31 percent, of their income, while those with income in the top 20 percent *gained* more than $11,500, or 15 percent, in annual income. Louisiana also had the poorest crime score in the Morgan Quitno[31] ranking and was designated "Most Dangerous State" because of its crime statistics. The relationship between the disparity index and crime must be considered preliminary at this time. Crime is a complicated problem and no single index can explain it; these figures do provide food for thought, however, and should focus more attention on income disparity, which appears to be an unanticipated by-product of externalities.

COMPETITIVENESS

Some economists worry that spending on pollution control, and preventing externalities in general, is not a good investment and may make industries less competitive. Their concern is not well founded. One of the rarely acknowledged benefits of environmental regulation, apparent from this analysis, is that environmental strategies like waste reduction require more cooperation, integration, and diversity of industry and increase industrial efficiency and competitive advantage. A study by the Organization for Economic Cooperation and Development[32] has shown that competitiveness is not affected by pollution control spending, primarily because pollution control spending is such a small part of total industrial sales or expenditures. In addition, the OECD found that there are offsetting positive and negative effects and that environmental policies "may spur innovation, improve efficiency and confer competitive advantage." I have found the same effect in this study and in a study of how economic systems change over time.[33]

LOUISIANA CASE STUDY

If, as I propose, there are positive economic effects from environmental improvements, there ought to be cases where it can be demonstrated. Indeed there are. During the years 1988–1992, new environmental laws and regulations and rigorous enforcement, policies, and programs in Louisiana brought emissions down 50 percent. Over the same period, investment in Louisiana increased two and a half times and unemployment dropped from 12 percent, the nation's highest, to about 6 percent, the nation's average. Cleaning up the environment occurred concurrently with more investment and more jobs.

Why should this be so? The connections between economy and environment are often subtle, indirect and difficult to quantify. What, for example, is the effect on economic development of the "Cancer Alley" label applied to the industrial corridor along the Mississippi River between Baton Rouge and New Orleans? Undoubtedly, having that kind of reputation is detrimental to development, even if the label is not deserved, but it is difficult to put a dollar value on it. How can we measure the effect on Louisiana of an entire on-site segment of an Oprah Winfrey show on Louisiana's Cancer Alley?

One direct economy-environment connection that can be demonstrated and quantified in dollars is that of spending on pollution control[34] and its effect on job creation. The primary reason there was a 50 percent reduction in toxic emissions in Louisiana from 1988 to 1992 was that the Louisiana manufacturing industry increased its capital outlay on pollution control from about $144 million per year in 1988 to about $1.06 billion by 1992—greater than a sixfold increase. The impetus for increased spending was environmental laws passed by the Congress and the legislature and agency regulations and programs designed to bring Louisiana's pollution in line with national averages. Concurrent with the increased spending, employment in the manufacturing sector increased by about 14,000 direct new jobs by 1991, excluding construction and contract jobs. Prior to 1988 employment in the manufacturing sector in Louisiana was slowly declining. The chemical industry's multiplier of 4.6 related jobs for each new direct job[35] yields an additional 64,000 new jobs caused by pollution control spending and partially accounts for the current low unemployment in Louisiana. Pollution control spending creates jobs; the U.S. average is 23 new jobs created for each $1 million spent.[36]

RECOMMENDATIONS FOR STATES OR PARISHES

A number of specific policy or management recommendations are suggested by these analyses.

1. A state or parish should set ambient environmental standards based on the assimilation capacity of the environment. Since assimilation capacity is a variable rate process and difficult to determine we can use the relationship of ambient pollutant concentrations to federal or state standards, or a standard based on health risk, to assess whether an area has exceeded its capacity. For example, if an area exceeds a federal ambient standard or health risk standard, we can assume that the assimilation capacity has also been exceeded and emissions should be reduced. In deciding which types of facilities should reduce emissions, the U.S. average E/J ratios for various industry types can provide guidance. These ratios are available for all two-digit and some four-digit SIC manufacturing classifications[37] and can point policy-makers in the direction of those dischargers that exceed U.S. average emissions/job by the widest margin. Rigorous enforcement of the standards is necessary, but flexibility is also important. That flexibility should include economic incentives.
2. Use direct control (command and control) to maintain a threshold level of ambient standards, but use economic incentives to achieve the facility discharges determined by E/J ratios, i.e., a hybrid regulatory system incorporating both command and control and economic tools, at least for the transition to a purely economic system. Examples of economic pollution control tools are the emission tax, tradable permits, or the environmental scorecard concept implemented in Louisiana for one year,[38] which conditioned tax exemptions on environmental compliance and the E/J ratio.
3. The emission tax, if used, should at least equal the pollution subsidy.[39] Both the tax and the subsidy can be converted to a dollar/pound figure, which would then be assessed so that the cost of the tax is the same as the cost of avoided pollution control at the margin. This means that each state's emission tax would vary depending on the size of the subsidy relative to the U.S. average. Those states that currently grant large pollution subsidies and have high emission levels would have relatively high total emission taxes, though the tax may not be high on a per-pound basis. This should eliminate the wide variance in E/J across states, which is not envisioned by federal law, and it addresses the equity issue.[40] It would also give some flexibility to states and allow an emissions reduction program to be tailored for a particular state situation, within limits.
4. Combine or link the environmental quality functions (or agency) with

the economic development agency. Since these two functions are related, having them together would ensure consistent policies. Set a goal for both functions based on reducing the E/J ratio. Decreasing emissions, the function of the environmental agency, and increasing jobs, the function of the economic development agency, will both reduce the E/J ratio.

5. Reduce a state's energy usage and encourage efficiency. This will reduce costs and pollution and increase competitiveness. Reasonable prices for industrial energy should be set and maintained. A reasonable energy price for industry relative to residents will promote efficiency and conservation; the U.S. average energy ratio can provide a guide.[41] State policies should encourage conservation, efficiency, and alternative renewable energy sources for all sectors. The energy intensity (energy necessary to generate a dollar of GSP) of a state or economic sector is a useful inverse measure of efficiency. A tax incentive system to promote energy efficiency would help reduce pollution and improve a state's public welfare.[42]

6. Eliminate direct tax subsidies designed to attract industry. These analyses indicate that they will not work and may be harmful.

7. State tax policies should reflect a reasonable balance of progressive and regressive taxes. Use the U.S. average tax ratio as an example.[43]

8. It is unlikely that all state political structures can withstand a determined effort by multinational corporations to externalize their costs. To help prevent undue influence on state policy and processes, preventive measures should be enacted or strengthened. Campaign reforms, including term limits and public financing of campaigns, seem to be useful ways to limit unhealthy political influence that negatively affects the environment and the economy.

THE FLORIDA PARISHES

To apply this analysis to the eight Florida Parishes we must return to the concept of the "three capitals," which was presented in this chapter's introduction. The three capitals refer to social, natural, and financial capital. Social capital is a measure of the quality of our communities' institutions, including schools and government, our participation in them, and so on. Natural capital is the value of the services provided by the environment, and financial capital is the composite of man-made capital, such as factories, goods, GNP, and income. The sum of the three is our total wealth or quality of life. Each can be estimated by a number of indicators. This kind of analysis allows us to see how a loss of one capital can affect the others and forces us to think about the real costs of development.[44]

SOCIAL CAPITAL

One of the most important forms of social capital is population, the number of people living in an area. A small population in a parish is an indication that the parish is rural; a large population indicates that a parish is highly developed and may be experiencing growth pains. Traffic problems may indicate a loss of social capital, and some natural capital may be lost as natural areas are converted to human uses. If natural areas are covered with impervious surfaces like roads, parking lots, and houses, then the area will be hotter in summers and flooding may occur because natural hydrology is interrupted. In this example, the increase in development (financial capital) leads to a loss of social and natural capital. Whether overall quality of life is improved or not will depend on the size of the gains and losses, but at least we are made aware of the effects of development on our quality of life.

Table 6 contains the data on population in the Florida Parishes for the period 1950–1999. East Baton Rouge has the largest population, followed by St. Tammany. The fastest-growing parishes are St. Tammany and Livingston; the East Baton Rouge Parish population growth rate has fallen below that of the average for the Florida Parishes. The growth rate for the Florida Parishes is higher than that of the state as a whole. This pace has been set by St. Tammany and Livingston, but Tangipahoa has recently begun to grow faster than the Louisiana average, too. East and West Feliciana, St. Helena, and Washington Parishes are growing, if at all, at rates below the Louisiana average. The Louisiana population as a whole is growing very slowly.

The population analysis indicates that East Baton Rouge Parish is fully developed and no longer growing. St. Tammany and Livingston Parishes are in the rapid-development stage, during which they can expect both social and natural capital to be affected. Tangipahoa may be in the very early stages of rapid growth, and the rural parishes of East and West Feliciana, Washington, and St. Helena are growing only slowly. There are subtle indications that West Feliciana is beginning to develop at a pace higher than the other three rural parishes and can expect growth pains. Planned

TABLE 6. POPULATION TRENDS, 1950–99

	1950	1960	1970	1980	1990	1999 (est.)	% increase 1950–99
E. Baton Rouge	158,236	230,058	285,142	366,191	380,105	393,294	148.55
E. Feliciana	19,133	20,198	17,657	19,015	19,211	21,119	10.38
Livingston	20,054	26,974	36,511	58,806	70,526	91,182	354.68
St. Helena	9,013	9,162	9,937	9,827	9,874	9,607	6.59
St. Tammany	26,988	38,643	63,585	110,869	144,508	192,945	614.93
Tangipahoa	53,218	59,434	65,875	80,698	85,709	98,285	84.68
Washington	38,371	44,015	41,987	44,207	43,185	43,162	12.49
W. Feliciana	10,169	12,395	11,376	12,186	12,915	13,833	36.03
Total	335,182	440,879	532,070	701,799	766,033	863,427	157.60
Louisiana	2,683,516	3,257,022	3,640,442	4,205,900	4,219,973	4,372,035	62.92

growth, in which steps are taken to protect social and natural capital, can mitigate the effects of unplanned development and preserve the quality of life for current residents as well as for future generations.

Education is an important factor in building social capital. It also improves natural capital because educated people tend to support environmental initiatives and financial capital, and businesses, in search of an educated work force, tend to locate where education is higher. An educated citizenry also participates more in government and supports measures to preserve capital through planned growth. Figure 1 shows high school and college graduates as percentages of the population. The percentage of high school graduates in the developed parishes of East Baton Rouge and St. Tammany is above both the Louisiana and the U.S. average.[45] The rural parishes of East and West Feliciana, St. Helena, Tangipahoa, and Washington are below the average of the Florida Parishes in high school graduates. For college graduates, the picture is much the same with some exceptions. The two developed parishes are above the U.S. and Louisiana averages, followed by the developing parishes of Livingston and Tangipahoa. The increase in college graduates in Tangipahoa over its neighbors can be attributed to the presence of Southeastern Louisiana University in the parish.

Infant deaths and poverty by parish are shown in tables 7 and 8. The infant death rate is a useful indicator because it tracks poverty, rural areas, and quality and accessibility of health care, especially for the poor. St. Tammany is the only parish with an infant death rate below the U.S. average, and it also has the lowest poverty of the Florida Parishes. Livingston is below the Louisiana rate but above the U.S. rate. The highest infant death rate is in East Feliciana and St. Helena Parishes. Poverty is highest in the rural parishes and lowest in St. Tammany. Only East Baton Rouge, Livingston, and St. Tammany Parishes are below the Louisiana average of 23.9 percent of the population living below the poverty line—considerably above the U.S. average of 15.5 percent. We see a correlation between low population, poor educational level, high infant death rates, and poverty in the rural parishes. These are parishes in which work is needed to improve social capital. This analysis indicates that social capital is highest in the developed parishes and lowest in the undeveloped parishes of the Florida Parishes.

NATURAL CAPITAL

We would expect the opposite in terms of natural capital, i.e., that the developed parishes have sacrificed some of their natural capital to build fi-

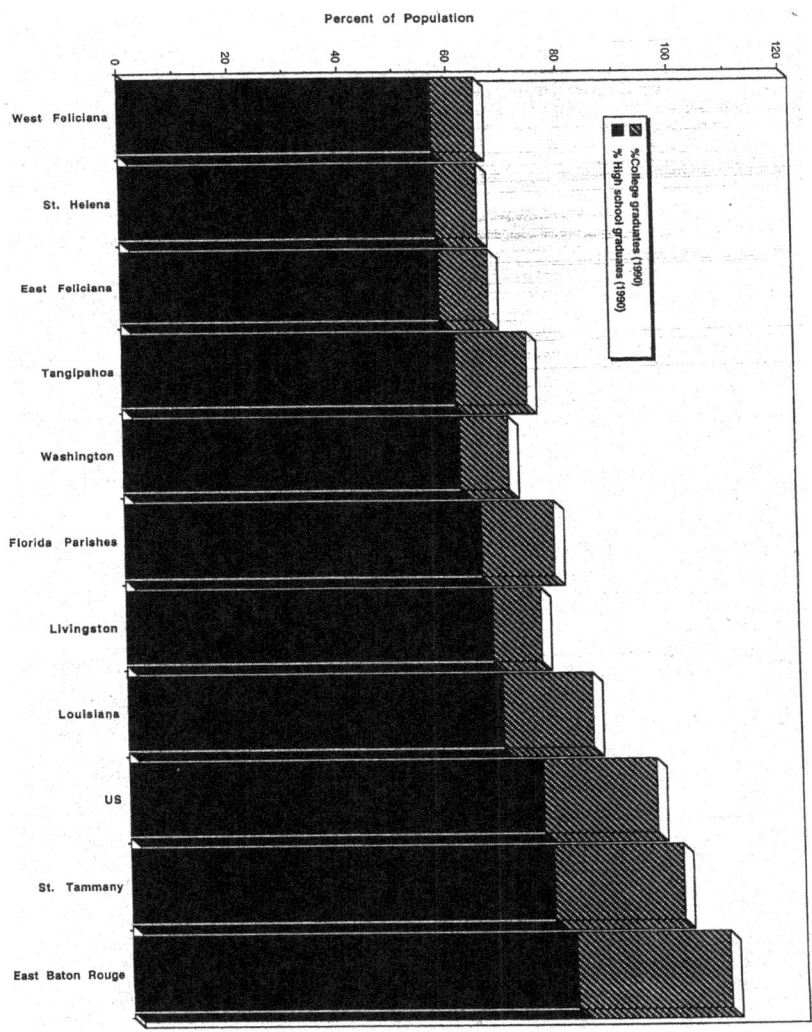

FIGURE 1. 1990 EDUCATIONAL ATTAINMENT IN THE FLORIDA PARISHES

TABLE 7. INFANT DEATHS/1,000 BIRTHS

St. Tammany	6.4
U.S.	8.0
Livingston	10.2
Louisiana	10.6
E. Baton Rouge	11.1
Washington	11.3
Tangipahoa	11.6
Florida Parishes	13.5
W. Feliciana	13.7
E. Feliciana	20.1
St. Helena	23.4

nancial and social capital. Is the tradeoff worthwhile? Probably so, if one asked the citizens; but since an accounting of what has been lost and what has been gained is never undertaken, we can only *assume* that this is true. A better question would be to ask how we might reduce the loss of natural capital while we are trying to build social and financial capital.

In the case of the Florida Parishes, East Baton Rouge Parish has the largest amount of toxic releases,[46] about 5.6 million pounds, contributing well over half the total discharges per year (see table 9). The amount of East Baton Rouge's discharges is so large because of the presence of heavy manufacturing, primarily chemicals and oil refining. The parish exceeded federal standards for ozone eleven times in 2000. Next is Washington Par-

TABLE 8. POVERTY RATE, 1993 (% OF POPULATION BELOW POVERTY LEVEL)

St. Tammany	14.2
U.S.	15.1
Livingston	15.3
E. Baton Rouge	19.7
Louisiana	23.9
Florida Parishes	24.3
E. Feliciana	25.6
W. Feliciana	28.7
Tangipahoa	29.8
St. Helena	30.1
Washington	31.0

TABLE 9. FLORIDA PARISHES MANUFACTURING TOXIC RELEASES, 1998 (LBS)

E. Feliciana	0
St. Helena	10,981
Livingston	15,923
St. Tammany	19,213
Tangipahoa	135,288
W. Feliciana	815,871
Washington	1,474,034
E. Baton Rouge	<u>5,592,140</u>
Total	8,063,450

ish (1.5 million pounds), followed by West Feliciana at 0.8 million pounds. Tangipahoa, St. Tammany, Livingston, St. Helena, and East Feliciana are fairly low in emissions, reflecting their lack of heavy manufacturing. Table 10 gives the intensive variable toxic releases/manufacturing jobs in the parish. West Feliciana moves to the fore, indicating that its small amount of industry, principally paper mills, has 1,088 pounds of releases per job, higher than the U.S., Louisiana, and Florida Parish averages. Washington Parish is second, and East Baton Rouge Parish at third is below the Louisiana average but above the U.S. and Florida Parish average. St. Helena, Tangipahoa, Livingston, St. Tammany, and East Feliciana are below the U.S. average. Natural capital could be improved in East Baton Rouge by tighter restrictions on industrial releases. Because St. Tammany and Livingston are

TABLE 10. FLORIDA PARISHES TOXIC MANUFACTURING RELEASES (LBS/JOB), 1998

E. Feliciana	0
St. Tammany	7
Livingston	12
Tangipahoa	47
St. Helena	70
U.S.	84
Florida Parishes	368
E. Baton Rouge	454
Louisiana	691
Washington	974
W. Feliciana	1,088

developing rapidly, the loss of open space and green areas is a concern. For example, residents of Central in East Baton Rouge Parish actively opposed the siting of a Wal-Mart facility in their rural community. One thing that attracts people to rural parishes is the open character of the landscape, but the development that occurs often reduces the amenities that attracted people in the first place. Good planning can mitigate some of these losses.

The only data presented here for natural capital are the toxic releases and the toxic releases per job for the parishes. Other useful data would be the amount of recreational space per citizen, the miles of streams out of compliance with water quality standards, the number of days per year that air quality does not meet federal standards, the acreage of farmlands, the trends in forest lands, the number of endangered species, and the loss of wilderness. Some of these data are available, but others would have to be developed.

FINANCIAL CAPITAL

A principal component of financial capital is a parish's average annual per capita income. Income determines the amount of dollars available for necessities and for wants, such as education. If income is too low, all is spent on necessities and wants go unsatisfied. The income per capita for all parishes in the Florida Parish area is below the U.S. average (see table 11). This fact is not surprising, given that Louisiana's average per capita income is more than $4,000 (19 percent) below the U.S. average. Of the Florida Parishes, only East Baton Rouge and St. Tammany are above the Louisiana

TABLE 11. INCOME PER CAPITA, 1994

W. Feliciana	$11,558
St. Helena	12,224
Tangipahoa	14,556
E. Feliciana	14,747
Washington	14,780
Florida Parishes	15,497
Livingston	15,631
Louisiana	17,622
St. Tammany	19,965
E. Baton Rouge	20,484
U.S.	21,696

average; Livingston is above the Florida Parish average. The rural parishes of Washington, East and West Feliciana, Tangipahoa, and St. Helena are all below the average for the Florida Parishes.

Unemployment (table 12) is a measure of the availability of jobs. Again, only East Baton Rouge and St. Tammany are below the U.S. average of 5.4 percent. The Louisiana and Florida Parish average unemployment rates (6.7 percent and 7.4 percent, respectively) are considerably higher than the U.S. average, and the remaining Florida Parishes have higher rates. Tangipahoa is the highest at 9.5 percent, nearly double the St. Tammany unemployment rate. Some of the differences could be caused by the seasonal unemployment characteristic of agricultural parishes. A clearer picture emerges when we examine the change in the number of businesses from 1990 to 1995 (table 13). This information is a measure of how rapidly businesses are being created in a parish. Each of the Florida Parishes exceeds the U.S. and Louisiana averages except for West Feliciana and Washington Parishes. The surprises are East Feliciana and St. Helena, which appear to be gaining businesses the most rapidly, followed by Livingston, St. Tammany, Tangipahoa, and East Baton Rouge. These parishes are above the Louisiana and U.S. averages for the percent of new establishments created in the period. More mature, developed areas tend to slow down in the rate of business creation, so it is not surprising that the rate of new business development in East Baton Rouge is low.

The service sector is becoming more important as a source of payroll in most of the Florida Parishes, reflecting the change from rural to more urban communities. In East Baton Rouge, for example, the service sector

TABLE 12. 1996 UNEMPLOYMENT, %

St. Tammany	4.9
E. Baton Rouge	5.3
U.S.	5.4
Louisiana	6.7
Florida Parishes	7.4
W. Feliciana	7.6
St. Helena	7.6
E. Feliciana	7.7
Livingston	7.7
Washington	8.5
Tangipahoa	9.5

TABLE 13. CHANGE IN NO. OF BUSINESS ESTABLISHMENTS, 1990–95 (%)

W. Feliciana	2.4
Washington	4.4
U.S.	6.6
Louisiana	8.1
E. Baton Rouge	10.8
Tangipahoa	13.5
Florida Parishes	14.2
St. Tammany	22.4
Livingston	24.7
St. Helena	27.1
E. Feliciana	27.4

as a source of payrolls grew to more than 50 percent in the period 1980–99 while manufacturing declined from about 36 percent to about 20 percent. Retail sales and finance stayed relatively constant while mining (oil and gas, primarily) and agriculture were low and unchanging over the period. In St. Tammany Parish the percentage of payrolls contributed by services increased over the period to a high of nearly 55 percent. In the same period retail sales and manufacturing payroll shares fell while finance and agriculture and mining remained about the same. Agriculture and mining were low and unchanging. In Livingston Parish services accounted for some 30 percent of payrolls but had declined somewhat in recent years, while retail sales were declining slightly as a share of payrolls. Manufacturing declined from 1980 to 1985 but has been increasing since then. Finance, mining, and agriculture are relatively constant over time and remain fairly low. Considering both services and retail as percentages of payroll in the Florida Parishes, West Feliciana has the highest total, 69 percent, and St. Helena the lowest, 46 percent, reflecting its rural status. The U.S. average contribution to payrolls from services and retail is 60 percent, the Louisiana average is 61 percent, and the Florida Parishes' average is 60 percent, or about the same as the U.S. average.

The three capitals data presented here are intended to be an example of how to measure each of the capitals and not a definitive analysis of the Florida Parishes. That is a larger task than can be undertaken here, but such an analysis would provide a good start to the information necessary for improving the quality of life of the Florida Parishes. By way of illustration, consider the number of merchant power plants slated for Louisiana, at least one of which is planned for Washington Parish. (A merchant power plant is a generator of electricity to be sold on the wholesale market.) How will this plant affect the three capitals? The plant will use natural gas to generate electricity. It will require water for cooling and will generate heated water and air pollution that will be put into the environment. The electricity will be sold principally outside of Louisiana, because it already has one of the highest generating capacities in the United States for its population. The ownership of the plant is outside the state, so profits should not be expected to stay in Louisiana. It will provide jobs during construction and a small number of permanent jobs. Initially the owners of the plant wanted to use groundwater for cooling, but a public outcry may have changed those plans. The plant could probably apply for tax exemptions—easy to get in Louisiana—and would not contribute much to the tax rolls even though it will rely on public services such as roads, school, sewers, and drinking water. In summary, while the plant will create a few jobs and some small tax revenues, it will require considerable use of natural capital in the form of water, air, and gas and would discharge heated water to streams. Social capital will not be improved, and financial capital will be improved only a little. On balance, merchant power plants appear to be a bad deal for the area.

CONCLUSION

It has become abundantly clear that there is little or no supporting evidence for the supposition that progressive environmental policies are detrimental to a state's economy. There is substantial and growing evidence, much of it practical empirical evidence, that the converse is true—that a clean environment not only is good for business, but is probably a necessary condition for a healthy economy over the long term. The statistical evidence is such that it would be difficult for a state to become prosperous economically while simultaneously abusing its environment. The efforts we make to improve our environment can only benefit our quality of life, including our economic life, and improve our chances of being sustainable. A sustainable society follows a path that includes low pollution and conserved resources with more equity,[47] leading to a higher quality of life for all of its citizens.

The Florida Parishes of Louisiana stand at a crossroads. In one direction lies traditional economic development that does not value environmental amenities and sacrifices them to gain financial capital at the expense of quality of life. The other direction recognizes that conserving natural capital is important for the long term and that sustainable economic development results in better communities and a higher quality of life. The choice of which path to take belongs to the people and is critical to the future of the area. Making citizens aware that there is a choice must be among our highest priorities.

Notes

1. Paul H. Templet, "The Energy Transition in International Economic Systems: An Empirical Analysis of Change during Development," Louisiana State University Institute for Environmental Studies report, February 22, 1995.

2. Sierra Business Council, *The Sierra Nevada Wealth Index* (Truckee, Calif.: Sierra Business Council, 1999).

3. Garrett Hardin, "The Tragedy of the Commons," *Science* 162 (1968): 1243–48.

4. H. E. Daly, "On Economics as a Life Science," *Journal of Political Science* 76 (1968): 392–406; C. Perrings, *Economy and Environment: A Theoretical Essay on the Interdependence of Economics and Environmental Systems* (Cambridge: Cambridge University Press, 1987); C. A. Tisdell, "The Environment and Economic Welfare," in *Energy, the Environment, and Public Policy: Issues for the 1990s*, ed. David L. McKee (New York, 1991), 6–18; W. Ophuls and S. A. Boyan Jr., *Ecology and the Politics of Scarcity Revisited: The Unraveling of the American Dream* (New York: W. H. Freeman, 1992), 195–216.

5. D. W. Bromley, "Land and Water Problems: An Institutional Perspective," *American Journal of Agricultural Economics* 64 (1982): 834–44.

6. Perrings, *Economy and Environment*, 84.

7. Arthur C. Pigou, *Economics of Welfare*, 3rd ed. (London: Macmillan, 1932); T. Cowen, *The Theory of Market Failure: A Critical Examination* (Fairfax, Va.: George Mason University Press, 1988), 3.

8. S. Farber, R. Moreau, and P. H. Templet, "A Tax Incentive Tool for Environmental Management: An Environmental Scorecard," *Ecological Economics* 12 (1995): 183–89.

9. Paul H. Templet, "The Positive Relationship between Jobs, Environment, and the Economy: An Empirical Analysis," *Spectrum* 68 (spring 1995): 37–49.

10. Paul H. Templet, "The Emissions-to-Jobs Ratio: A Tool for Evaluating Pollution Control Programs," *Environmental Science and Technology* 27 (May 1993): 810–12; Paul H. Templet, "Chemical Industry Pollution Control Spending and Its Relationship to the Emission-to-Jobs Ratio," *Environmental Science and Technology* 27 (October 1993): 1983–85.

11. Standard Industrial Classification (SIC) 20–39.

12. The emissions data used in this analysis are from EPA's Toxic Release Inventory (1992) and are data submitted by manufacturing industries across the United States. Economics and energy data come from the U.S. Bureau of the Census, *Annual Survey of Manufactures, Statistics for Industry Groups and Industries, 1989* (Washington, D.C., 1991); U.S. Bureau of the Cen-

sus, *Statistical Abstract of the United States,* 11th ed. (Washington, D.C., 1991); U.S. Bureau of the Census, *State and Metropolitan Area Data Book, 1991* (Washington, D.C., 1991).

13. Templet, "Chemical Industry Pollution Control Spending," 1983–85.

14. SIC 28.

15. Paul H. Templet and S. Farber, "The Complementarity between Environmental and Economic Risk: An Empirical Analysis," *Ecological Economics* 9 (1994): 153–65.

16. Corporation for Enterprise Development, *The 1992 Development Report Card for the States: Executive Summary* (Washington, D.C., 1992).

17. Paul H. Templet, "Grazing the Commons: An Empirical Analysis of Externalities, Subsidies, and Substainability," Louisiana State University Institute for Environmental Studies report, 1995.

18. J. R. Wright, "PACs, Contributions, and Roll Calls: An Organizational Perspective," *American Political Science Review* 79 (1984): 400–14.

19. U.S. Bureau of the Census, *Statistical Abstract of the United States* (Washington, D.C., 1988), table 444.

20. S. M. Meyer, *Environmentalism and Economic Prosperity: Testing the Environmental Impact Hypotheses,* Project on Environmental Politics and Policy (Cambridge, Mass.: Massachusetts Institute of Technology, 1992).

21. F. Cannon, "Economic Growth and the Environment," in *Economic and Business Outlook* (San Francisco: Bank of America Economics-Policy Research Department, 1993).

22. B. Hall, *Gold and Green* (Durham, N.C.: Institute for Southern Studies, 1994).

23. World Commission on Economic Development, *Our Common Future,* Brundtland Report (Oxford: Oxford University Press, 1987).

24. H. E. Daly, "Toward Some Operational Principles of Sustainability," *Ecological Economics* 2 (1990): 1–6.

25. Templet, "Grazing the Commons."

26. S. Barancik and I. Shapiro, *Where Have All the Dollars Gone?* (Washington, D.C.: Center on Budget and Policy Priorities, 1992).

27. Daly, "Toward Some Operational Principles of Sustainability," 1–6.

28. B. Hall and M. L. Kerr, *Green Index* (Durham, N.C.: Island Press, 1992).

29. Barancik and Shapiro, *Where Have All the Dollars Gone?*

30. *Crime State Rankings, 1994* (Lawrence, Kans.: Morgan Quitno, 1994).

31. Ibid.

32. Organization for Economic Cooperation and Development, *Environmental Policies and Industrial Competitiveness* (Paris: Organization for Economic Cooperation and Development, 1993).

33. Templet, "Energy Transition."

34. U.S. Bureau of the Census, *Current Industrial Reports, Pollution Abatement Costs, and Expenditures* (Washington, D.C., 1992).

35. S. C. Scott, *The Chemical Industry in Louisiana: Economic Profile,* prepared for the Louisiana Chemical Association, Baton Rouge (September 1989).

36. "Management Information Services," *Environmental Science and Technology* (May 1993): 771.

37. Templet, "Emissions-to-Jobs Ratio," 810–12.

38. Paul H. Templet, J. Glenn, and S. Farber, "Louisiana Ties Environmental Performance to Tax Rates," *Environmental Finance* (autumn 1991): 271–77; Farber, Moreau, and Templet, "Tax Incentive Tool," 183–89.

39. Templet, "Grazing the Commons."

40. Paul H. Templet, "Equity and Sustainability: An Empirical Analysis," *Society and Natural Resources* 8 (October 1995): 509–23.

41. Templet, "Grazing the Commons."

42. Templet, "Energy Transition."

43. Templet, "Grazing the Commons."

44. Census Bureau, *USA Counties*.

45. East Baton Rouge Parish is home to two universities, Louisiana State University and Southern University. St. Tammany has recently become a haven for members of the white-collar community from New Orleans and Jefferson Parishes, who are wont to leave the urban environment.

46. Environmental Protection Agency, *Toxic Release Inventory* (1998). Feliciana has the highest total, 69 percent, and St. Helena the lowest, 46 percent, reflecting its rural status. The U.S. average contribution to payrolls from services and retail is 60 percent; the Louisiana average is 61 percent, and the Florida Parishes' average is 60 percent, or about the same as the U.S. average.

47. Templet, "Grazing the Commons."

CONTRIBUTORS

Hodding Carter III is president and chief executive officer of the John S. and James I. Knight Foundation and was assistant secretary of state for public affairs in the Jimmy Carter administration.

Gilbert C. Din is professor emeritus at Fort Lewis College. He is the author of *Spaniards, Planters, and Slaves: The Spanish Regulation of Slavery in Louisiana, 1763–1803*; *The Canary Islanders of Louisiana*; *Francisco Bouligny: A Bourbon Soldier in Spanish Louisiana*; *The New Orleans Cabildo: Colonial Louisiana's First City Government, 1769–1803*; and *Imperial Osage: Spanish-Indian Diplomacy in the Mississippi Valley*.

Charles N. Elliott is an instructor of Louisiana history at Southeastern Louisiana University.

Robin F. A. Fabel is professor of history at Auburn University. Among his many publications are *The Economy of British West Florida, 1763–1783*; *Bombast and Broadsides: The Lives of George Johnstone*; and *Shipwreck and Adventure of Monsieur Pierre Viaud*.

Adam Fairclough is professor of history at the University of East Anglia, United Kingdom. He is the author of *Race and Democracy; The Civil Rights Struggle in Louisiana*; *To Redeem the Soul of America: The Southern Christian Leadership Conference and Martin Luther King Jr.*; and *The Star Creek Papers: Washington Parish and the Lynching of Jerome Wilson*.

Samuel C. Hyde Jr. holds the Leon Ford Chair, is the director for the Center for Southeast Louisiana Studies, and is associate professor of history at Southeastern Louisiana University. He is the author of *Pistols and Politics: The Dilemma of Democracy in Louisiana's Florida Parishes, 1810–1899* and editor of *Plain Folk of the South Revisited* and *Sunbelt Revolution: The Historical Progression of the Civil Rights Struggle in the Gulf South, 1866–2000*.

Richard H. Kilbourne Jr. lives in Clinton, Louisiana. He is the author of *Debt, Investments, Slaves: Credit Relations in East Feliciana Parish, Louisiana, 1825–1885*.

Gene A. Smith is associate professor of history at Texas Christian University. He is the author of *Historical Memoir of the War in West Florida and Louisiana in 1814–15*; *"For the Purpose of Defense": The Politics of the Jefferson Gunboat Program*; *Filibusters and Expansionists: Jeffersonian Manifest Destiny, 1800–1821*; *Thomas ap Catesby Jones: Commodore of Manifest Destiny*; and *Iron and Heavy Guns: The Monitor and Merrimac*.

Latimore Smith is a state ecologist with the Louisiana Natural Heritage Program, Louisiana Department of Wildlife and Fisheries.

Paul H. Templet is a professor with the Environmental Studies Institute at Louisiana State University and former director of the Louisiana Department of Environmental Quality.

Bill Wyche is professor emeritus in the Department of History and Political Science at Southeastern Louisiana University.

INDEX

Acollapissas Indians, 18, 19, 31–37
agriculture: 140, 187; credit system and, 126–38; pine forests and, 143–45, 147, 150, 152; environmental impact of, 193, 218
Aitchison, Robert, 98
Allain, Francisco, 70
Allen, C. M., 121
Alligator, 99, 100
Alligator Bayou, 16, 25
Alston, Santiago, 70, 71
Amacker, Abigail, 112, 121
American Federation of Labor, 167
Amite River: 1, 17, 18, 25, 49, 50, 53, 54, 55, 63, 132; exploration of, 31, 47; pine forests along, 140, 142
Apalachicola River, 44, 95
Armide, 99
Association of Southern Women for the Prevention of Lynching, 177
Attakapa Indians, 70
Aubry, Charles-Philippe, 46
Avoyelles Parish, 36

Bacon, Edward, 116
Badine, 22
bahia grass, 151
Ball, John, 179
Balltown riot, 179, 180
Baratarians, 94, 96, 97, 102
Barings, the, 127
Baton Rouge: 4, 18, 24, 61, 64, 65, 69, 78, 173, 188; slavery in, 62, 63, 68, 72–77; Civil War in, 112, 115, 117; environmental quality of, 207

Bautista, Juan, 74
Bay St. Louis, Miss., 99, 100
Bayou Bienvenu, 98
Bayou Choupic, 27
Bayou Fountain, 16, 25
Bayou Jasemine, 16
Bayou Lafourche, 23, 31, 36
Bayou Manchac: 1, 16, 17, 18, 33, 34, 35, 37, 60, 61; exploration of, 24, 25, 26, 30–31; land speculation around, 46–55, 61, 62, 64; slavery in, 62, 64, 69, 70
Bayou St. John, 31, 33, 34, 35, 36, 98
Bayou Sara, 74, 121
Bayou Terrebonne, 36
Bayougoula Indians, 4, 18, 20, 22–26, 28, 30, 33, 36, 37
Beauregard, P. G. T., 113
bermuda grass, 151
Bertonière, Pierre, 76
sieur de Bienville, Jean Baptiste Lemoyne, 25–28, 30–32, 34
Bienville, Juan Baptista, 63
Biloxi, Miss., 24, 26, 29
Biloxi Bay, 22, 25, 26
Biloxi Indians, 23, 47
Biscayenne, 22
blackjack oak, 141
Blackwell, Jacob, 48
Bloomington, George, 162, 163
bobwhite, 142, 154
Bogalusa, La.: 18; lumber industry in, 148, 161, 164; race relations in, 163–70, 173, 174
Bond, Horace Mann, 9–10, 174–88
Bond, William, 21, 27

Bouchillon, Porter, 168
Bowling Green Plantation, 117
Breton Sound, 23
Broad River, 51
Brock, J. L., 177
Brooks-Scanlon Lumber Company, 148
Brotherhood of Carpenters and Joiners of America, 167–68
Brown Brothers, 127, 128
Browne, Montfort, 49
Bruce, James, 53–54
Bruce, Philip A., 185
Burke, Charles, 69
Burris, William, 182
Butler, Benjamin, 115

Cabo, Joseph, 74
Caddo Indians, 31
Cadillac, Antoine de la Mothe, 34
Calhoun, Arthur W., 185
Camp Moore, 111, 113, 115, 119
Campbell, James, 46
Canary Islanders, 64. *See also* Isleños
Cane River, 182
Carlos III, 45, 56
barón de Carondelet, Francisco Luis Hector, 66–68, 70–72, 75–78, 80
marqués de Casa-Calvo, Sebastián Nicolás Calvo de la Puerta y O'Farrill, 76–79
Cat Island, 98, 99
cattle industry: 150–51; environmental impact of, 193–94
Causey, R. J., 121
Chalmette, Ignacio Delinó, 65
Chandeleur Sound, 23
Charles Town (Charleston), S.C., 21, 27, 28, 29, 128
Chef Menteur Road, 98
Chester, Peter, 47–53, 56
Chickasaw Bluffs, 21
Chickasaw Indians, 6, 21, 28–30, 32–34, 37
Chitimacha Indians, 31, 33, 45
Choctaw Indians, 5, 19, 27, 29, 32, 34, 35, 36, 45, 55, 95
Chozeta Indians, 22

Chrystie, Adam, 54, 57
Chubby Bottoms, 18
Civil War: 4, 8, 109, 173, 179; irregular operations during, 110–22; economic impact of, 126, 129. *See also* Confederate army; Union army
Claiborne, W. C. C., 3
Clinton, La., 132
Cochrane, Alexander Forrester Inglis, 94–99, 102, 103
Code Noir, 65–66
Cohn, David, 185
Coles Creek Culture (Indian), 16
Comite River, 47, 49, 50, 54, 55
Concepción, 64
Confederate army: 8; irregular operations of, 109–21; Ninth Louisiana Partisan Rangers, 115; First Louisiana Cavalry, 117; Second Arkansas Cavalry, 121
Constitution of 1898 (Louisiana), 180
Corinth, Miss., 113
corn, 53, 54, 69, 70, 144
cotton, 50, 77, 112, 132, 133, 136, 137, 180, 187
Coxe, Daniel, 21
Craigue, N. F., 119
Creek Indians, 47, 55, 94
Creek-Choctaw war, 56
Crosby, Columbus, 166
Crozat, Antoine, 34

Dacus, Sol, 168
Daly, H. E., 203
Daniels, Mandy, 184, 188
Dartmouth, La., 50–51, 52
Dauphine Island, 99
Davis, Allison, 175
de Moscoso, Luis, 17
de Soto, Hernando, 17
Deacons for Defense, 174
DeClouet, Alexandre, 70
Dendenger (mill), 164
Department of Economic Development, 201
Department of Environmental Quality, 10, 193, 194, 195

Department of Southwestern Mississippi and East Louisiana, 114
Department of Wildlife and Fisheries, 154
Desautel, Antonio, 72
Domett, William, 94
Donaldsonville, La., 36
Doyle, J. M., 116
Du Bois, W. E. B., 186
Dunbar, William, 62, 68
Duparc, Guillermo, 69, 70
Duplantier, Armand, 63
Durnford, Elias, 61

East Baton Rouge Parish: 2, 16, 118, 140, 163, 173; environmental quality of, 210, 212, 214, 215, 216, 217
East Feliciana Parish: 2, 133, 134, 135, 140, 142; environmental quality of, 210, 212, 215, 217
East Louisiana Lumber Company, 148
eastern bluebird, 142
eastern white pine, 146
Ellis, Lucy, 182
Environmental Protection Agency, 195

Favrot, Pierre Joseph, 65
Feliciana (New Feliciana), 61, 64, 77, 78
Fitzpatrick, John, 57
Florida Parishes: ix, x, xii, 44; distinctiveness of, 1–10; Indian nations of, 15–19; British involvement in, 2, 3, 5, 26–30, 33, 36, 37, 44, 45, 49, 51, 56, 60; French exploration of, 23–25, 29; European interaction with Indians in, 22, 26–37; land speculation in, 44–57; slavery in, 63–81; War of 1812 in, 91, 92, 95, 97–100, 102–105; Civil War in, 111, 112, 115, 117, 120, 122; agriculture in, 131–34, 136, 137, 138; longleaf pine forests in, 140–55; timber industry in, 161, 163, 164, 165, 168, 169, 170; environmental quality of, 191, 192, 209–19
Flowers, Samuel, 78–79
Fluker, Joseph, 116
Fort Bowyer, 104
Fort Bute, 71
Fort de la Boulaye, 27, 28, 30, 31, 34

Fort James, 51
Fort Manchac, 34, 47
Fort Maurepas, 26, 28, 29
Fort Petites Coquilles, 91, 98, 99
Fort St. John, 31, 34
Fort San Gabriel, 55
Fort Toulouse, 47
Franklinton, La., 174, 176, 177, 180, 181, 182, 187
Frazier, E. Franklin, 178, 181, 183, 186, 187
free people of color: 7, 36, 61, 63, 64, 72, 182; War of 1812 and, 93, 95
Fremaux, Celine, 116
French and Indian War, 4, 6, 36, 44, 45, 49, 56

Gabriel's rebellion, 78
Galveston, Tex., 125, 128
Gálvez, Bernardo de, 4, 6, 62, 63
Gálvez, José de, 80
Gayoso de Lemos, Manuel, 65, 73, 74
Georgia, 28, 51, 95, 143, 164
Gill, G. Wray, 176
Golden, Louis William, 166, 167
Goodyear family, 148
gopher tortoise, 142
Gould, Jay, 133
Grand Terre, 96
Grand-Pré, Carlos de, 64, 65, 73, 74, 75, 76, 77, 78, 79
Grange organization, 132
Graves, Nathaniel, 182
Gravier, Jacques, 30
Great Northern Lumber Company, 180
Great Southern Lumber Company, 148, 150, 151, 162, 163, 167, 168, 173
Greensburg, La., 119
Greenville, Miss., ix, xi

Hair, William Ivy, 183
Hall, Elihu Bay, 51
Hall, Gwendolyn Midlo, 185
Halleck, Henry W., 110
Hammond, La., ix, 162
Harrison, William Henry, 93

Harwich, 47, 48, 50, 51, 52, 53
Heard, William, 180
Henslow's sparrow, 142, 154
Hickey, Daniel, 69
Hoover site (archaeological), 17
Hotham, Henry, 93
Houma, La., 4
Houma Indians, 18, 20, 24, 30, 33, 34, 36, 37, 45, 47
Hyde, Samuel C., 132, 137, 138

sieur d'Iberville, Pierre LeMoyne, 1, 15, 21, 22, 23, 24–30, 32, 33, 34, 36, 37
Iberville Canal, 46, 56
Iberville River, 46, 47, 48, 49, 50, 54, 63. *See also* Bayou Manchac
Illinois Central Railroad, 146, 147, 150. *See also* New Orleans, Jackson, and Great Northern Railroad
indigo, 53, 54, 57, 69, 77
International Monetary Fund, 131
International Union of Timber Workers, 167
International Workers of the World, 168
Isabell, La., 162
Isle of Orleans, 7, 44, 61, 98
Isleños, 3. *See also* Canary Islanders
Istrouma, La., 24

Jackson, Andrew, 4, 7, 91, 94, 95, 97, 98, 101, 103, 105
Jackson, Miss., 148
Jackson Military Road, 7
Jamaica, 94
Jaynes, Gerald, 126
Johnson, William, 99, 100
Johnston, Joseph E., 120
Johnstone, George, 45–47, 54, 56
Johnstone, William, 54
Jones, Thomas ap Catesby, 7, 91, 92, 98–105

Kent, Amos, 147, 148, 162, 164, 165
Kentwood, La.: 147, 148, 151; lumber industry in, 164
Kentwood, Greensburg, and Southwestern Railroad, 148

Kentwood and Eastern Railroad, 148
Kilbourne, James G., 133
Killian, La., 166
Kleinpeter site (archaeological), 16, 17
Koch, Annette, 119
Ku Klux Klan, 174

La Salle, René Robert Cavalier de, 1, 20–21, 22, 23, 25–27
Lacombe, La., 164
Lacombe Lumber, 164
Lafitte, Jean, 96
Lake Borgne: 4, 25; battle of, 91, 98–105
Lake Maurepas, 1, 18, 20, 46, 48, 50, 63
Lake Pontchartrain: 1, 4, 15, 16, 18, 20, 28, 31, 35, 37, 48, 50, 71, 191; War of 1812 and, 98; Civil War and, 121; lumber industry and, 146, 147
Law, John, 35
Le Blanc, Valentin, 75
LeBlond, Marie Bara, 75–77, 80
Lee, Robert E., 114, 120
Lehman Brothers, 127
Levi, Henry, 166
Liberty, Miss., 119
Liberty Place, Battle of, 131
little blue-stem, 154
Livingston, Philip, Jr., 51, 53, 56
Livingston Parish: 2, 112, 118, 140, 173; environmental quality of, 210, 212, 215, 217, 218
Lockyer, Nicholas, 96, 100, 102
Loftus, Arthur, 45
Long, George, 166
Long, Huey P., xi, 177, 183
longleaf pine, 140–45, 147–55, 162
Louis XIV, 20–21, 22, 26, 27
Louisiana Natural Heritage Program, 155
Louisiana Purchase, 2, 3, 5, 92, 104
Louisiana State University, Baton Rouge, 135, 150, 194, 195
Lovell, Mansfield, 111, 112, 113, 114
Loyalists, 52, 53, 54, 55, 62
Lydia, 64
lynching, 168, 173, 174, 177, 178, 179, 183, 187, 188

Macullagh, Alexander, 51
Madisonville, La.: 18, 98; lumber industry in, 164
Magee, Fleet, 182
Magee, Hezekiah, 179, 188
Magee, John, 182
Magee, Wade Hampton, 180, 182
malaria, 45
Malheureux Island, 100
Manchac Point, 25, 57
Mandeville, La., 31, 148
Marion, Francis, 109, 113
Marksville, La., 36
maroons, 70, 71, 73
Marshall, William, 54, 63, 68
Massacre Island, 22
Matagorda Bay, 20
McClellan, George B., 112, 113
McGehee family, 117
Melville, Viscount, 93, 94
Memphis, Tenn., 21, 27
Meyer, Stephen, 201
Meyer Brothers, 135, 136
Miró, Esteban, 63, 64, 68, 73
miscegenation, 176, 179, 181–84
Mississippi: 29, 49, 60, 64, 79, 95, 128, 143, 147, 148, 164, 173, 174, 179, 183, 191; Civil War and, 111, 112, 114, 120
Mississippi River: 1, 3, 7, 27, 29, 31, 33, 34, 35, 36, 37, 45, 48, 49, 79, 191; Indian nations along, 15–20; exploration of, 20–23, 25, 26, 27, 60; land speculation along, 46, 47, 50, 51, 56, 63; slavery along, 60–61, 62, 64, 66, 70, 73, 74; War of 1812 and, 92, 93, 94, 98, 104; Civil War and, 111, 112, 113, 117, 121; postbellum agriculture and, 125, 129, 130, 134; environment and, 207
Mississippian Culture (Indian), 16–19, 28
Missouri River, 25
Mobile, Ala.: 26, 29, 30, 31, 34, 35, 44, 48, 50, 51, 56, 125; War of 1812 in, 92, 97, 98, 102, 104
Mobile Bay: 22, 26; War of 1812 in, 104
mockernut hickory, 141

Moore, Thomas, 112, 114
Morganza, La., 116
Morris, Bill, 179
Mosby, John Singleton, 110

Nairne, Thomas, 34
Napoleon Bonaparte, 92, 93, 109
Natalbany, La., 148, 165
Natalbany Lumber Company, 148, 162, 166, 167
Natchez, Miss., 45, 47, 48, 55, 61, 63, 65, 73, 74, 75, 132, 175
Natchez Indians, 6, 19, 33, 34, 35
Natchitoches, La., 35
Natchitoches Indians, 31, 32, 33, 34, 35
National Association for the Advancement of Colored People, 169, 176–78
Native Americans. *See* names of individual tribes
Nature Conservancy, 155
naval stores, 145–46
Negril Point, 94
Neshoba County, Miss., 36
New Feliciana. *See* Feliciana
New Orleans: ix, 2, 6, 7, 15, 23, 35, 36, 37, 44, 45, 46, 48, 60, 62, 66, 173, 178; fire in, 64; slavery in, 68–71, 73, 74, 75, 76, 77, 80; War of 1812 and, 91, 92, 93, 94, 96, 97, 98, 101, 102, 103, 104, 105; Civil War and, 111, 112, 113, 114, 126; credit in, 125, 128, 130, 135; environmental quality of, 207
New Orleans–Jackson Railroad, 115
New Orleans, Jackson, and Great Northern Railroad, 147, 148
New Orleans, Natalbany, and Natchez Railroad, 148
Nichols, Ruth Connor, 53

Office of State Lands, 154
Ofogoulas Indians, 45
Oglethorpe, James, 28
Ohio River, 25, 48
O'Reilly, Alejandro, 62
O'Rourke, S. L., 168
Osyka, Miss., 119, 120

Page, Thomas Nelson, 185
Pakenham, Edward Michael, 94, 103
Park, Robert E., 175, 178, 182, 186
Parker, George, 101
Pascagoula Indians, 47
Pass Christian, Miss., 99
Pass Manchac, 112
Patin, Alejandro, 69–70
Patterson, Daniel Todd, 91, 96, 105
Pearl River: 15, 18, 19, 20, 25, 31, 36, 140; Civil War and, 111, 118–19
Pearl River Valley Lumber Company, 166
Pénicaut, André, 31, 32, 33
Pensacola, Fla.: 21, 22, 26, 27, 49, 50, 51, 53; War of 1812 in, 92, 97, 98, 102
Percy, William Alexander, ix
Perry, Oliver Hazard, 93
Philadelphia, Miss., 29, 36
Philibert (slave), 69, 70
Pigot, Hugh, 95
Pinckney's Treaty, 65
Pine Grove, Miss., 148
Pointe Coupée, La.: 24, 30, 50, 69, 70; slave conspiracy in, 71, 72, 75–77, 80
Poitevent-Favre Lumber Company, 148
Ponchatoula, La., 17, 18, 116
post oak, 141
Pratt, George, 101
Precieux, 22

Quinipissas-Mugalashas Indians, 18, 20, 24, 25, 26, 30 36, 37
Quinto, Morgan, 206

Ransom, Roger, 137
Raoul, W. Greene, 118
Rea, Robert R., 63
Reconstruction, 4, 5, 8, 180, 182
red-cockaded woodpecker, 142, 154, 155
red oak, 141
Red River, 18, 24, 25, 31, 33, 35, 36
Reddix, Jacob L., 182
Republican party, 180
Revolutionary War, 52, 54, 61, 63, 73, 109
rice, 50, 53

Richmond, Va., 112, 114, 128
Rigolets, the, 91, 98, 99
Rivas, Francisco, 69, 71
Robertson, Archibald, 47
Roemer, Buddy, 194, 195
Rosenwald Fund, 175, 176, 178
Ross, Robert, 94, 96
Rothschilds, the, 127, 128
Ru, Paul du, 30
Ruggles, Daniel, 114
Rural School Exploration Project, 175
rye grass, 151

St. Francisville, La., 74, 121
St. Helena Parish: 2, 119, 121, 134, 140; lumber industry in, 146; environmental quality of, 210, 212, 215, 217, 218
St. Mary's Island, 99
St. Tammany Parish: 2, 36, 91, 103, 140, 173; environmental quality of, 210, 212, 215, 216, 217, 218; lumber industry in, 146, 148, 151, 152, 154
Salmen Lumber Company, 148, 166
San Malo, Juan, 71
Santo Domingo, 22, 23
Scott, John S., 117, 118, 120, 121
Seahorse, 99, 100
segregation, xi, 134, 168, 184
sharecropping, 8, 126, 130, 133, 134, 136, 137, 176, 187
Ship Island, 22, 99
Sigu, Lorenzo, 71
Simmons, Si, 166
slash pine, 150–52
slavery: 6, 21, 49, 50, 53, 54, 55, 60, 181, 185, 186, 187, 188; involving Indians, 28, 29, 32, 33; under British rule, 61–62, 80; under French rule, 60–61, 65, 66, 80; under Spanish rule, 63–81; War of 1812 and, 92, 94, 95, 96, 97, 102, 104; Civil War and, 115; economic consequences of, 128, 129, 130, 134
Slidell, La.: 18, 25, 148; lumber industry in, 166, 167
Smith, Jep, 161

Sophia, 99
South Carolina, 21, 28, 29, 34, 143
Southeastern Louisiana University, x, 5, 212
Southern Pine Association, 166
Spanish colonialism, 3, 6, 15, 17, 21, 28, 34, 36, 37, 44, 45, 50, 65
Sparks, William H., 143
Stamps, John O., 166
Star Creek, 174, 175, 176, 177, 178, 187, 188
State Office of Forestry, 155
Steer, Samuel, 63, 68
Stirling, James, 93
sugar, 77, 98, 129
Sullivan, William H., 167
Sutch, Richard, 137
sweet gum, 142

Tadman, Michael, 134
Talapoosa River: 47; pollution in, 193
Tangipahoa Indians, 18, 19, 36, 37
Tangipahoa Parish: 2, 16, 17, 140, 173; Civil War in, 112; lumber industry in, 146, 150, 152, 162, 163, 164, 166; environmental quality of, 210, 212, 215, 217
Tchefuncte Culture (Indian), 16
Tennessee: 29, 93, 125; Civil War in, 112, 117
Tensas Indians, 32, 33, 34, 35
Terrasco, John, 47
Terrebonne Parish, 36
Texas, 20, 114, 140, 164, 166, 188
Thomas, John, 55, 56
Thompson, M. Jeff, 113
Thompson's Creek, 50, 54, 55, 56, 121
timber industry: 8–9, 53, 57, 145–50, 153, 161, 162, 180; railroads and, 145–49; black workers in, 162–69
tobacco, 77
Tolnay, Stewart, 187
Tombigbee River, 19
Tonti, Henri de, 20, 26
Treaty of Fontainbleau (1762), 15
Treaty of Ghent (1815), 104
Treaty of Paris (1763), 15, 44, 61
Treaty of San Lorenzo, 65
tung-oil, 151, 152

Tunica Indians, 5, 19, 33, 34, 35, 45, 55, 56
Tupelo, Miss., 21, 27
Turnbull, John, 63
turpentine, 145, 146, 153
Tyson, Robert, 116

Union army: 8, 109–13, 115–22, 126; General Orders Number 100, p. 110; Thirtieth Massachusetts Regiment, 115; General Orders Number 33, p. 119; Fourth Wisconsin Cavalry, 119
University of Chicago, 175
University of Louisiana in New Orleans, 133
Unzaga, Luis de, 62
U.S. Fish and Wildlife Service, 154

Vahamonde, José Vázquez, 65, 68, 69, 70, 72
Van Dorn, Earl, 114
Vergés, Francisco de, 65, 73
Vicksburg, Miss., 16, 19, 65
Vidal, Jose, 74
Vidal, Nicolás María, 71
Vidalia, La.., 74
Virginia: 78, 93, 105, 140; Civil War in, 110, 112, 113, 117

Walker, Ollie, 166
Walker, William, 55
Wallace, George C., 8
War of 1812: 4, 6, 91–104; battle of the Thames, 93; battle of Horseshoe Bend, 95; Plain of Gentilly, 98; Spanish and, 93, 95, 96, 97, 102, 103; Plains of Chalmette, 102, 103, 105
Warren, John Borlase, 93, 94
Washington, Booker T., 181, 186, 187
Washington, D.C.: ix, 101, 102, 162, 168, 184; Civil War and, 112, 120
Washington Parish: 2, 10, 140, 168, 173, 188; timber industry in, 9, 151, 161–64; race relations in, 174–87; environmental quality of, 210, 212, 214, 215, 217, 219
Washington Parish Training School, 187
water oak, 142
Weatherford, Willis D., 185

Weiss, Carl, 183
West Feliciana Parish: 2, 121, 133; environmental quality of, 210, 212, 215, 217, 218
West Florida law, 61–62
West Florida Revolution, 4
Wickliffe, Robert, 121
Wilcox County, Ala., 183
Wilkins, Roy, 177
Wilkinson County, Miss., 18
Williams, L. E., 161, 168–69
Williams, Thomas, 115
Willing, James, 62
Wilson, Isom, 184, 188
Wilson, Jerome, 173, 174, 176, 177, 183, 187, 188
Wilson, John, 176, 178, 179, 180, 181, 183, 188
Wood, Delos, 176, 183
Woodbine, George, 95
Woodville, Miss., 117, 119
Woodward, C. Vann, 133–34
World War I, 163, 164
World War II, 5, 8, 179
Wright, Gavin, 134

Yazoo River, 19, 33
yellow fever, 45

www.ingramcontent.com/pod-product-compliance
Lightning Source LLC
Chambersburg PA
CBHW070758230426
43665CB00017B/2413